CUET

(UG) & Integrated PG

2022

Mathematics

DU | BHU | JNU | JMI | TISS & etc.

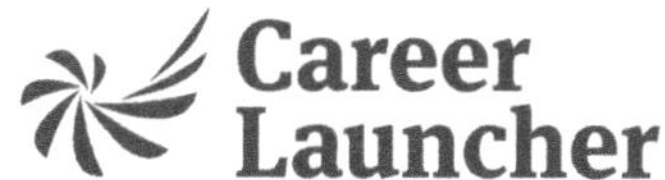

Title   : CUET 2022 : Mathematics

Language   : English

Editor's Name   : Amit singh

Copyright ©   : 2022 CLIP

Typeset & Published by :

Career Launcher Infrastructure (P) Ltd.

A-45, Mohan Cooperative Industrial Area, Near Mohan Estate Metro Station, New Delhi - 110044

Marketed by :

G.K. Publications (P) Ltd.

Plot No. 9A, Sector-27A, Mathura Road, Faridabad, Haryana-121003

ISBN   : **978-93-95101-29-5**

For product information :

Visit ***www.gkpublications.com*** or email to ***gkp@gkpublications.com***

CONTENTS

About CUET

A year ago, it would have been unimaginable that cut-offs in Delhi University would skyrocket to 100% for some of the undergraduate courses! While DU has always been known for its high cut-offs, there are several other universities where the story is no different.

However, the National Education Policy 2020 (NEP) aims to do away with the tyranny of the ever-rising cut-offs by introducing a Common Entrance Test for all the Central Universities in the country. NEP not only proposes a holistic approach in evaluating the students by giving them the option to select subjects based on their interest, but it also aims to simplify the process of admission to higher-education institutes.

To start with, there would be a Common Entrance Test for all the Central Universities, which would be conducted twice a year from 2022. While this might sound like a new concept to many, the fact is, there is already a CUET, which is conducted for the Central Universities established in or after 2009. As many as 14 of them already admit students based on their performance in the entrance test. The CUET scores are also accepted by four state universities of the country.

The proposed CUET aims to assess conceptual understanding and application of knowledge; and also, to lessen the burden of appearing in multiple tests.

CUET Eligibility

Getting into a premier University is every student's dream. The brand value of the University not only facilitates securing a seat in a master's program in a national/international institute, but also helps in getting job offers through campus placements.

Entry to a Central University, in most cases earlier, was based on merit, i.e., marks secured in Class XII Board exams. However, from the academic year 2021, all Central Universities will also consider the CUET score for admissions into their Undergraduate programs.

CUET 2022: Eligibility Criteria

While the official criteria will be learnt once the CUET 2021 notification is released, the stipulations are not expected to change much from those of previous years.

- A candidate must have passed Class XII (10+2) or equivalent from a recognized education Board.
- If the respective Board awards grades (or CGPA), the conversion factor given by the Board must be used to compute the percentage of marks.
- Candidates, who have completed their Class XII in 2021, and have passed the Board exams, will also be eligible to apply for CUET 2022.

Eligibility: Class XII Students

While CUET is for students who have passed the Class XII (or equivalent) Board exams, any student who is appearing for the Class XII Board exam in 2022 is also eligible to apply for CUET 2021. The candidate would be required to produce the marksheets and relevant certificates as mandated by the participating Central University, and follow the timelines provided for admissions.

Key Points

- Each participating Central University is free to decide its own eligibility criteria for admissions.

- The weightages for CUET and Class XII Board exam results(if, applicable) will be at the sole discretion of the Central University, to which admission is being sought.

- As of date, CUET does not have an age limit. However, Central Universities can fix minimum & maximum age limit for admissions to all (or any) of the programs on offer.

Reservation of Seats

As CUET is an entrance exam for admissions to Undergraduate courses at the Central Universities, which have been established under an Act of the Parliament, each Central University must follow the norms set by the Government of India, with respect to intake and reservation of seats.

Generally, the following break-up is followed:

Category	Reservation
Scheduled Castes	15%
Scheduled Tribes	7.5%
Other Backward Classes (Non-Creamy)	27%
Persons with Disability	5%

Some institutions might even have provisions for the Economically Weaker Sections, which can account for 10% of the total seats. These EWS seats are carved out from the Open Category.

To avail of the reservation benefit based on caste (or any other category as specified), a candidate must be able to produce valid documents/certificates to support such claims.

Conclusion

It is essential for every candidate to check the validity of their candidature for CUET, as well as the Central University he/she is applying to. The candidate should be aware of the documents that might be required while applying for the exam, or during the admissions.

CUET 2022 notification is expected in March 2022, and registration is also going to start then.

CUET: Exam Pattern

Examination Structure for CUET (UG) -2022:

CUET (UG) –2022 will consist of the following 4 Sections:

 Section IA –13 Languages
 Section IB –19 Languages
 Section II –27 Domain specific Subjects
 Section III –General Test

Choosing options from each Section is not mandatory. Choices should match the requirements of the desired University.

Broad features of CUET (UG) -2022 are as follows:

Section	Subjects/ Tests	Questions to be Attempted	Question Type	Duration
Section IA – Languages	There are 13* different languages. Any of these languages may be chosen.	40 questions to be attempted out of 50 in each language	Language to be tested through Reading Comprehension (based on different types of passages–Factual, Literary and Narrative, [Literary Aptitude and Vocabulary]	45 Minutes for each language
Section IB – Languages	There are 19** Languages. Any other language apart from those offered in Section I A may be chosen.			
Section II - Domain	There are 27*** Domains specific subjects being offered under this Section. A candidate may choose a maximum of Six (06) Domains as desired by the applicable University/Universities.	40 Questions to be attempted out of 50	• Input text can be used for MCQ Based Questions • MCQs based on NCERT Class XII syllabus only	
Section III- General Test	For any such undergraduate programme/ programmes being offered by Universities where a General Test is being used for admission.	60 Questions to be attempted out of 75	• Input text can be used for MCQ Based Questions • General Knowledge, Current Affairs, General Mental Ability, Numerical Ability, Quantitative Reasoning (Simple application of basic mathematical concepts arithmetic/algebra geometry/mensuration/s tat taught till Grade 8), Logical and Analytical Reasoning	

*** Languages (13):** Tamil, Telugu, Kannada, Malayalam, Marathi, Gujarati, Odiya, Bengali, Assamese, Punjabi, English, Hindi and Urdu

**** Languages (19):** *French, Spanish, German, Nepali, Persian, Italian, Arabic, Sindhi, Kashmiri, Konkani, Bodo, Dogri, Maithili, Manipuri, Santhali, Tibetan, Japanese, Russian, Chinese.*

***** Domain Specific Subjects (27):** 1. Accountancy/ Book Keeping 2. Biology/ Biological Studies/ Biotechnology/Biochemistry 3. Business Studies 4. Chemistry 5. Computer Science/ Informatics Practices 6. Economics/ Business Economics 7. Engineering Graphics 8.Entrepreneurship 9. Geography/Geology 10. History 11. Home Science 12.Knowledge Tradition and Practices of India 13. Legal Studies 14. Environmental Science 15. Mathematics 16. Physical Education/ NCC /Yoga 17.Physics 18.Political Science 19. Psychology 20. Sociology 21. Teaching Aptitude 22. Agriculture 23. Mass Media/ Mass Communication 24. Anthropology 25. Fine Arts/Visual Arts (Sculpture/ Painting)/Commercial Arts, 26. Performing Arts – (i) Dance (Kathak/ Bharatnatyam/Oddisi/ Kathakali/Kuchipudi/ Manipuri (ii) Drama- Theatre (iii) Music General (Hindustani/ Carnatic/ RabindraSangeet/ Percussion/ Non-Percussion), 27. Sanskrit *[For all Shastri (Shastri 3 years/ 4 years Honours) Equivalent to B.A./B.A. Honours courses i.e. Shastri in Veda, Paurohitya (Karmakand), Dharamshastra, Prachin Vyakarana, Navya Vyakarana, Phalit Jyotish, Siddhant Jyotish, Vastushastra, Sahitya,Puranetihas, Prakrit Bhasha,Prachin Nyaya Vaisheshik, Sankhya Yoga, Jain Darshan, Mimansa, AdvaitaVedanta, Vishihstadvaita Vedanta, Sarva Darshan, a candidate may choose Sanskrit as the Domain].*

- A Candidate can choose a maximum of **any 3 languages** from Section IA and Section IB taken together. (One of the languages chosen needs to be in lieu of Domain specific subjects)
- Section II offers 27 Subjects, out of which a candidate may choose a **maximum of 6 Subjects.**
- Section III comprises **General Test.**
- For choosing Languages (upto 3) from Section IA and IB and a maximum of 6 Subjects from Section II and General Test under Section III, the Candidate must refer to the requirements of his/her intended University.

Mode of the Test	Computer Based Test-CBT
Test Pattern	Objective type with Multiple Choice Questions
Medium	13 languages (*Tamil, Telugu, Kannada, Malayalam, Marathi, Gujarati, Odiya, Bengali, Assamese, Punjabi, English, Hindi and Urdu)*
Syllabus	**Section IA & IB:** Language to be tested through Reading Comprehension (based on different types of passages–Factual, Literary and Narrative [Literary Aptitude & Vocabulary]
	Section II : As per NCERT model syllabus as applicable to Class XII only
	Section III : General Knowledge, Current Affairs, General Mental Ability, Numerical Ability, Quantitative Reasoning (Simple application of basic mathematical concepts arithmetic/algebra geometry/mensuration/stat taught till Grade 8), Logical and Analytical Reasoning

Level of questions for CUET (UG) -2022:

All questions in various testing areas will be benchmarked at the level of Class XII only. Students having studied Class XII Board syllabus would be able to do well in CUET (UG) – 2022.

Number of attempts:

If any University permits students of previous years of class XII to take admission in the current year also, such students would also be eligible to appear in CUET (UG) – 2022.

Choice of Languages and Subjects:

Generally the languages/subjects chosen should be the ones that a student has opted in his latest Class XII Board examination. However, if any University permits any flexibility in this regards, the same can be exercised under CUET (UG) -2022 also. Candidates must carefully refer to the eligibility requirements of various Central Universities in this regard. Moreover, if the subject to be studied in the Undergraduate course is not available in the list of **27 Domain Specific Subject** being offered, the Candidate may choose the Subject closest to his choice for e.g. For Biochemistry the candidate may choose Biology.

Candidates are advised to visit the NTA CUET (UG)-2022 official website **https://cuet.samarth.ac.in/** for latest updates regarding the Examination.

CUET Syllabus

CUET Syllabus

Before you start your preparation for any entrance exam, it is important to understand the syllabus. Otherwise, your prep will be directionless, and you might be left wondering where things might have gone wrong!

With more than 1.68 lakh seats on offer for the undergraduate courses at the 54 Central Universities, CUET is one the most competitive examinations. For this very reason, while preparing for the exam, you will need to adopt a structured approach. And in doing that, understanding the syllabus is a critical step.

CUET 2022 Overview

CUET 2022 will be a Computer-Based Test (CBT), commonly referred to as an online exam. However, there is a difference between the two terms: CBT and online. In CBT, the questions are kept constant and simply presented in an online format; whereas in an Online Test, questions are stored as a bank, and the system decides which questions are to be presented to the candidate, based on a pre-defined logic.

CUET 2022 is likely to be a General Ability Test, with focus on English Language, Numerical Ability, Logical & Analytical Reasoning, along with General Awareness and Current Affairs.

CUET 2022 Syllabus

The CUET 2022 exam pattern gives a good idea about what is in store for the candidate and how one needs to prepare for the exam.

- **English Language:** The questions in this section will test one's proficiency in the language, based on comprehension passages, fundamentals of grammar, and vocabulary. In the Comprehension section, candidates will be evaluated on their understanding of a passage and its central theme, meanings of words used therein, etc. The Grammar section entails correcting grammatically incorrect sentences, filling of blanks in sentences with appropriate words, etc. Questions on synonyms & antonyms will check one's command over English vocabulary.
- **Numerical Ability:** Questions on Numerical Ability will test the candidate's knowledge of elementary mathematics. Areas like arithmetic, number system, basics of algebra, and modern maths will be central to these types of questions.
- **Logical & Analytical Reasoning:** This section tests the candidate's ability to identify patterns & logical links, and rectify illogical arguments. It can include a variety of Logical Reasoning questions, such as those on syllogisms, logical sequences, analogies, etc., along with Analytical Reasoning questions on series, directions, clocks & calendars, arrangements, and puzzles to name a few.
- **General Awareness and Current Affairs:** The General Awareness section includes static general knowledge, while questions on Current Affairs will gauge a candidate's knowledge of national & international current affairs.

CUET 2022 may or may not have a section on subject knowledge. Once the exam notification is out in March, there will be more clarity on this matter.

While there is no syllabus explicitly mentioned by CUET, the broad idea is always presented. One must look at the previous years' papers and solve the sample papers available to form a basic understanding.

About University of Delhi

University of Delhi (commonly known as DU) was established in 1922 and is one of the largest Universities in the country. With 16 faculties, 86 academic departments, 90 colleges and 540 programs on offer, Delhi University is no doubt one of the sought-after University in the country.

With 1, 96,000 students enrolled in UG programs, Delhi University is a valued university and constantly ranked among the top in the country. DU bagged 11th Rank in NIRF 2020 and ranked 6th in QS India Rankings 2020. The University has two Campuses: North and South.

DU UG Programs

Delhi University offers several programs at the undergraduate level. With more than 60 constituent colleges, the Delhi University offers many undergraduate courses.

Please refer to the table below for the important undergraduate courses offered by the DU and the intake across each program.

Program	Intake
B. A (Pass)	11249
B. A (Hons) Geography	788
B. A (Hons) Economics	2754
B. A (Hons) History	2791
B. A (Hons) Political Science	3657
B. A (Hons) Sociology	596
B. A (Hons) Psychology	670
B. A (Hons) Applied Psychology	252
B. A (Hons) Social Work	133
B. A (Hons) Philosophy	783
B. A (Hons) English	2886
B. A (Hons) Hindi	2829
B. A (Hons) Sanskrit	1407
B. A (Hons) Punjabi	214
B. A (Hons) Urdu	207
BA(Hons) French	49

Program	Intake
BA(Hons) German	49
BA(Hons) Spanish	49
BA(Hons) Italian	49
B. Com (Hons)	7953
B.Com (Pass)	7854
Program	Intake
B.Sc. (H) Biomedical Science	162
B.Sc. (H) Botany	937
B.Sc. (H) Chemistry	1487
B.Sc. (H) Computer Science	1265
B.Sc. (H) Electronics	624
B.Sc. (H) Mathematics	2428
B.Sc. (H) Physics	1659
B.Sc. (H) Zoology	944
B.Sc. Life Sciences	1515
B.Sc. Physical Science with Chemistry	703
B.Sc. Physical Science with Computer Science	553
B.Sc. Physical Science with Electronics	247
B. Sc (Hons.) Statistics	476
B. Sc. (Prog.) Applied Physical Science Industrial Chemistry	96
B.Sc. (Hons.) Home Science	900
B. Sc. (Hons.) Psychology	57
B.Sc. (H) Food Technology	179
B.Sc. (H)Instrumentation	99
B.Sc. (H) Microbiology	238
B.Sc. (H) Polymer Science	59
B.SC. Mathematical Science	224
B.SC. (Hons.) Biochemistry	146
B.SC. Industrial Chemistry	78
B.Sc. (Prog.) Physical Science	940
B.SC. (Hons.) Geology	98

DU UG Programs Eligibility:

As the University offers multiple programs and separate intake for male and female candidates, it is important to check the university official website regularly to keep oneself updated about the eligibility for each program, which can change.

DU UG Admissions:

Until 2021, Delhi University admitted students on the basis of class XII marks. From the academic year 2022, admissions to UG programs offered Delhi University will be based on CUET. CUET will be a common entrance for admissions to UG programs offered by all the Central Universities in the country.

Delhi University UG Programs Reservation:

DU being a Central University offers reservations in admissions according to central government rules.

Schedule Caste (SC): 15% of the total seats are reserved for students who belong to SC category.

Schedule Tribe (ST): 7.5% of the total seats are reserved for students belonging to ST Category.

Other Backward Classes (OBC): 27% of the total intake is reserved for students from Other Backward Classes (OBC), excluding those from creamy layer.

Economically Weaker Section (EWS): The University has reserved 10% seats for EWS category, in accordance with the directive of Ministry of Education.

Persons with Disability (PWD): 5% of the seats are reserved on horizontal basis for students from PWD category.

About BHU

Banaras Hindu University (BHU), situated in the holy city of Varanasi, was founded by Pandit Madan Mohan Malviya in cooperation with Dr. Annie Besant, in 1916 under the act of Parliament-B.H.U Act, 1915. BHU, which is a Central University, comprises of 6 Institutes, 14 Faculties, 144 academic departments, and 4 Inter-disciplinary centers, spread over 1300 acres. The University consists of 15,000 students, 1700 teachers and 8000 non-teaching staff.

BHU was ranked 3rd among the Universities in India in 2020. According to university submissions for NIRF 2021, BHU has 10, 585 students pursuing UG programs, of which 236 students are foreign nationals.

BHU UG Programs

BHU offers a host of undergraduate programs including medical and engineering. Through its various faculties, BHU offers a range of programs which caters to students learning abilities. The University along with its main campus, also offers the undergraduate courses from the following colleges: Mahila Mahavidyalaya (MMV); Arya Mahila Post Graduate College (AMPGC), Vasant Kanya Mahavidyalaya (VKM); Vasanta College for Women (VCW); DAV Post Graduate College (DAVPGC) and Rajiv Gandhi South Campus (RGSC).

Please refer to the table below for the important undergraduate courses offered by BHU and the intake across each program/campuses.

Faculty of Arts				
Course	Campus	Intake	Status	Duration
B.A (Hons) Arts	Faculty of Arts	765	Co-Ed	3 Years
	Mahila Mahavidyalaya	286	Women	3 Years
	Arya Mahila Post Graduate College	383	Women	3 Years
	Vasant Kanya Mahavidyalaya	286	Women	3 Years
	Vasanta College for Women	412	Women	3 Years
	DAV Post Graduate College	309	Co-Ed	3 Years
Faculty of Social Sciences				
Course	Campus	Intake	Status	Duration
B.A (Hons) Social Sciences [incl. B. A (Hons) Economics]	Faculty of Social Sciences	573	Co-Ed	3 Years
	Mahila Mahavidyalaya	193	Women	3 Years
	Arya Mahila Post Graduate College	383	Women	3 Years
	Vasant Kanya Mahavidyalaya	249	Women	3 Years
	Vasanta College for Women	210	Women	3 Years
	DAV Post Graduate College	326	Co-Ed	3 Years

Faculty of Commerce				
Course	Campus	Intake	Status	Duration
B. Com (Hons)	Faculty of Commerce	286	Co-Ed	3 Years
	Vasant Kanya Mahavidyalaya	96	Women	3 Years
	Arya Mahila Post Graduate College	96	Women	3 Years
	DAV Post Graduate College	227	Co-Ed	3 Years
	Rajiv Gandhi South Campus, Mirzapur	114	Co-Ed	3 Years
B. Com (Hons) Financial Markets Management	Faculty of Commerce	62	Co-Ed	3 Years
	Rajiv Gandhi South Campus, Mirzapur	62	Co-Ed	3 Years
Institute of Science				
Course	Campus	Intake	Status	Duration
B.Sc (Hons) Maths Group	Faculty of Science	573	Co-Ed	3 Years
	Mahila Mahavidyalaya	96	Women	3 Years
B.Sc (Hons) Bio Group	Faculty of Science	383	Co-Ed	3 Years
	Mahila Mahavidyalaya	193	Women	3 Years

Faculty of Visual Arts				
Course	Campus	Intake	Status	Duration
B.F.A (Bachelor of Fine Arts)	Faculty of Visual Arts	96	Co-Ed	4 Years
Faculty of Arts				
Bachelor of Vocation (Retail and Logistics Management)	Rajiv Gandhi South Campus	62	Co-Ed	3 Years
Bachelor of Vocation (Hospitality & Tourism Management)	Rajiv Gandhi South Campus	62	Co-Ed	3 Years
Bachelor of Vocation (Fashion Designing and Event Management)	Rajiv Gandhi South Campus	62	Co-Ed	3 Years
Bachelor of Vocation (Modern Office Management)	Rajiv Gandhi South Campus	62	Co-Ed	3 Years
Bachelor of Vocation (Food Processing & Management)	Rajiv Gandhi South Campus	62	Co-Ed	3 Years
Bachelor of Vocation (Medical Lab. & Technology)	Rajiv Gandhi South Campus	62	Co-Ed	3 Years

BHU UG Programs Eligibility:

Each of the courses have different eligibility for admissions. To be eligible for admissions, one must fulfil all the criteria as laid down by the respective faculties of the University.

B.A (Hons) Arts/ B.A (Hons) Social Sciences: Candidate must not be more than 22 years of age and must have passed class XII or equivalent with minimum 50% marks in aggregate.

B.A (Hons) Economics: Candidate must not be more than 22 years of age and must have passed class XII or equivalent with minimum 50% marks in aggregate along with mathematics as one of the papers.

B. Com (Hons)/B. Com (Hons) Financial Markets Management: Candidate must not be more than 22 years of age and must have passed class XII or equivalent with minimum 50% marks in aggregate with Commerce/ Economics/Maths/Computer Science/Finance/Financial Markets Management as one of the subjects.

B. Sc (Hons) Maths Group: Candidate must not be more than 22 years of age and must have passed class XII or equivalent with minimum 50% marks in aggregate in the subjects Physics, Maths plus any one of the following: Chemistry, Statistics, Geology, Computer Science, Information Technology and Geography and must have passed in each of the concerned three subjects.

B. Sc (Hons) Bio Group: Candidate must not be more than 22 years of age and must have passed class XII or equivalent with minimum 50% marks in aggregate in the subjects Physics, Chemistry plus any one of the following: Biology, Geology and Geography and must have passed in each of the concerned three subjects.

B. F. A (Bachelor of Fine Arts): Candidate must not be more than 22 years of age and must have passed class XII or equivalent with minimum 50% marks in aggregate.

Bachelor of Vocation: Candidate must have passed class XII or equivalent in any stream (Science for Food Processing and Medical Lab Technology) or level 4 NSQF certificate.

BHU UG Admissions:

Until 2021, admissions to BHU UG courses were based on Undergraduate Entrance Test (UET) conducted by the University. From the academic year 2022, admissions to UG programs offered by BHU will be based on CUET, which will replace the UET. CUET will be a common entrance for admissions to UG programs offered by all the Central Universities in the country.

BHU UG Programs Reservation:

BHU being a Central University offers reservations in admissions according to central government rules.

Schedule Caste (SC): 15% of the total seats are reserved for students who belong to SC category.

Schedule Tribe (ST): 7.5% of the total seats are reserved for students belonging to ST Category.

Other Backward Classes (OBC): 27% of the total intake is reserved for students from Other Backward Classes (OBC), excluding those from creamy layer.

Economically Weaker Section (EWS): The University has reserved 10% seats for EWS category, in accordance with the directive of Ministry of Education.

Persons with Disability (PWD): 5% of the seats are reserved on horizontal basis for students from PWD category.

About JNU

Ever wondered which University, the cadets from National Defence Academy (NDA) graduate from? Yes. It is Jawaharlal Nehru University (JNU). JNU started in the year 1969, three years after the act of Parliament in 1966. With several academic centres of JNU declared "Centres of Excellence" by the University Grants Commission, JNU has been ranked No. 1 by National Assessment and Accreditation Council (NAAC). JNU has been ranked No. 2 by National Institutional Ranking Framework (NIRF) 2020 and has been awarded the Best University Award by the President of India in 2017. The European Commission has awarded the Jean Monnet Centre of Excellence for European Union Studies in India (CEEUSI) to Jawaharlal Nehru University in 2018. This is one of the highest international recognition for any European Studies programme.

JNU was the first University to start integrated five-year Master of Arts in Language Courses. JNU actively collaborates with National and International Universities for student and faculty exchange programs.

According to university submissions for NIRF 2020, JNU has 1,048 students pursuing UG programs, of which 46 are foreign nationals.

JNU UG Programs

JNU offers a limited program at the undergraduate level, unlike other universities. The focus at undergraduate has been largely on language courses. In 2018, JNU started two programs in engineering and plans to add a few more specializations in future.

Please refer to the table below for the important undergraduate courses offered by JNU and the intake across each program.

School	Program	Intake	Duration
School of Language, Literature and Cultural Studies	B. A (Hons) Pashto	19	3 Years
	B. A (Hons) Persian	39	3 Years
	B. A (Hons) Arabic	39	3 Years
	B. A (Hons) Japanese	48	3 Years
	B. A (Hons) Korean	39	3 Years
	B. A (Hons) Chinese	44	3 Years
	B. A (Hons) French	48	3 Years
	B. A (Hons) German	48	3 Years
	B. A (Hons) Russian	68	3 Years
	B. A (Hons) Spanish	39	3 Years

School of Sanskrit and Indic Studies	B. Sc - M. Sc Integrated Program in Ayurveda Biology	20	5 Years
School of Engineering	B. Tech in Computer Science and Engineering & MS/M. Tech in Social Sciences/Humanities/Science/Technology	25	5 Years
	B. Tech in Electronics and Communication Engineering & MS/M. Tech in Social Sciences/Humanities/Science/Technology	25	5 Years

JNU UG Programs Eligibility:

Each of the courses have different eligibility for admissions. To be eligible for admissions, one must fulfil all the criteria as laid down by the respective faculties of the University.

B.A (Hons) Language Courses: Candidate must not be less than 17 years of age and must have passed Senior School Certificate (10+2) or equivalent examination with minimum of 45% marks.

B. Sc - M. Sc Integrated Program in Ayurveda Biology: Candidate must not be less than 17 years of age and must have passed Senior School Certificate (10+2) or equivalent examination with minimum of 45% marks.

B. Tech-M. Tech: Based on JEE Mains

JNU UG Admissions:

Until 2021, admissions to JNU UG courses were based on JNU Entrance Examination (JNUEE) conducted by the National Testing Agency (NTA). From the academic year 2022, admissions to UG programs offered by JNU will be based on CUET, which will replace the JNUEE. CUET will be a common entrance for admissions to UG programs offered by all the Central Universities in the country.

JNU UG Programs Reservation:

JNU being a Central University offers reservations in admissions according to central government rules.

Schedule Caste (SC): 15% of the total seats are reserved for students who belong to SC category.

Schedule Tribe (ST): 7.5% of the total seats are reserved for students belonging to ST Category.

Other Backward Classes (OBC): 27% of the total intake is reserved for students from Other Backward Classes (OBC), excluding those from creamy layer. Also, Central List of Caste to be followed.

Economically Weaker Section (EWS): The University has reserved 10% seats for EWS category, in accordance with the directive of Ministry of Education.

Persons with Disability (PWD): 5% of the seats are reserved on horizontal basis for students from PWD category.

About Jamia Milia Islamia

Jamia Milia Islamia (JMI) was founded in 1920 in Aligarh and became a Central University in 1988 by the act of Parliament. Jamia in Urdu stands for University and Milia means National, making Jamia Milia Islamia a National University. Jamia Milia Islamia moved to Delhi in 1925 and shifted to its present campus in Okhla in 1935.

Jamia Milia Islamia is a NAAC accredited University with grade "A" and was placed 10th in NIRF Rankings 2020. According to submissions made by University for NIRF 2021, Jamia Milia Islamia has a total of 5,911 students pursuing undergraduate courses at the University, of which 105 are foreign nationals. The University also manage to place a total of 681 UG students with an average salary ranging 4.2 Lacs-6.0 Lacs.

JMI UG Programs

Jamia Milia Islamia (JMI) offers a host of undergraduate programs for students. Through its various faculties, JMI offers a range of programs which caters to students learning abilities.

Please refer to the table below for the important undergraduate courses offered by Jamia Milia Islamia and the intake across each program.

Faculty	Course	Intake	Duration
Faculty of Humanities and Language	B. A (Hons) English	60	3 Years
	B. A (Hons) Hindi	40	3 Years
	B. A (Hons) Mass Media-Hindi	40	3 Years
	B. A (Hons) History	60	3 Years
	Bachelor of Hotel Management (BHM)	40	3 Years
	Bachelor of Tourism and Travel Management	40	3 Years
	B. Voc (Food Production)	40	3 Years
Faculty of Social Sciences	Bachelor of Arts (B. A)	68	3 Years
	B. Com (Hons)	55	3 Years
	BBA (Bachelor of Business Administration)	44	3 Years
	B. A (Hons) Economics	53	3 Years
	B. A (Hons) Sociology	42	3 Years
	B. A (Hons) Political Science	42	3 Years
	B. A (Hons) Psychology	42	3 Years
Faculty of Natural Sciences	B. Sc (Bachelor of Science)	50	3 Years
	B. Sc Biosciences	40	3 Years
	B. Sc Biotechnology	35	3 Years
	B. Sc (Hons) Chemistry	40	3 Years
	B. A/B. Sc (Hons) Geography	60	3 Years
	B. Sc (Hons) Mathematics	45	3 Years
	B. Sc (Hons) Applied Mathematics	45	3 Years
	B. Sc (Hons) Physics	45	3 Years
Faculty of Fine Arts	Bachelor of Fine Arts (Applied Art)	30	4 Years
	Bachelor of Fine Arts (Art Education)	20	4 Years
	Bachelor of Fine Arts (Painting)	20	4 Years
	Bachelor of Fine Arts (Sculpture)	10	4 Years

JMI UG Programs Eligibility:

Each of the courses have different eligibility for admissions. To be eligible for admissions, one must fulfil all the criteria as laid down by the respective faculties of the University.

B. Com (Hons) /BBA /B. A (Hons) Economics: Candidate must have passed class XII or equivalent with a minimum of 50% marks in five subjects.

BHM/BTTM/B. Voc (Food Production): Candidate must have passed class XII or equivalent with a minimum of 45% marks in five subjects.

B. A (Hons) Mass Media/B. A (Hons) Hindi: Candidate must have passed class XII or equivalent with a minimum of 45% marks in five subjects.

B. Sc/B. Sc (Hons): Candidate must have passed class XII or equivalent with minimum 50% marks in each of the science subjects i.e. Physics, Chemistry and Mathematics and 50% marks in aggregate of best 5-subjects.

JMI UG Admissions:

Until 2021, admissions to JMI UG courses were based on Entrance Test (JMI-ET) conducted by the University. From the academic year 2022, admissions to UG programs offered by JMI will be based on CUET, which will replace the JMI-ET. CUET will be a common entrance for admissions to UG programs offered by all the Central Universities in the country.

JMI UG Programs Reservation:

JMI is a minority reservation-based University and accordingly, seats are reserved for candidates as per the norms laid down by the University.

Muslim Minority: 30% of the total seats are reserved for Muslim applicants; 10% of the total seats are reserved for women applicants who are Muslim; 10% of the total intake is for OBC-NC candidates who are Muslims.

Persons with Disability (PWD): 5% of the seats are reserved for students from PWD category.

Jamia Students: 5% seats in all Undergraduate Programs shall be filled by internal students of Jamia who have passed their qualifying examination of the concerned programme (X or XII) from Jamia Schools as regular students.

In addition, Jamia Milia Islamia has supernumerary seats for Kashmiri Migrants and students from Jammu and Kashmir.

About Aligarh Muslim University

Aligarh Muslim University also referred as AMU was established by Sir Syed Ahmad Khan in 1875. The University started as Muhammadan Anglo-Oriental College and became a University (AMU) in 1920. The university has been ranked 801–1000 in the QS World University Rankings of 2021 and 17 in India by the National Institutional Ranking Framework in 2020.

Aligarh Muslim University is institution of national importance, under the seventh schedule of the Constitution of India.

AMU UG Programs

Aligarh Muslim University offers several programs at the undergraduate level. With 7 constituent colleges, the Aligarh Muslim University offers many undergraduate courses.

Please refer to the table below for the important undergraduate courses offered by the AMU and the intake across each program.

Course	Intake	Duration
B. Sc (Hons) Home Science	30*	3 Years
B.Sc (Hons) Agriculture	40	4 Years
B. A (Hons) Arabic	20+10*	3 Years
B. A (Hons) Communicative English	15+20*	3 Years
B. A (Hons) English	40+35*	3 Years
B. A (Hons) Hindi	40+25*	3 Years
B. A (Hons) Geography	50+20*	3 Years
B. A (Hons) Linguistics	20+25*	3 Years
B. A (Hons) Persian	15+25*	3 Years
B. A (Hons) Philosophy	20+10*	3 Years
B. A (Hons) Quaranic Studies	10+10*	3 Years
B. A (Hons) Sanskrit	15+10*	3 Years
B. A (Hons) Urdu	40+50*	3 Years
Bachelor of Fine Arts	15+15*	3 Years
B. Com (Hons)	180+100*	3 Years
B. Voc Production Technology	50	3 Years
B Voc Polymer and Coating Technology	50	3 Years
B. Voc Fashion Design and Garment Technology	50	3 Years
B. A (Hons) Chinese	20	3 Years
B. A (Hons) French	20	3 Years
B. A (Hons) German	20	3 Years

B. A (Hons) Russian	20	3 Years
B. A (Hons) Spanish	20	3 Years
B. Sc (Hons) Biochemistry	30+30*	3 Years
B. Sc (Hons) Botany	60+40*	3 Years
B. Sc (Hons) Zoology	60+45*	3 Years
B. Sc (Hons) Physics	120+35*	3 Years
B. Sc (Hons) Chemistry	120+65*	3 Years
B. Sc (Hons) Mathematics	120+40*	3 Years
B. Sc (Hons) Geography	45+30*	3 Years
B. Sc (Hons) Geology	100+30*	3 Years
B. Sc (Hons) Statistics	60+30*	3 Years
B. Sc (Hons) Industrial Chemistry	20+10*	3 Years
B. Sc (Hons) Computer Applications	40+20*	3 Years

AMU UG Programs Eligibility:

As the University offers multiple programs and separate intake for male and female candidates, it is important to check the university official website regularly to keep oneself updated about the eligibility for each program, which can change.

AMU UG Admissions:

Until 2021, AMU conducted its own entrance test to admit students for the UG programs. From the academic year 2022, admissions to UG programs offered by Aligarh Muslim University will be based on CUET. CUET will be a common entrance for admissions to UG programs offered by all the Central Universities in the country.

University of Allahabad UG Programs Reservation:

Allahabad University being a Central University offers reservations in admissions according to central government rules. Kindly check the university website for further details.

MATHEMATICS

CHAPTER 1

Relations and Functions

Concept of Relations and Functions

Relation

Definition: If $(a, b) \in R$, we say that a is related to b under the relation R and we write it as aRb.

Domain of a relation: The set of first components of all the ordered pairs which belong to R is the domain of R.

$$\text{Domain } (R) = \left\{a \in A : (a,b) \in R \,\forall\, b \in B\right\}$$

Range of a relation: The set of second components of all the ordered pairs which belong to R is the domain of R.

$$\text{Range of } R = \left\{b \in B : (a,b) \in R \,\forall\, a \in A\right\}$$

Types of relations:

- **Empty relation:** Empty relation is the relation R from X to Y if no element of X is related to any element of Y, it is given by $R = \varphi \subset X \times Y$.

  For example, let $X = \{2,4,6\}, Y = \{8,10,12\}$

  $R = \left\{(a,b) : a \in X, b \in Y \text{ and } a + b \text{ is odd}\right\}$

  R is an empty relation.

- **Universal relation:** Universal relation is a relation R from X to Y if each element of X is related to every element of Y it is given by $R = X \times Y$.

  For example, let $X = \{x, y\}$, $Y = \{x, z\}$

  $R = \{(x, x), (y, z), (y, x), (y, z)\}$

  $R = X \times Y$, so relation R is a universal relation.

- **Reflexive relation:** Reflexive relation R in X is a relation with $(a, a) \in R \,\forall a \in X$.

  For example, let $X = \{x, y, z\}$ and relation R is given as

  $R = \{(x, x), (y, y), (z, z)\}$

  Here, R is a reflexive relation on X.

- **Symmetric relation:** Symmetric relation R in X is a relation satisfying $(a, b) \in R$ implies $(b, a) \in R$.

  For example, let $X = \{x, y z\}$ and relation R is given as

  $R = \{(x, y), (y, x)\}$

  Here, R is a symmetric relation on X.

- **Transitive relation:** Transitive relation R in X is a relation satisfying $(a, b) \in R$ and $(b, c) \in R$ implies that $(a, b) \in R$.

  For example, let $X = \{x, y, z\}$ and relation R is given as

  $R = \{(x, z), (z, y), (x, y)\}$

  Here, R is a transitive relation on X.

- **Equivalence relation:** It is a relation R in X which is reflexive, symmetric and transitive.

  For example, let $X = \{x, y, z\}$ and relation R is given as

  $R = \{(x, y), (x, x), (y, x), (y, y), (z, z), (x, z), (z, x), (y, z)\}$

  Here, R is reflexive, symmetric and transitive. So R is an equivalence relation on X.

- **Equivalence class** $[a]$ containing $a \in X$ for an equivalence relation R in X is the subset of X containing all elements b related to a.

Function

Definition: A rule f which associates each element of a non-empty set A with a unique element of another non-empty set B is called a function.

Types of functions:

- **Injective function:** A function $f : X \to Y$ is one-one (or injective) if $f(x_1) = f(x_2) \Rightarrow x_1 = x_2 \,\forall x_1, x_2 \in X$.

- **Surjective function:** A function $f : X \to Y$ is onto (or surjective) if given any $y \in Y$, $\exists x \in X$ such that $f(x) = y$.

- **Bijective function:** A function $f : X \to Y$ is one-one and onto (or bijective), if f is both one-one and onto.

- **Composite function:** The composition of functions $f : A \to B$ and $g : B \to C$ is the function $gof : A \to C$ given by $gof(x) = g(f(x)) \,\forall\, x \in A$

- **Invertible function:** A function $f : X \to Y$ is invertible if $\exists g : Y \to X$ such that $gof = I_X$ and $fog = I_Y$.

  A function $f : X \to Y$ is invertible if and only if f is one-one and onto.

- **Steps to find inverse of a function**

  Let $f(x) = y$ where $x \in X$ and $y \in Y$

  Solve $f(x) = y$ for x in terms of y.

  Now replace x with $f^{-1}(y)$ in the expression obtain from the above step.

  Finally to find the inverse function of $ff^{-1}(x)$ replace y with x in the expression obtained from the above step.

Binary Operations

- **Binary Operation:** A binary operation * on a set A is a function * from $A \times A$ to A. We denote $*(a, b)$ by $a * b$.

- An element $e \in X$ is the identity element for binary operation $* : X \times X \to X$, if $a * e = a = e * a \,\forall a \in X$.

- An element $a \in X$ is invertible for binary operation $* : X \times X \to X$, if there exists $b \in X$ such that $a * b = e = b * a$ where, e is the identity for the binary operation *. The element b is called inverse of a and is denoted by a^{-1}.

- An operation * on X is commutative if $a * b = b * a \,\forall a, b$ in X.

- An operation * on X is associative if $(a * b) * c = a * (b * c) \forall a, b, c$ in X.

Exercise

1. Let A = {1, 2, 3}. Then, the relation R = { (1, 1), (2, 2), (3, 3), (1, 2), (2, 1), (2, 3), (3, 2)} on A is-

   (a) Reflexive and transitive but not symmetric.

   (b) Symmetric and transitive but not reflexive.

   (c) Reflexive and symmetric but not transitive.

   (d) Reflexive, symmetric & transitive.

2. Let R be a relation on the set N of all natural numbers, defined by a R b $\Leftrightarrow$ a is a factor of b. Then, R is

   (a) Reflexive and symmetric, but not transitive.

   (b) Symmetric and transitive, but not reflexive.

   (c) Reflexive and transitive, but not symmetric.

   (d) An equivalence relation.

3. If R = {(x, y) : x + 2y = 8} is a relation on N, then, the range of R is

   (a) {1, 2, 3}   (b) {1, 2, 3, 4}

   (c) {1, 2, 3, 4, 5}   (d) {1}

4. If $R \to R$ is defined by f(x) = 3x + 2, then find f[f(x)]

   (a) 9x + 6   (b) 9x + 8

   (c) 6x + 8   (d) 6x + 9

5. A relation R on A reflexive, only when

   (a) $R^{-1} = R$

   (b) $RoR \subseteq R$

   (c) $I_A \subseteq R$, where I_A is the identity relation on A.

   (d) None of these

6. A relation R on A is symmetric, if

   (a) $I_A \subseteq R$ (b) $RoR \subseteq R$

   (c) $R^{-1} = R$ (d) None of these

7. A relation R on a set A is transitive, if

   (a) $R^{-1} = R$ (b) $I_A \subseteq R$

   (c) $RoR \subseteq R$ (d) None of these

8. Let $f : R \to R : f(x) = x^3$, then f is

   (a) One - one, onto

   (b) One - one, into

   (c) Many - one, onto

   (d) Many - one, into

9. If $f : Q \to Q : f(x) = 3x + 5$, then $f^{-1}(x) = ?$

   (a) $3x - 5$ (b) $\dfrac{1}{(3x - 5)}$

   (c) $\dfrac{1}{3}(x - 5)$ (d) None of these

10. If $f(x) = (x^2 - 1)$ and $g(x) = (3x + 1)$, then $(gof)(x) = ?$

    (a) $9x^2 + 6x$ (b) $3x^2 - 1$

    (c) $2x^2 - 1$ (d) $3x^2 - 2$

11. If the function $f : R \to R$ be defined by $f(x) = 2x - 3$ and $g : R \to R$ by $g(x) = x^3 + 5$, then find the value of $(fog)^{-1}(x)$

    (a) $\sqrt[3]{\dfrac{y-7}{2}}$ (b) $\sqrt[3]{\dfrac{2}{y-7}}$

    (c) $\sqrt{\dfrac{y-7}{7}}$ (d) None of these

12. If $f(x) = [x]$ and $g(x) = |x|$, then $(gof)\left(-\dfrac{5}{3}\right) - (fog)\left(-\dfrac{5}{3}\right) = ?$

    (a) 0   (b) 1

    (c) 2   (d) $\dfrac{1}{2}$

13. If $f\left(x + \dfrac{1}{x}\right) = x^2 + \dfrac{1}{x^2}, x \neq 0$, then $f(x) = ?$

    (a) x^2 (b) $(x^2 - 1)$

    (c) $(x^2 - 2)$ (d) None of these

14. If $f = \{(1, 2), (3, 5), (4, 1)\}$ and $g = \{(2, 3), (5, 1), (1, 3)\}$, then gof = ?

   (a) $\{(1, 3), (3, 1), (4, 3)\}$ (b) $\{(1, 5), (2, 5), (5, 2)\}$

   (c) $\{(3, 1), (1, 3), (3, 4)\}$ (d) $\{(5, 1), (5, 2), (2, 5)\}$

15. Let $f(x) = \dfrac{x}{\left(x^2 - 3x + 2\right)}$, then Dom (f) = ?

   (a) R   (b) $R - \{1\}$

   (c) $R - \{1, 2\}$ (d) None of these

16. Let $A = \{a, b, c\}$ and $R = \{(a, a), (b, b), (c, c) (b, c), (a, b)\}$ be a relation on A, then R is

   (a) Symmetric   (b) Transitive

   (c) Reflexive   (d) Equivalence

17. If $A = \{1, 2, 3\}$ and f, g, h are relations corresponding to the subsets of $A \times A$ indicated against them, which of f, g, h is a function?

   (a) $f = \{(1, 2), (3, 2)\}$

   (b) $g = \{(1, 2), (1, 3), (2, 3), (3, 2)\}$

   (c) $h = \{(1, 3), (2, 1), (3, 2)\}$

   (d) None of any f, g, h

18. Range of the function $f(x) = {}^{7-x}P_{x-3}$ is given by

   (a) $\{3, 4, 5\}$

   (b) $[1, 3]$

   (c) $\{1, 2, 3\}$

   (d) R

19. For real x, let $f(x) = x^3 + 5x + 1$, then

   (a) f is one-one but not onto R .

   (b) f is onto R not one-one

   (c) f is one-one and onto R

   (d) f is neither one-one nor onto R

20. Set A has 3 elements and set B has 4 elements. The number of injections that can be defined from A to B is

   (a) 144

   (b) 12

   (c) 24

   (d) 64

Answer Keys

1. (c)	2. (c)	3. (a)	4. (b)	5. (c)	6. (c)	7. (c)	8. (a)	9. (c)	10. (d)
11. (a)	12. (b)	13. (c)	14. (a)	15. (c)	16. (c)	17. (c)	18. (c)	19. (c)	20. (c)

Solutions

1. Since (1, 1), (2, 2), (3, 3) are in R,

   ∴ R is reflexive.

   Also, $(a, b) \in R \Rightarrow (b, a) \in R$.

   ∴ R is symmetric.

   But $(3, 2) \in R, (2, 1) \in R$, while $(3, 1) \notin R$.

   ∴ R is not transitive.

2. $a \,|\, a \Rightarrow R$ is is reflexive.

   $2 \,|\, 6$ but 6 is not a factor of 2.

   $a \,|\, b, b \,|\, c \Rightarrow c = bm, b = an$ for some m,n∈N

   $\Rightarrow c = amn$ for some m, n∈N $\Rightarrow a \,|\, c$

   ∴ R is reflexive and transitive but not symmetric.

3. $R = \{(x, y) : x + 2y = 8\}$ is a relation on N Then, we can say, $2y = 8 - x$

   $\Rightarrow y = \dfrac{8 - x}{2} = 4 - \dfrac{x}{2}$

   So, we can put the value of x, x = 2, 4, 6 only we get y = 3 at x = 2,

   y = 2 at x = 4

   and y = 1 at x = 6

   Hence, required range = $\{1, 2, 3\}$

4. According to the question,

   $f(x) = 3x + 2$

   Now, $f[f(x)] = 3(3x + 2) + 2$

   $= 9x + 6 + 2$

   $= 9x + 8$

5. A relation R on A is reflexive only when $I_A \subseteq R$.

6. A relation R on A is symmetric only when $R^{-1} = R$.

7. A relation R on A is transitive, if $RoR \subseteq R$.

8. $f(x_1) = f(x_2) \Rightarrow x_1^3 = x_2^3$

   $\Rightarrow x_1 = x_2$

   ∴ f is one - one.

   for each x∈R there exists

   $x^{\frac{1}{3}} \in R \Rightarrow f\left(x^{\frac{1}{3}}\right) = \left(x^{\frac{1}{3}}\right)^3 = x.$

   ∴ f is onto.

   Hence, f is one-one and onto.

9. Let $f(x) = y$, then

$x = f^{-1}(y)$

$y = 3x + 5 \Rightarrow x = \dfrac{1}{3}(y - 5)$

$\Rightarrow f^{-1}(y) = \dfrac{1}{3}(y - 5)$

$\therefore f^{-1}(x) = \dfrac{1}{3}(x - 5)$

10. $\because f(x) = (x^2 - 1)$ and $g(x) = (3x + 1)$

$\therefore (gof)(x) = g[f(x)]$

$= g[x^2 - 1]$

$= 3(x^2 - 1) + 1$

$= 3x^2 - 3 + 1$

$= 3x^2 - 2$

11. Let $y = (fog)(x)$ and $y = h(x)$

$\therefore y = f[g(x)] = f[x^3 + 5]$

$= 2x^3 + 7$

$\Rightarrow x = \sqrt[3]{\dfrac{y - 7}{2}} = h^{-1}(y)$

$\Rightarrow (fog)^{-1}(x) = \sqrt[3]{\dfrac{y - 7}{2}}$

12. $(gof)\left(-\dfrac{5}{3}\right) = g\left[f\left(-\dfrac{5}{3}\right)\right]$

$= g\left[-2 + \dfrac{1}{3}\right] = g(-2) = |-2| = 2$

and $(fog)\left(-\dfrac{5}{3}\right) = f\left[g\left(-\dfrac{5}{3}\right)\right] = f\left(\left|-\dfrac{5}{3}\right|\right)$

$= f\left(\dfrac{5}{3}\right) = f\left(1 + \dfrac{2}{3}\right)$

$= \left[1 + \dfrac{2}{3}\right] = 1$

$\therefore$ Given expression $= 2 - 1 = 1$

13. Let $x + \dfrac{1}{x} = z$, then

$f(z) = f\left(x + \dfrac{1}{x}\right) = \left(x^2 + \dfrac{1}{x^2}\right)$

$= \left(x + \dfrac{1}{x}\right)^2 - 2 = \left(z^2 - 2\right)$

$\therefore f(x) = (x^2 - 2)$

14. Dom (gof) = Dom (f)

$\therefore (gof)(1) = f(f(1)] = g(2) = 3$

$(gof)(3) = f(f(3)] = g(5) = 1$

$(gof)(4) = f[f(4)] = g(1) = 3$

$\therefore gof = \{(1,3), (3, 1), (4, 3)\}$

15. Given $f(x) = \dfrac{x}{(x - 1)(x - 2)}$

Clearly, $f(x)$ is not defined when

$x - 1 = 0$ or $x - 2 = 0$

i.e. when $x = 1$ or $x = 2$

$\therefore$ Dom $(f) = R - \{1, 2\}$.

16. Reflexive, $R = \{(a, 0) \forall a \varepsilon A\}$

17. Each and every elements of set A have different imager in set A

18. $f(x) = {}^{7-x}P_{x-3}$

$7 - x \in I$

$\& \ x - 3 \in I$

$7 - x \geq 0$

$x - 3 \geq 0$

$\Rightarrow 3 \leq x \leq 7$

$7 - x \geq x - 3$

$x \leq 5$

$x = 3, 4, 5$

Range $= \{f(3), f(4), f(5)\}$

$= \left\{{}^4P_0, {}^3P_1, {}^2P_2\right\}$

$= \{1, 3, 2\}$

19. $f(x) = x^3 + 5x + 1$

$f'(x) = 3x^2 + 5 > 0$

function is increasing

$\Rightarrow$ function is one-one range is R

20. Number of injective functions $= {}^4P_3 = 24$

CHAPTER 2

Inverse Trigonometric Functions

Inverse Trigonometric Functions

Definition of inverse trigonometric functions:

Inverse trigonometric functions are the inverse of trigonometric functions, we can represents them by using "-1" or arc on trigonometric functions. Also the Range of trigonometric function becomes the Domain of Inverse trigonometric function.

For ex: $x = \sin y$ will be represented as $y = \arcsin x$ or $y = \sin^{-1} x$.

Range of $x = \sin y$ is $[-1, 1]$ and Domain of $y = \arcsin x$ is $[-1, 1]$.

- The inverse trigonometric functions are also called as Inverse Circular Functions.
- Function: $y = \sin^{-1}x$

  Domain: $[-1, 1]$

  Range: $\left[\dfrac{-\pi}{2}, \dfrac{\pi}{2}\right]$

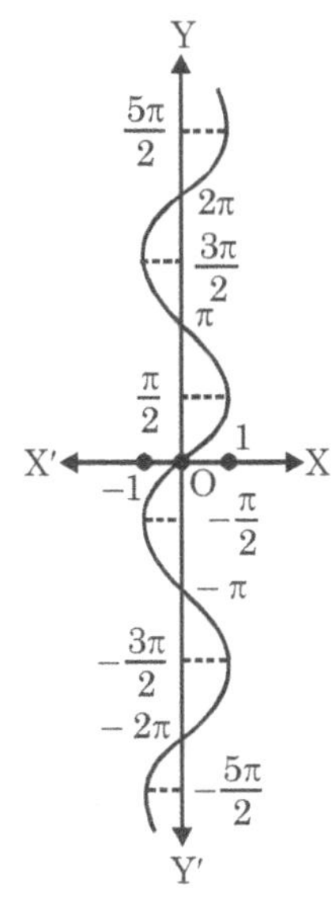

$$y = \sin^{-1} x$$

- Function: $y = \cos^{-1}x$

  Domain: $[-1, 1]$

  Range: $[0, \pi]$

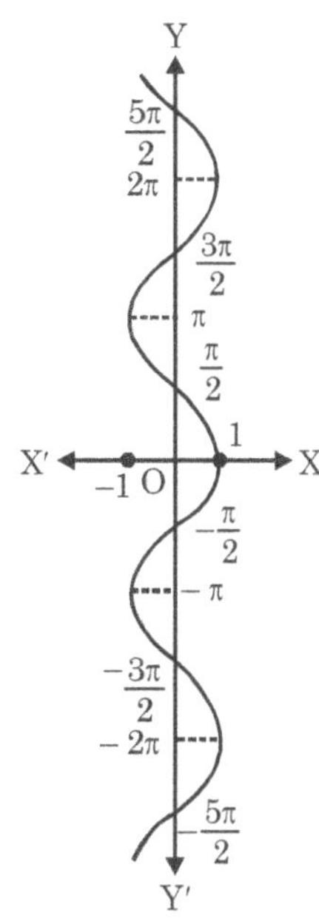

$$y = \cos^{-1} x$$

- Function: $y = \operatorname{cosec}^{-1}x$

  Domain: $R - (-1, 1)$

  Range: $\left[\dfrac{-\pi}{2}, \dfrac{\pi}{2}\right] - \{0\}$

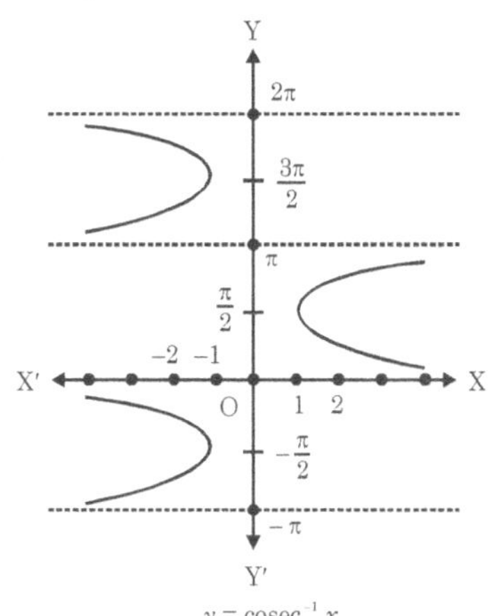

$$y = \operatorname{cosec}^{-1} x$$

- **Function:** $y = \sec^{-1}x$

  Domain: $R - (-1, 1)$

  Range: $[0, \pi] - \left\{\dfrac{\pi}{2}\right\}$

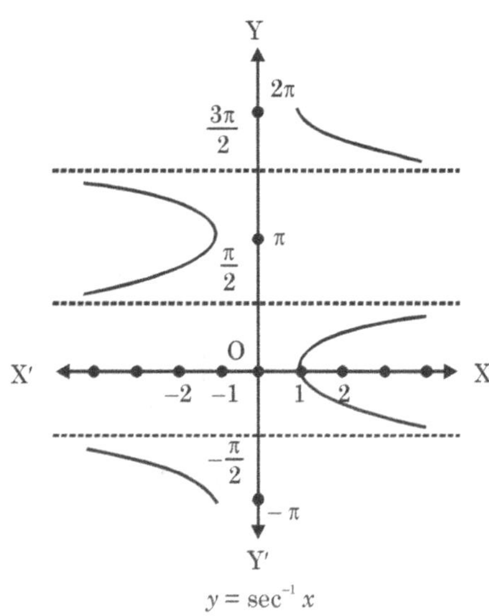

$$y = \sec^{-1}x$$

- **Function:** $y = \tan^{-1}x$

  Domain: R

  Range: $\left(\dfrac{-\pi}{2}, \dfrac{\pi}{2}\right)$

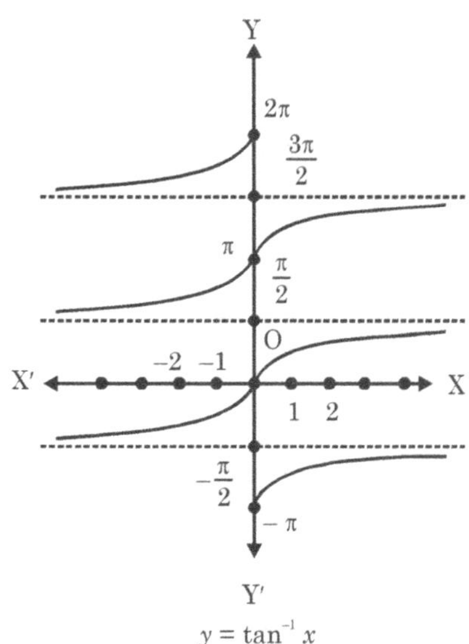

$$y = \tan^{-1}x$$

- **Function:** $y = \cot^{-1}x$

  Domain: R

  Range: $(0, \pi)$

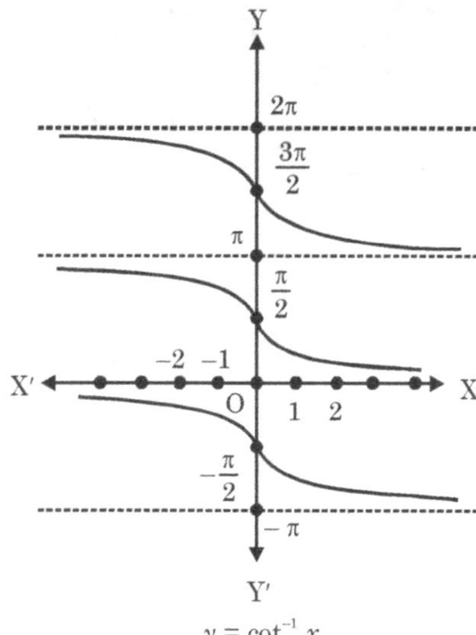

$$y = \cot^{-1}x$$

- **Properties:**

  - $\sin^{-1}(\sin x) = x$

  - $\cos^{-1}(\cos x) = x$

  - $\tan^{-1}(\tan x) = x$

  - $\operatorname{cosec}^{-1}(\operatorname{cosec} x) = x$

  - $\sec^{-1}(\sec x) = x$

  - $\cot^{-1}(\cot x) = x$

  - $\sin^{-1}(x) = \operatorname{cosec}^{-1}\left(\dfrac{1}{x}\right),\ x \in [-1, 1]$

  - $\operatorname{cosec}^{-1}(x) = \sin^{-1}\left(\dfrac{1}{x}\right),\ x \in (-\infty, -1] \cup [1, \infty)$

  - $\cos^{-1}(x) = \sec^{-1}\left(\dfrac{1}{x}\right),\ x \in [-1, 1]$

  - $\sec^{-1}(x) = \cos^{-1}\left(\dfrac{1}{x}\right),\ x \in (-\infty, -1] \cup [1, \infty)$

  - $\tan^{-1}(x) = \begin{cases} \cot^{-1}\left(\dfrac{1}{x}\right), & x > 0 \\[2mm] -\pi + \cot^{-1}\left(\dfrac{1}{x}\right), & x < 0 \end{cases}$

  - $\cot^{-1}(x) = \begin{cases} \tan^{-1}\left(\dfrac{1}{x}\right), & x > 0 \\[2mm] \pi + \tan^{-1}\left(\dfrac{1}{x}\right), & x < 0 \end{cases}$

  - $\sin^{-1}x + \cos^{-1}x = \dfrac{\pi}{2},\ x \in [-1, 1]$

  - $\tan^{-1}x + \cot^{-1}x = \dfrac{\pi}{2},\ x \in R$

  - $\operatorname{cosec}^{-1}x + \sec^{-1}x = \dfrac{\pi}{2},\ |x| \geq 1$

- $\sin^{-1}(-x) = -\sin^{-1}x$
- $\cos^{-1}(-x) = \pi - \cos^{-1}x$
- $\tan^{-1}(-x) = -\tan^{-1}x$
- $\cot^{-1}(-x) = \pi - \cot^{-1}x$
- $\sec^{-1}(-x) = \pi - \sec^{-1}x$
- $\operatorname{cosec}^{-1}(-x) = -\operatorname{cosec}^{-1}x$
- $\tan^{-1}x + \tan^{-1}y = \tan^{-1}\dfrac{x+y}{1-xy}$

- $\tan^{-1}x - \tan^{-1}y = \tan^{-1}\dfrac{x-y}{1+xy}$

- $2\tan^{-1}x = \begin{cases} \sin^{-1}\left(\dfrac{2x}{1+x^2}\right), & |x| \le 1 \\[2mm] \cos^{-1}\left(\dfrac{1-x^2}{1+x^2}\right), & |x| \ge 0 \\[2mm] \tan^{-1}\left(\dfrac{2x}{1-x^2}\right), & -1 < x < 1 \end{cases}$

Exercise

1. The principal value of $\cos^{-1}\left(\dfrac{-1}{2}\right)$ is

(a) $-\dfrac{\pi}{3}$

(b) $\dfrac{2\pi}{3}$

(c) $\dfrac{5\pi}{3}$

(d) None

2. The principal value of $\cot^{-1}\left(-\sqrt{3}\right)$ is

(a) $\dfrac{\pi}{6}$

(b) $-\dfrac{\pi}{6}$

(c) $\dfrac{5\pi}{6}$

(d) None

3. The value of $\sin^{-1}\left(\sin\dfrac{2\pi}{3}\right)$ is

(a) $\dfrac{2\pi}{3}$

(b) $-\dfrac{2\pi}{3}$

(c) $-\dfrac{\pi}{3}$

(d) $\dfrac{\pi}{3}$

4. The value of $\sin\left[2\tan^{-1}\left(\dfrac{8}{15}\right)\right]$ is

(a) $\dfrac{240}{289}$

(b) $\dfrac{230}{289}$

(c) 120

(d) None

5. If $\sec^{-1}\dfrac{1}{\sqrt{1-x^2}} + \cot^{-1}\dfrac{\sqrt{1-x^2}}{x} = \sin^{-1}K$, then the value of K is:

(a) $x\sqrt{1-x^2}$

(b) $2x\sqrt{1-x^2}$

(c) $\sqrt{1-x^2}$

(d) $2x$

6. The value of $[\tan^{-1}(\cot x) - \tan^{-1}(\cot 2x)]$ is

(a) $2x$

(b) x

(c) $3x$

(d) None

7. The value of $\sin^{-1}(\sin 750°)$ is

(a) $750°$

(b) $30°$

(c) $-30°$

(d) $150°$

8. $\tan^{-1}\left(\dfrac{1-\cos x}{\sin x}\right) = ?$

(a) x

(b) $\dfrac{x}{2}$

(c) $2x$

(d) None

9. $\tan^{-1}\sqrt{\dfrac{1-\cos x}{1+\cos x}} = ?$

(a) x

(b) $\dfrac{x}{2}$

(c) $2x$

(d) None

10. The value of $\cot^{-1}\left(\dfrac{1-x}{1+x}\right) = ?$

(a) $\dfrac{\pi}{4} - \tan^{-1}x$

(b) $\dfrac{\pi}{2} - \tan^{-1}x$

(c) $\dfrac{\pi}{4} + \tan^{-1}x$

(d) None of these

11. The value of $\cos^{-1}(4x^3 - 3x) = ?$

(a) $3x$

(b) $3\cos^{-1}x$

(c) $\cos^{-1}(3x)$

(d) None of these

12. The value of $\tan^{-1}\left(\dfrac{a\cos x - b\sin x}{b\cos x + a\sin x}\right)$ is

  (a) $\tan^{-1}\left(\dfrac{a}{b}\right) - x$ (b) $\tan^{-1}\left(\dfrac{a}{b}\right) + x$

  (c) $\tan^{-1}\left(\dfrac{b}{a}\right)$ (d) None of these

13. If $\sin^{-1}x + \sin^{-1}y = \dfrac{2\pi}{3}$, then $\cos^{-1}x + \cos^{-1}y = ?$

  (a) π (b) $\dfrac{2\pi}{3}$

  (c) $\dfrac{\pi}{3}$ (d) $\dfrac{\pi}{6}$

14. The range of $\sin^{-1}x$ is

  (a) $[0, \pi]$ (b) $\left[0, \dfrac{\pi}{2}\right]$

  (c) $\left[-\dfrac{\pi}{2}, \dfrac{\pi}{2}\right]$ (d) None

15. The domain of $\cos^{-1}x$ is

  (a) $[0, \pi]$ (b) $[-1, 1]$

  (c) $[0, 1]$ (d) None of these

16. Value of $\cos^{-1}\left(\cos\dfrac{7\pi}{6}\right)$ is equal to

  (a) $\dfrac{7\pi}{6}$ (b) $\dfrac{5\pi}{6}$

  (c) $\dfrac{\pi}{6}$ (d) $\dfrac{\pi}{3}$

17. $\sin(\cot^{-1}x)$ is equal to

  (a) $\sqrt{1+x^2}$ (b) x

  (c) $\left(1+x^2\right)^{-3/2}$ (d) $\left(1+x^2\right)^{-1/2}$

18. The range of $4\sin^{-1}(2x)$ is equal to

  (a) $\left[-\dfrac{\pi}{2}, \dfrac{\pi}{2}\right]$ (b) $[-2\pi, 2\pi]$

  (c) $[-\pi, \pi]$ (d) R

19. The value of $\cos(\tan^{-1}(\tan 2))$ is equal to

  (a) $\dfrac{1}{\sqrt{5}}$ (b) $-\dfrac{1}{\sqrt{5}}$

  (c) $\cos 2$ (d) $-\cos 2$

20. The value of $\sin\left[2\cos^{-1}\dfrac{\sqrt{5}}{3}\right]$ is equal to

  (a) $\dfrac{\sqrt{5}}{3}$ (b) $\dfrac{2\sqrt{5}}{3}$

  (c) $\dfrac{4\sqrt{5}}{3}$ (d) $\dfrac{4\sqrt{5}}{9}$

Answer Keys

1. (b)   2. (c)   3. (d)   4. (a)   5. (b)   6. (b)   7. (b)   8. (b)   9. (b)   10. (c)

11. (b)   12. (a)   13. (c)   14. (c)   15. (b)   16. (b)   17. (d)   18. (b)   19. (d)   20. (d)

Solutions

1. The range of $\cos^{-1}x$ is $[0, \pi]$

$$\therefore \cos^{-1}\left(-\dfrac{1}{2}\right) = \pi - \cos^{-1}\left(\dfrac{1}{2}\right)$$

$$= \left(\pi - \dfrac{\pi}{3}\right) = \dfrac{2\pi}{3}$$

2. The range of $\cot^{-1}x$ is $]0, \pi[$.

Let $\cot^{-1}\left(-\sqrt{3}\right) = y$, where $0 < y < \pi$.

Then, $\cot y = -\sqrt{3} = -\cot\dfrac{\pi}{6}$

$$= \cot\left(\pi - \dfrac{\pi}{6}\right) = \cot\dfrac{5\pi}{6}$$

$$\therefore y = \cot^{-1}\left(\cot\dfrac{5\pi}{6}\right) = \dfrac{5\pi}{6}$$

3. The range of $\sin^{-1}x$ is $\left[-\dfrac{\pi}{2}, \dfrac{\pi}{2}\right]$.

$$\therefore \sin\dfrac{2\pi}{3} = \sin\left(\pi - \dfrac{\pi}{3}\right) = \sin\dfrac{\pi}{3}.$$

and $\sin^{-1}\left(\sin\dfrac{2\pi}{3}\right) = \sin^{-1}\left(\sin\dfrac{\pi}{3}\right) = \dfrac{\pi}{3}$

4. We know that

$$2\tan^{-1}x = \sin^{-1}\left(\dfrac{2x}{1+x^2}\right)$$

$$\therefore\ 2\tan^{-1}\frac{8}{15} = \sin^{-1}\left\{\frac{2\times\dfrac{8}{15}}{1+\dfrac{64}{225}}\right\}$$

$$= \sin^{-1}\left(\frac{240}{289}\right)$$

Then, $\sin\left[2\tan^{-1}\dfrac{8}{15}\right] = \sin\left[\sin^{-1}\dfrac{240}{289}\right]$

$$= \frac{240}{289}$$

5. On putting $x = \sin\theta$, we get

L.H.S. $= \sec^{-1}(\sec\theta) + \cot^{-1}(\cot\theta)$

$= \theta + \theta = 2\theta = 2\sin^{-1}x$

$$= \sin^{-1}\left(2x\sqrt{1-x^2}\right)$$

$$\therefore\ k = 2x\sqrt{1-x^2}$$

6. Given expression

$$= \tan^{-1}\left[\tan\left(\frac{\pi}{2}-x\right)\right] - \tan^{-1}\left[\tan\left(\frac{\pi}{2}-2x\right)\right]$$

$$= \left(\frac{\pi}{2}-x\right) - \left(\frac{\pi}{2}-2x\right)$$

$$= \frac{\pi}{2}-x-\frac{\pi}{2}+2x = x$$

7. The range of $\sin^{-1}x$ is $\left[-\dfrac{\pi}{2},\dfrac{\pi}{2}\right]$

$\therefore\ \sin(750°) = \sin[2\times 360° + 30°] = \sin 30°$

$\Rightarrow \sin^{-1}[\sin(750°)] = \sin^{-1}(\sin 30°)$

$= 30°$

8. $\tan^{-1}\left(\dfrac{1-\cos x}{\sin x}\right) = \tan^{-1}\left\{\dfrac{2\sin^2\left(\dfrac{x}{2}\right)}{2\sin\left(\dfrac{x}{2}\right)\cos\left(\dfrac{x}{2}\right)}\right\}$

$$= \tan^{-1}\left(\tan\frac{x}{2}\right) = \frac{x}{2}$$

9. $\tan^{-1}\sqrt{\dfrac{1-\cos x}{1+\cos x}} = \tan^{-1}\sqrt{\dfrac{2\sin^2\left(\dfrac{x}{2}\right)}{2\cos^2\left(\dfrac{x}{2}\right)}}$

$$= \tan^{-1}\left(\tan\frac{x}{2}\right)$$

$$= \frac{x}{2}$$

10. On puting $x = \tan\theta$, we get

$$\cot^{-1}\left(\frac{1-x}{1+x}\right) = \cot^{-1}\left(\frac{1-\tan\theta}{1+\tan\theta}\right)$$

$$= \cot^{-1}\left[\tan\left(\frac{\pi}{4}-\theta\right)\right]$$

$$= \cot^{-1}\left[\cot\left(\frac{\pi}{2}-\left(\frac{\pi}{4}-\theta\right)\right)\right]$$

$$= \cot^{-1}\left[\cot\left(\frac{\pi}{4}+\theta\right)\right] = \left(\frac{\pi}{4}+\theta\right)$$

$$= \frac{\pi}{4}+\tan^{-1}x$$

11. On putting $x = \cos\theta$, we get

$\cos^{-1}(4x^3 - 3x) = \cos^{-1}(4\cos^3 x - 3\cos x]$

$= \cos^{-1}(\cos 3x) = 3x$

$= 3\cos^{-1}x$

12. On putting $a = r\sin\theta$ and $b = r\cos\theta$.

We get,

$$\tan^{-1}\left(\frac{a\cos x - b\sin x}{b\cos x + a\sin x}\right) = \tan^{-1}\left[\frac{\sin(\theta - x)}{\cos(\theta - x)}\right]$$

$= \tan^{-1}[\tan(\theta - x)]$

$= \theta - x$

$$= \tan^{-1}\left(\frac{a}{b}\right) - x$$

13. $\because\ \sin^{-1}x + \sin^{-1}y = \dfrac{2\pi}{3}$

$$\Rightarrow \left(\frac{\pi}{2}-\cos^{-1}x\right) + \left(\frac{\pi}{2}-\cos^{-1}y\right) = \frac{2\pi}{3}$$

$$\Rightarrow \cos^{-1}x + \cos^{-1}y = \left(\pi - \frac{2\pi}{3}\right) = \frac{\pi}{3}$$

14. The range of $\sin^{-1}x$ is $\left[-\dfrac{\pi}{2},\dfrac{\pi}{2}\right]$

15. The domain of $\cos^{-1}x$ is $[-1, 1]$.

16. $\cos^{-1}\left(\cos\dfrac{7\pi}{6}\right) = \cos^{-1}\cos\left(2\pi - \dfrac{7\pi}{6}\right)$

$$= \cos^{-1}\left(\cos\dfrac{5\pi}{6}\right) = \dfrac{5\pi}{6}$$

17. $\sin^{-1}\left(\cot^{-1}x\right) = \sin\left(\sin^{-1}\sqrt{\dfrac{1}{1+x^2}}\right) = \dfrac{1}{\sqrt{1+x^2}}$

$$= (1+x^2)^{-\frac{1}{2}}$$

18. $-\dfrac{\pi}{2} \le \sin^{-1}2x \le \dfrac{\pi}{2}$

$-2\pi \le 4\sin^{-1}2x \le 2\pi$

Range $[-2\pi, 2\pi]$

19. $\cos\left(\tan^{-1}\left(\tan^2\right)\right) = \cos\tan^{-1}\left(\tan(2-\pi)\right)$

$= \cos(2-\pi)$

$= \cos(\pi - 2)$

$= -\cos 2$

20. Let $\cos^{-1}\dfrac{\sqrt{5}}{3} = \theta$

$\cos\theta = \dfrac{\sqrt{5}}{3}$

$\sin\theta = \dfrac{2}{3}$

$\sin\left(2\cos^{-1}\dfrac{\sqrt{5}}{3}\right) = \sin 2\theta$

$= 2\sin\theta\cos\theta$

$= 2\times\dfrac{2}{3}\times\dfrac{\sqrt{5}}{3}$

$= \dfrac{4\sqrt{5}}{9}$

Matrices

CHAPTER 3

Matrix and Operations on Matrices

- A matrix is an ordered rectangular array of numbers or functions. The numbers are called the elements of the matrix.

$$A = \begin{bmatrix} a_{11} & a_{12} & a_{13} & \cdots & \cdots & a_{1n} \\ a_{21} & a_{22} & a_{23} & \cdots & \cdots & a_{2n} \\ a_{31} & a_{32} & a_{33} & \cdots & \cdots & a_{3n} \\ \cdot & \cdot & \cdot & \cdots & \cdots & \cdot \\ \cdot & \cdot & \cdot & \cdots & \cdots & \cdot \\ a_{m1} & a_{m2} & a_{m3} & \cdots & \cdots & a_{mn} \end{bmatrix}_{m \times n}$$

Example: $A = \begin{bmatrix} 4 & \frac{1}{2} & -2 \\ 0 & 3 & 5 \\ 1 & \sqrt{6} & -7 \end{bmatrix}$

- The order of the matrix is determined by $m \times n$ where m is the number of rows and n is the number of columns.
- The matrix with $m \times n$ order can be represented as $A = \left[a_{ij}\right]_{m \times n}; i, j \notin \mathbb{N}$ also $1 \le i \le m, 1 \le j \le n,$.

Types of Matrices

- Column matrix is a matrix which has only 1 column. It is defined as $A = [a_{ij}]_{m \times 1}$.

Example: $\begin{bmatrix} 2 \\ 3 \\ 4 \end{bmatrix}_{3 \times 1}$

- Row matrix is a matrix which has only row. It is defined as $B = [b_{ij}]_{1 \times n}$.

Example: $\begin{bmatrix} \sqrt{2} & -1 & 3 \end{bmatrix}_{1 \times 3}$

- The square matrix is the matrix which has equal number of rows and columns i.e. the matrix in which $m = n$. It is defined as $A = [a_{ij}]_{m \times m}$.

Example: $\begin{bmatrix} 3 & 9 & 1 \\ 7 & 6 & 3 \\ 9 & 0 & 2 \end{bmatrix}_{3 \times 3}$

- The square matrix $A = [a_{ij}]_{m \times m}$ is said to be a diagonal matrix if all its non-diagonal elements are zero. It is defined as $A = [a_{ij}]_{m \times m}$ if $a_{ij} = 0$, when $i \ne j$.
- A scalar matrix is the one in which the diagonal elements of a diagonal matrix are equal. It is defined as $A = [a_{ij}]_{m \times m}$ if $a_{ij} = 0$, when $i \ne j$ and $a_{ij} = k$, when $i = j$, where k is some constant.

Example: $\begin{bmatrix} 3 & 0 \\ 0 & 3 \end{bmatrix}$

- Identity matrix is the square matrix where the diagonal elements are all 1 and rest are all zero. It is defined as $A = [a_{ij}]_{m \times m}$ where $a_{ij} = 1$ if $i = j$ and $a_{ij} = 0$ if $i \ne j$.

Example: $\begin{bmatrix} 1 & 0 \\ 0 & 1 \end{bmatrix}_{2 \times 2}$

- A zero matrix is the one in which all the elements are zero.

Example: $\begin{bmatrix} 0 & 0 & 0 \\ 0 & 0 & 0 \\ 0 & 0 & 0 \end{bmatrix}_{3 \times 3}$

- Two matrices $A = [a_{ij}]$ and $B = [b_{ij}]$ are equal if they are of the same order and also each element of matrix A is equal to the corresponding element of Matrix B.
- The sum of the two matrices $A = [a_{ij}]$ and $B = [b_{ij}]$ of same order $m \times n$ is defined as $C = [c_{ij}]_{m \times n}$ where $c_{ij} = a_{ij} + b_{ij}$.
- If x is a scalar and $A = [a_{ij}]_{m \times n}$ is a matrix, then xA is the matrix obtained by multiplying each element of the matrix by the scalar x. It can be defined as $xA = x[a_{ij}]_{m \times m} = [x(a_{ij})]_{m \times n}$.
- $-A$ denotes the negative of a matrix. $-A = (-1)A$.
- The difference of the two matrices $A = [a_{ij}]$ and $B = [b_{ij}]$ of same order $m \times n$ is defined as $C = [c_{ij}]_{m \times n}$ where $c_{ij} = a_{ij} - b_{ij}$.

- If $A = [a_{ij}]$ and $B = [b_{ij}]$ are matrices of the same order, say $m \times n$ then $A + B = B + A$. It is called the commutative law.
- If $A = [a_{ij}]$, $B = [b_{ij}]$ and $C = [c_{ij}]$ are the three matrices of same order, say $m \times n$, then $(A + B) + C = A + (B + C)$. It is called the associative law.
- If $B = [b_{ij}]$ is a matrix of order $m \times n$ and O is a zero matrix of the order $m \times n$, then $B + O = O + B = B$. O is the additive identity for matrix addition.
- If $B = [b_{ij}]$ is a matrix of order $m \times n$ then we have another matrix as $-B = [-b_{ij}]$ of the order $m \times n$ such that $B + (-B) = (-B) + B = O$. So, $-B$ is the additive inverse of B.
- If $A = [a_{ij}]$ and $B = [b_{ij}]$ are matrices of the same order, say $m \times n$, and x and y are the scalars, then
  - $x(A + B) = xA + xB$
  - $(x + y)A = xA + yA$
- If $A = [a_{ij}]$ is a matrix of order $m \times n$ and $B = [b_{jk}]$ is a matrix of order $n \times p$ then the product of the matrices A and B is a matrix C of order $m \times p$. It can be denoted as $AB = C = [C_{ik}]_{m \times p}$, where

$$c_{ik} = \sum_{j=1}^{n} a_{ij} b_{jk}$$

- Properties of multiplication of matrices are as follows:
  - The associative law: If there are 3 matrices X, Y and Z we have $(XY)Z = X(YZ)$
  - Distributive law: If there are 3 matrices X, Y and Z then:
    $X(Y + Z) = XY + XZ$
    $(X + Y)Z = XZ + YZ$
  - The existence of multiplicative identity: For every square matrix X, there exists an identity matrix of the same order such that $IX = XI = X$.
  - Multiplication is not commutative: $AB \neq BA$

Transpose of a Matrix and Symmetric and Skew Symmetric Matrices

- The transpose of the matrix $A = [a_{ij}]_{m \times n}$ is denoted by $A^T = [a_{ji}]_{n \times m}$ and is obtained by interchanging the rows with columns of matrix A.

Example: If $A = \begin{bmatrix} -4 & 1 \\ 2 & 0 \end{bmatrix}$, then $A^T = \begin{bmatrix} -4 & 2 \\ 1 & 0 \end{bmatrix}$.

- Some properties of transpose of the matrices are as follows:
  If A and B are matrices of suitable orders then
  - $(A^T)^T = A$
  - $(kA)^T = kA^T$ (Where k is any constant)
  - $(A + B)^T = A^T + B^T$
  - $(AB)^T = B^T A^T$

- If $A^T = A$ then the square matrix $A = [a_{ij}]$ is said to be symmetric matrix for all possible values of i and j.

Example: $\begin{bmatrix} 1 & 2 & 4 \\ 2 & 3 & 7 \\ 4 & 7 & 0 \end{bmatrix}$

- If $A^T = -A$ then the square matrix $A = [a_{ij}]$ is said to be skew symmetric matrix for all the possible values of i and j. All the diagonal elements of a skew symmetric matrix are zero.

Example: $A = \begin{bmatrix} 1 & 2 & -4 \\ -2 & 3 & 7 \\ 4 & -7 & 0 \end{bmatrix}$ then

$$A^T = \begin{bmatrix} 1 & -2 & 4 \\ 2 & 3 & -7 \\ -4 & 7 & 0 \end{bmatrix} = -\begin{bmatrix} 1 & 2 & -4 \\ -2 & 3 & 7 \\ 4 & -7 & 0 \end{bmatrix} = -A$$

- For any square matrix A with real number entries, $A + A^T$ is a symmetric matrix and $A - A^T$ is a skew symmetric matrix.
- Any square matrix can be expressed as the sum of a symmetric matrix and a skew symmetric matrix

  i.e $A = \dfrac{1}{2}\left(A + A^T\right) + \dfrac{1}{2}\left(A - A^T\right)$

Inverse of matrices by Elementary row transformation

- Elementary operation of a matrix are as follows:
  - Interchanging of two rows or columns: $R_i \leftrightarrow R_j$ or $C_i \leftrightarrow C_j$ represents that the ith row or column is interchanged with j^{th} row or column.
  - Multiplying the row or column of matrix by non- zero scalar: $R_i \rightarrow lR_j$ or $C_i \rightarrow lC_j$ where I is any non- zero number, represents the ith row or column is multiplied by I.
  - Adding the elements of any row or column to another row or column: $R_i \rightarrow R_i + lR_j$ or $C_i \rightarrow C_i + lC_j$, where I is any non-zero number, represents that the jth row or column is multiplied by I and added to respective element of ith row or column.
- If X is a square matrix of order n and if there exists another square matrix Y of the same order n, such that $XY = YX = I$, then Y is called the inverse matrix of X and it is denoted by X^{-1}.
- The inverse of a matrix can be found using row or column operations.
- If Y is the inverse of X, then X is also the inverse of Y. Also, $(XY)^{-1} = Y^{-1}X^{-1}$
- Inverse of a square matrix, if it exists, is unique.

Exercise

1. If $A = \begin{bmatrix} 1 & K & 3 \\ 3 & K & -2 \\ 2 & 3 & -4 \end{bmatrix}$ is a singular matrix, then $K = ?$

(a) $\dfrac{16}{3}$

(b) $\dfrac{34}{5}$

(c) $\dfrac{33}{2}$

(d) None

2. If $\begin{bmatrix} 1 & -2 \\ 3 & 6 \end{bmatrix} + 2X = \begin{bmatrix} 5 & -6 \\ -7 & 4 \end{bmatrix}$, then $X = ?$

(a) $\begin{bmatrix} -2 & 2 \\ -5 & 1 \end{bmatrix}$

(b) $\begin{bmatrix} 2 & -2 \\ 5 & -1 \end{bmatrix}$

(c) $\begin{bmatrix} 2 & -2 \\ -5 & -1 \end{bmatrix}$

(d) None of these

3. If $A = \begin{bmatrix} \alpha & \beta \\ \gamma & \delta \end{bmatrix}$, then adj $A = ?$

(a) $\begin{bmatrix} \delta & -\gamma \\ -\beta & \alpha \end{bmatrix}$

(b) $\begin{bmatrix} \delta & -\beta \\ -\gamma & \alpha \end{bmatrix}$

(c) $\begin{bmatrix} -\delta & \beta \\ \gamma & -\alpha \end{bmatrix}$

(d) $\begin{bmatrix} -\delta & -\beta \\ \gamma & \alpha \end{bmatrix}$

4. If A and B are square matrices of the same order, then $(A + B)^2 = ?$
   (a) $A^2 + 2AB + B^2$
   (b) $A^2 + 2AB + B$
   (c) $A^2 + AB + BA + B^2$
   (d) None of these

5. If A and B are square matrices of the same order, then $(A - B)^2 = ?$
   (a) $A^2 - 2AB + B^2$
   (b) $A^2 - 2BA + B^2$
   (c) $A^2 - AB - BA + B^2$
   (b) None of these

6. If $A = \begin{bmatrix} \cos\theta & \sin\theta \\ \sin\theta & \cos\theta \end{bmatrix}$, then $A^2 = ?$

(a) $\begin{bmatrix} \cos^2\theta & \sin^2\theta \\ \sin^2\theta & \cos^2\theta \end{bmatrix}$

(b) $\begin{bmatrix} \cos2\theta & \sin2\theta \\ \sin2\theta & \cos2\theta \end{bmatrix}$

(c) $\begin{bmatrix} \cos^2\theta & \sin2\theta \\ \sin^2\theta & \cos2\theta \end{bmatrix}$

(d) None of these

7. If matrix $A = \begin{bmatrix} 1 & -1 \\ -1 & 1 \end{bmatrix}$ and $A^2 = KA$, then what is the value of K?
   (a) 2
   (b) 3
   (c) 4
   (d) 5

8. If $\begin{bmatrix} 2 & 3 \\ 5 & 7 \end{bmatrix}\begin{bmatrix} 1 & -3 \\ -2 & 4 \end{bmatrix} = \begin{bmatrix} -4 & 6 \\ -9 & x \end{bmatrix}$, then what is the value of x?
   (a) 11
   (b) 13
   (c) 9
   (d) 17

9. If matrix $A = \begin{bmatrix} 0 & 2b & -2 \\ 3 & 1 & 3 \\ 3a & 3 & -1 \end{bmatrix}$ is symmetric, then what is the value of a and b?

(a) $\dfrac{-2}{3}, \dfrac{3}{2}$

(b) $\dfrac{3}{2}, \dfrac{2}{3}$

(c) $\dfrac{2}{3}, \dfrac{-3}{2}$

(d) None of these

10. If A is a square matrix, then $(A - A^T)$ is
    (a) a null matrix
    (b) an identity matrix
    (c) a symmetric matrix
    (d) a skew-symmetric matrix

11. If A is a square matrix, then $(A + A^T)$ is
    (a) a null matrix
    (b) an identity matrix
    (c) a symmetric matrix
    (d) a skew-symmetric matrix

12. If the matrix $A = \begin{bmatrix} 0 & a & -3 \\ 2 & 0 & -1 \\ b & 1 & 0 \end{bmatrix}$ is a skew symmetric matrix, then what is the value of a and b?
    (a) −2, 3
    (b) 3, 2
    (c) 4, −5
    (d) 2, −3

13. For what value of x, is the matrix

$$A = \begin{bmatrix} 0 & 1 & -2 \\ -1 & 0 & 3 \\ x & -3 & 0 \end{bmatrix}$$ a skew symmetric matrix?

  (a) 4   (b) 3
  (c) 2   (d) 5

14. If $A = \begin{bmatrix} 3 & -1 \\ -2 & 5 \end{bmatrix}$, then adj $(A^T) = ?$

  (a) $\begin{bmatrix} 5 & 1 \\ 2 & 3 \end{bmatrix}$ (b) $\begin{bmatrix} 5 & 2 \\ 3 & 1 \end{bmatrix}$

  (c) $\begin{bmatrix} 5 & 2 \\ 1 & 3 \end{bmatrix}$ (d) $\begin{bmatrix} -5 & 2 \\ 1 & 3 \end{bmatrix}$

15. If $A = \begin{bmatrix} 5 & 2 \\ 3 & 1 \end{bmatrix}$, then $A^{-1} = ?$

  (a) $\begin{bmatrix} -1 & 2 \\ 3 & -5 \end{bmatrix}$ (b) $\begin{bmatrix} 1 & -2 \\ -3 & 5 \end{bmatrix}$

  (c) $\begin{bmatrix} -1 & -2 \\ -3 & -5 \end{bmatrix}$ (d) $\begin{bmatrix} 1 & 2 \\ 3 & 5 \end{bmatrix}$

16. If $|A| = 3$ and $A^{-1} = \begin{bmatrix} 3 & -1 \\ \dfrac{-5}{3} & \dfrac{2}{3} \end{bmatrix}$, then adj $A = ?$

  (a) $\begin{bmatrix} 9 & -3 \\ -5 & 2 \end{bmatrix}$ (b) $\begin{bmatrix} -9 & 3 \\ 5 & -2 \end{bmatrix}$

  (c) $\begin{bmatrix} 9 & 3 \\ -5 & -2 \end{bmatrix}$ (d) $\begin{bmatrix} 9 & -3 \\ 5 & -2 \end{bmatrix}$

17. If A and B are invertible square matrices of the same order, then

  (a) $(AB)^{-1} = (A^{-1})(B^{-1})$
  (b) $(AB)^{-1} = (B^{-1})(A^{-1})$
  (c) $(AB)^{-1} = A^{-1}B$
  (d) $(AB)^{-1} = AB^{-1}$

18. If A is an invertible square matrix and k is a non-negative real number, then $(kA)^{-1} = ?$

  (a) kA^{-1}

  (b) $\dfrac{1}{k}A^{-1}$

  (c) $2kA$
  (d) None

19. If $A = [1\ 2\ 3]$ and $B = \begin{bmatrix} -5 & 4 & 0 \\ 0 & 2 & -1 \\ 1 & -3 & 2 \end{bmatrix}$, then $AB =$

  (a) $\begin{bmatrix} -5 & 4 & 0 \\ 0 & 4 & -2 \\ 3 & -9 & 6 \end{bmatrix}$

  (b) $[3\ 1\ 1]$
  (c) $[-2\ -1\ 4]$
  (d) $[-2\ 1\ 4]$

20. A square matrix $A = [a_{ij}]$ in which $a_{ij} = 0$ for $i \neq j$ and $a_{ij} = k$ (constant) for $i = j$ is called a
  (a) Unit matrix
  (b) scalar matrix
  (c) Null matrix
  (d) Diagonal matrix

Answer Keys

1. (c)	2. (c)	3. (b)	4. (c)	5. (c)	6. (d)	7. (a)	8. (b)	9. (a)	10. (d)
11. (c)	12. (a)	13. (c)	14. (c)	15. (a)	16. (a)	17. (b)	18. (b)	19. (c)	20. (d)

Solutions

1. $\because$ A is a singular matrix,

$\Rightarrow$ $|A| = 0$

$\therefore$ $\begin{vmatrix} 1 & k & 3 \\ 3 & k & -2 \\ 2 & 3 & -4 \end{vmatrix} = 0$

$\Rightarrow$ $1 . (-4k + 6) - k(-12 + 4) + 3 (9 - 2k) = 0$

$\Rightarrow$ $-4k + 6 + 12k - 4k + 27 - 6k = 0$

$\Rightarrow$ $12k - 14k + 33 = 0$

$\Rightarrow$ $-2k = -33$

$\Rightarrow$ $2k = 33$

$\therefore$ $k = \dfrac{33}{2}$

2. Given,

$\begin{bmatrix} 1 & -2 \\ 3 & 6 \end{bmatrix} + 2X = \begin{bmatrix} 5 & -6 \\ -7 & 4 \end{bmatrix}$

$\Rightarrow 2X = \begin{bmatrix} 5 & -6 \\ -7 & 4 \end{bmatrix} - \begin{bmatrix} 1 & -2 \\ 3 & 6 \end{bmatrix}$

$= \begin{bmatrix} 4 & -4 \\ -10 & -2 \end{bmatrix}$

$\therefore$ $X = \dfrac{1}{2}\begin{bmatrix} 4 & -4 \\ -10 & -2 \end{bmatrix} = \begin{bmatrix} 2 & -2 \\ -5 & -1 \end{bmatrix}$

3. $\because$ $A = \begin{bmatrix} \alpha & \beta \\ \gamma & \delta \end{bmatrix}$

$\therefore$ $M_{11} = \delta$. $M_{12} = \gamma$, $M_{2} = \beta$, $M_{22} = \alpha$

and $C_{11} = \delta$, $C_{12} = -\gamma$, $C_{21} = -\beta$, $C_{22} = \alpha$.

$\therefore$ Adj A $= \begin{bmatrix} \delta & -\beta \\ -\gamma & \alpha \end{bmatrix}$

4. $(A + B)^2 = (A + B)(A + B)$

$= A^2 + AB + BA + B^2$

[by distributive law]

5. $A - B)^2 = (A - B)(A - B)$

$= A^2 - AB - BA + B^2$

[By distributive law]

6. $\because$ $A = \begin{bmatrix} \cos\theta & \sin\theta \\ \sin\theta & \cos\theta \end{bmatrix}$

$\therefore$ $A^2 = \begin{bmatrix} \cos\theta & \sin\theta \\ \sin\theta & \cos\theta \end{bmatrix}\begin{bmatrix} \cos\theta & \sin\theta \\ \sin\theta & \cos\theta \end{bmatrix}$

$= \begin{bmatrix} \cos^2\theta + \sin^2\theta & 2\sin\theta\cos\theta \\ 2\sin\theta\cos\theta & \sin^2\theta + \cos^2\theta \end{bmatrix}$

$= \begin{bmatrix} 1 & \sin 2\theta \\ \sin 2\theta & 1 \end{bmatrix}$

7. Given $A^2 = kA$

$\Rightarrow \begin{bmatrix} 1 & -1 \\ -1 & 1 \end{bmatrix}\begin{bmatrix} 1 & -1 \\ -1 & 1 \end{bmatrix} = k\begin{bmatrix} 1 & -1 \\ -1 & 1 \end{bmatrix}$

$\Rightarrow \begin{bmatrix} 2 & -2 \\ -2 & 2 \end{bmatrix} = \begin{bmatrix} k & -k \\ -k & k \end{bmatrix}$

$\therefore$ $k = 2$

8. Given,

$\begin{bmatrix} 2 & 3 \\ 5 & 7 \end{bmatrix}\begin{bmatrix} 1 & -3 \\ -2 & 4 \end{bmatrix} = \begin{bmatrix} -4 & 6 \\ -9 & x \end{bmatrix}$

$\Rightarrow \begin{bmatrix} 2-6 & -6+12 \\ 5-14 & -15+28 \end{bmatrix} = \begin{bmatrix} -4 & 6 \\ -9 & x \end{bmatrix}$

$\Rightarrow \begin{bmatrix} -4 & 6 \\ -9 & 13 \end{bmatrix} = \begin{bmatrix} -4 & 6 \\ -9 & x \end{bmatrix}$

$\therefore$ $x = 13$

9. $\because$ A is a symmetric matrix

$\Rightarrow A^T = A$

$\begin{bmatrix} 0 & 3 & 3a \\ 2b & 1 & 3 \\ -2 & 3 & -1 \end{bmatrix} = \begin{bmatrix} 0 & 2b & -2 \\ 3 & 1 & 3 \\ 3a & 3 & -1 \end{bmatrix}$

Therefore, $3a = -2$

$\therefore a = \dfrac{-2}{3}$

and $2b = 3$

$\therefore$ $b = \dfrac{3}{2}$

10. $(A - A^T)^T = A^T - (A^T)^T = A^T - A = -(A - A^T)$

$\therefore$ $(A - A^T)$ is a skew symmetric matrix.

11. $(A + A^T)^T = A^T + (A^T)^T = A^T + A = (A + A^T)$

$\therefore$ $(A + A^T)$ is a symmetric matrix.

12. Given that, A is a skew symmetric matrix.

$\Rightarrow A^T = -A$

$$\begin{bmatrix} 0 & 2 & b \\ a & 0 & 1 \\ -3 & -1 & 0 \end{bmatrix} = -\begin{bmatrix} 0 & a & -3 \\ 2 & 0 & -1 \\ b & 1 & 0 \end{bmatrix}$$

$$\Rightarrow \begin{bmatrix} 0 & 2 & b \\ a & 0 & 1 \\ -3 & -1 & 0 \end{bmatrix} = \begin{bmatrix} 0 & -a & 3 \\ -2 & 0 & 1 \\ -b & -1 & 0 \end{bmatrix}$$

On comparing the above matrices,

We get, a = –2 and b = 3

13. The value of determinants of skew symmetric matrix of odd order is always equal to zero.

$$\begin{bmatrix} 0 & 1 & -2 \\ -1 & 0 & 3 \\ x & -3 & 0 \end{bmatrix} = 0$$

$\Rightarrow -1(0 - 3x) - 2(3 - 0) = 0$

$\Rightarrow 3x - 6 = 0$

$\Rightarrow 3x = 6$

$\therefore x = \dfrac{6}{3} = 2$

14. $A^T = \begin{pmatrix} 3 & -2 \\ -1 & 5 \end{pmatrix}$

$\therefore M_{11} = 5, M_{12} = -1, M_{21} = -2, M_{22} = 3$
and $C_{11} = 5, C_{12} = 1, C_{21} = 2, C_{22} = 3$

$\therefore Adj\left(A^T\right) = \begin{bmatrix} 5 & 2 \\ 1 & 3 \end{bmatrix}$

15. $|A| = \begin{bmatrix} 5 & 2 \\ 3 & 1 \end{bmatrix} = (5 - 6) = -1$

and $M_{11} = 1, M_{12} = 3, M_{21} = 2, M_{22} = 5$
$C_{11} = 1, C_{12} = -3, C_{21} = -2, C_{22} = 5$

$\therefore Adj\,A = \begin{bmatrix} 1 & -2 \\ -3 & 5 \end{bmatrix}$

$\therefore A^{-1} = \dfrac{1}{|A|}.Adj\,A = \dfrac{1}{-1}\begin{bmatrix} +1 & -2 \\ -3 & +5 \end{bmatrix}$

$= \begin{bmatrix} -1 & 2 \\ 3 & -5 \end{bmatrix}$

16. We know that,

$A^{-1} = \dfrac{1}{|A|}.Adj\,A$

$\Rightarrow Adj\,A = |A| . A^{-1}$

$= 3\begin{bmatrix} 3 & -1 \\ \dfrac{-5}{3} & \dfrac{2}{3} \end{bmatrix}$

$= \begin{bmatrix} 9 & -3 \\ -5 & 2 \end{bmatrix}$

17. We have $(AB)^{-1} = B^{-1}A^{-1}$

18. We have $(KA)^{-1} = \dfrac{1}{KA} = \dfrac{1}{K}.(A)^{-1}$

19. $AB = [1\ 2\ 3]\begin{bmatrix} -5 & 4 & 0 \\ 0 & 2 & -1 \\ 1 & -3 & 2 \end{bmatrix}$

$= [-5+0+3 \quad 4+4-9 \quad 0-2+6]$

$= [-2 \quad -1 \quad 4]$

20. Use definition

CHAPTER 4

Determinants

Expansion of Determinants

- **Definition**: A determinant is a number (real or complex) that can be related to any square matrix $A = [a_{ij}]$ of order n. It is denoted as $det(A)$.

  Determinant of a matrix $A = \begin{bmatrix} a_{11} & a_{12} \\ a_{21} & a_{22} \end{bmatrix}$ can be given as:

  $$|A| = \begin{vmatrix} a_{11} & a_{12} \\ a_{21} & a_{22} \end{vmatrix} = a_{11}a_{22} - a_{12}a_{21}$$

  Determinant of a matrix $A = \begin{bmatrix} a_{11} & a_{12} & a_{13} \\ a_{21} & a_{22} & a_{23} \\ a_{31} & a_{32} & a_{33} \end{bmatrix}$ by expanding along R_1 can be given as:

  $$\det(A) = |A| = (-1)^{1+1} a_{11} \begin{vmatrix} a_{22} & a_{23} \\ a_{32} & a_{33} \end{vmatrix}$$

  $$+ (-1)^{1+2} a_{12} \begin{vmatrix} a_{21} & a_{23} \\ a_{31} & a_{33} \end{vmatrix} + (-1)^{1+3} a_{13} \begin{vmatrix} a_{21} & a_{22} \\ a_{31} & a_{32} \end{vmatrix}$$

- **Minors**: The minor M_{ij} of a_{ij} in A is the determinant of the square sub matrix of order $(n-1)$ obtained by deleting its ith row and j^{th} column in which a_{ij} lies. It is denoted by M_{ij}.

  Minor of an element of a determinant of order n (for all $n \geq 2$) is a determinant of order $n-1$.

- **Co-factors**: Co-factor of an element a_{ij} is defined by $A_{ij} = (-1)^{(i+j)} M_{ij}$, where M_{ij} is a minor of a_{ij}. Co-factor is denoted by A_{ij}.

Properties of Determinants

- **Properties of determinants**:
  - The value of the determinant remains unchanged if its rows and columns are interchanged.
  - If A is a square matrix, then $det(A) = det(A')$, where $A' =$ transpose of A.
  - If any two columns (or rows) of a determinant are interchanged, then the sign of the determinant changes.
  - The determinant of the product of two square matrices of same order is equal to the product of their respective determinants, that is $|AB| = |A||B|$.
  - If any two rows or columns of a determinant are identical (i.e. all corresponding elements are same), then value of determinant is zero.
  - If each element of a row or a column of a determinant is multiplied by a constant k, then its value gets multiplied by k.
  - If some or all elements of a row or column of a determinant are expressed as sum of two or more terms, then the determinant can be expressed as sum of two or more determinants.

    For example:

    $$\begin{vmatrix} a_1 + x & a_2 + y & a_3 + z \\ b_1 & b_2 & b_3 \\ c_1 & c_2 & c_3 \end{vmatrix} = \begin{vmatrix} a_1 & a_2 & a_3 \\ b_1 & b_2 & b_3 \\ c_1 & c_2 & c_3 \end{vmatrix} + \begin{vmatrix} x & y & z \\ b_1 & b_2 & b_3 \\ c_1 & c_2 & c_3 \end{vmatrix}$$

  - If we multiply each element of a row or a column of a determinant, by a constant k, then the value of the determinant is also multiplied by k.
  - Multiplying a determinant by k means multiply elements of any one row or any one column by k.
  - Adding or subtracting each element of any column or any row of a determinant with the equimultiples of corresponding elements of any other row or column, does not changes the value of the determinant, i.e., the value of

determinant remain same if we apply the operation $R_i \to R_i \to kR_j$.

- **Area of triangle:** If a triangle is given with its vertices at points (x_1, y_1), (x_2, y_2) and (x_3, y_3), then its area can be calculated as:

$$\Delta = \frac{1}{2}\begin{vmatrix} x_1 & y_1 & 1 \\ x_2 & y_2 & 1 \\ x_3 & y_3 & 1 \end{vmatrix}$$

  - Area is a positive quantity, so we always take the absolute value of the determinant.
  - If the area of the triangle is already given, use both positive and negative values of the determinant for calculation.
  - Area of triangle formed by three collinear points is always zero.

Adjoint and Inverse of a Matrix

- **Adjoint of a square matrix:**
  The adjoint of a square matrix $A = [a_{ij}]_{n \times n}$ is defined as the transpose of the matrix $[A_{ij}]_{n \times n}$, where A_{ij} is the cofactor of the element a_{ij}. Adjoint of the matrix A is denoted by "$adj(A)$".

  Example: $A = \begin{bmatrix} 1 & 4 \\ 2 & 3 \end{bmatrix}$ then, $adj\, A = \begin{bmatrix} 3 & -4 \\ -2 & 1 \end{bmatrix}$

  If A be any given square matrix of order n, then

$A(adj\, A) = (adj\, A)A = AI$, where I is the identity matrix of order n.

- **Inverse of a Matrix**
  - **Singular matrix:** It is a matrix with zero determinant value. i.e. $|A| = 0$.
  - **Non-singular matrix:** It is a matrix with a non-zero determinant value. i.e. $|A| \neq 0$.
    If A and B are nonsingular matrices of the same order, then AB and BA are also nonsingular matrices of the same order.
  - A square matrix A is invertible if and only if A is nonsingular matrix.
  - If A is a nonsingular matrix, then its **inverse** exists which is given by $A^{-1} = \dfrac{1}{|A|}adj(A)$

- **Consistent system:** A system of equations is said to be consistent if there exist one or more solution to the system of equation.
- **Inconsistent system:** If the solution to the system of equation does not exist, then it is termed as inconsistent system.
- For the square matrix A in the matrix equation $AX = B$
  - $|A| \neq 0$, there exists unique solution. The system of equation is consistent.
  - $|A| = 0$ and $(adj\, A)B \neq 0$ then there exists no solution. The system is inconsistent.
  - $|A| = 0$ and $(adj\, A)B = 0$, then system may or may not be consistent.

Exercise

1. The value of $\begin{vmatrix} \cos 15° & \sin 15° \\ \sin 15° & \cos 15° \end{vmatrix}$ is:

   (a) 1

   (b) $\dfrac{1}{2}$

   (c) $\dfrac{\sqrt{3}}{2}$

   (d) None

2. If $\begin{vmatrix} 3x & 7 \\ -2 & 4 \end{vmatrix} = \begin{vmatrix} 8 & 7 \\ 6 & 4 \end{vmatrix}$, then what is the value of x?

   (a) –2

   (b) 2

   (c) 4

   (d) 3

3. The value of $\begin{vmatrix} 67 & 19 & 21 \\ 39 & 13 & 14 \\ 81 & 24 & 26 \end{vmatrix}$ is:

   (a) –43

   (b) 43

   (c) 86

   (d) 0

4. If $\Delta = \begin{vmatrix} 5 & 3 & 8 \\ 2 & 0 & 1 \\ 1 & 2 & 3 \end{vmatrix}$, then the minor of the elements a_{23} is:

   (a) 5

   (b) 7

   (c) 3

   (d) 9

5. The value of the determinant $\begin{vmatrix} \cos 75° & -\sin 75° \\ \sin 30° & \cos 30° \end{vmatrix}$ is

   (a) $-\dfrac{1}{\sqrt{2}}$

   (b) $\dfrac{1}{\sqrt{2}}$

   (c) $\sqrt{2}$

   (d) None

6. If $x \neq 0$ and $\begin{vmatrix} 1 & x & 2x \\ 1 & 3x & 5x \\ 1 & 3 & 4 \end{vmatrix} = 0$, then x = ?

   (a) –1

   (b) 1

   (c) 2

   (d) –2

7. The value of

$$\cos\theta \begin{bmatrix} \cos\theta & \sin\theta \\ -\sin\theta & \cos\theta \end{bmatrix} + \sin\theta \begin{bmatrix} \sin\theta & -\cos\theta \\ \cos\theta & \sin\theta \end{bmatrix} \text{ is:}$$

(a) $\begin{bmatrix} 1 & 0 \\ 0 & 1 \end{bmatrix}$ (b) $\begin{bmatrix} 1 & 0 \\ 2 & 1 \end{bmatrix}$

(c) $\begin{bmatrix} 1 & 1 \\ 2 & 1 \end{bmatrix}$ (d) None

8. If a, b, c be positive district real number, then the

value of $\begin{vmatrix} a & b & c \\ b & c & a \\ c & a & b \end{vmatrix}$ is

(a) Positive   (b) Negative

(c) Perfect square   (d) zero

9. The maximum value of $\begin{vmatrix} 1 & 1 & 1 \\ 1 & (1+\sin\theta) & 1 \\ 1 & 1 & (1+\cos\theta) \end{vmatrix}$

is:

(a) 1   (b) $-\dfrac{1}{2}$

(c) $\dfrac{1}{2}$ (d) 0

10. The value of $\begin{vmatrix} a+ib & c+id \\ -c+id & a-ib \end{vmatrix}$ is:

(a) $(a^2 - b^2 + c^2 - d^2)$ (b) $(a^2 + b^2 - c^2 - d^2)$

(c) $(a^2 + b^2 + c^2 + d^2)$ (d) None of these

11. Using properties of determinants, find the value

of $\begin{vmatrix} -a^2 & ab & ac \\ ba & -b^2 & bc \\ ca & cb & -c^2 \end{vmatrix} = ?$

(a) $4\,a^2\,b^2\,c^2$ (b) $4\,a^2bc$

(c) $2\,a^2b^2c^2$ (d) None

12. If A is a 3×3 matrix and $|3A| = k|A|$, then the value of k is:

(a) 1   (b) 27

(c) 23   (d) None

13. If $\begin{vmatrix} (b+c) & (c+a) & (a+b) \\ (y+z) & (z+x) & (x+y) \\ (q+r) & (r+p) & (p+q) \end{vmatrix} = k\begin{vmatrix} a & b & c \\ x & y & z \\ p & q & r \end{vmatrix}$, then the

value of k is:

(a) $\dfrac{1}{2}$ (b) 2

(c) 1   (d) -2

14. $\begin{vmatrix} 0 & p-q & p-r \\ q-p & 0 & q-r \\ r-p & r-q & 0 \end{vmatrix} = ?$

(a) $(p + q + r)$ (b) $(p + q - r)$

(b) 1   (b) 0

15. $\begin{vmatrix} (a-b-c) & 2b & 2c \\ 2a & (b-c-a) & 2c \\ 2a & 2b & (c-a-b) \end{vmatrix} = ?$

(a) $a + b + c$ (b) $(a + b + c)^2$

(c) $(a + b + c)^3$ (d) None

16. The value of k for which the equations $9x + 4y = 9$ and $7x + ky = 5$ have no solution, is:

(a) $\dfrac{9}{5}$ (b) $\dfrac{9}{7}$

(c) $\dfrac{28}{9}$ (d) $\dfrac{9}{28}$

17. If for any 2×2 square matrix A, $A(\text{adj } A) = \begin{bmatrix} 8 & 0 \\ 0 & 8 \end{bmatrix}$,

then write the value of $|A|$.

(a) 8   (b) 6

(c) 5   (d) 10

18. For what values of k, the system of linear equations $x + y + z = 2$, $2x + y - z = 3$ and $3x + 2y + kz = 4$ has a unique solution?

(a) $R - \{0\}$ (b) R

(c) $R - \{0, 1\}$ (d) None

19. The system of linear equations $x + y + z = 0$, $2x + y - z = 0$ and $3x + 2y = 0$ has:

(a) No solution

(b) A unique solution

(c) Infinitely many solutions

(d) None of these

20. If the system of equations $x - ky - z = 0$, $kx - y - z = 0$ and $x + y - z = 0$ has a non-zero solution, then the possible values of k are:

(a) $-1, 2$ (b) 1, 2

(c) 0, 1   (d) $-1, 1$

21. If

$$f(x) = \begin{vmatrix} 1 & x & x+1 \\ 2x & x(x-1) & (x+1) \\ 3x(x-1) & x(x-1)(x-2) & (x+1)(x-1)x \end{vmatrix},$$

then $f(10) = ?$

(a) 90   (b) 9000

(c) -100 (d) 0

22. If $A = \begin{bmatrix} 2 & 5 \\ 1 & 3 \end{bmatrix}$, then $A^{-1} = ?$

    (a) $\begin{bmatrix} 3 & -5 \\ -1 & 2 \end{bmatrix}$ (b) $\begin{bmatrix} -3 & 5 \\ 1 & -2 \end{bmatrix}$

    (c) $\begin{bmatrix} 1 & 2 \\ 3 & 5 \end{bmatrix}$ (d) $\begin{bmatrix} 1 & 2 \\ 3 & 0 \end{bmatrix}$

23. For two determinants A and B of the same order $|AB| = ?$

    (a) $|A| + |B|$ (b) $\dfrac{|A|}{|B|}$

    (c) $|A||B|$ (d) None of these

Answer Keys

1. (c)	2. (a)	3. (a)	4. (b)	5. (b)	6. (a)	7. (a)	8. (b)	9. (c)	10. (c)
11. (a)	12. (b)	13. (b)	14. (d)	15. (c)	16. (c)	17. (a)	18. (a)	19. (c)	20. (d)
21. (d)	22. (a)	23. (c)							

Solutions

1. $\Delta = (\cos 15° \times \cos 15° - \sin 15° \times \sin 15°)$

   $= (\cos^2 15° - \sin^2 15°)$

   $= \cos 2 \times 15° = \cos 30° = \dfrac{\sqrt{3}}{2}$

2. Given, $\begin{vmatrix} 3x & 7 \\ -2 & 4 \end{vmatrix} = \begin{vmatrix} 8 & 7 \\ 6 & 4 \end{vmatrix}$

On expanding both determinants.

we get, $12x - (-14) = 8 \times 4 - 7 \times 6$

$\Rightarrow 12x + 14 = 32 - 42$

$\Rightarrow 12x = -10 - 14 = -24$

$\therefore x = \dfrac{-24}{12} = -2$

3. Given $\Delta = \begin{vmatrix} 67 & 19 & 21 \\ 39 & 13 & 14 \\ 81 & 24 & 26 \end{vmatrix}$

By $C_1 \to C_1 - 3C_2$ and $C_3 \to C_3 - C_2$

We get, $\Delta = \begin{vmatrix} 67 - 3 \times 19 & 19 & (21 - 19) \\ 39 - 3 \times 13 & 13 & (14 - 13) \\ 81 - 3 \times 24 & 24 & (26 - 24) \end{vmatrix}$

$= \begin{vmatrix} 10 & 19 & 2 \\ 0 & 13 & 1 \\ 9 & 24 & 2 \end{vmatrix}$

$= 10 (26 - 24) + 9(19 - 26)$

$= 10 \times 2 + 9 \times (-7)$

$= 20 - 63$

$= -43$

4. Minor of $a_{23} = \begin{vmatrix} 5 & 3 \\ 1 & 2 \end{vmatrix}$

   $= 10 - 3 = 7$

5. $\Delta = \cos 75° \cos 30° + \sin 75° \sin 30°$

   $= \cos (75° - 30°)$

   $= \cos 45° = \dfrac{1}{\sqrt{2}}$

6. Given, $\begin{vmatrix} 1 & x & 2x \\ 1 & 3x & 5x \\ 1 & 3 & 4 \end{vmatrix} = 0$

By $R_2 \to R_2 - R_1$ and $R_3 \to R_3 - R_1$

We get, $\begin{vmatrix} 1 & x & 2x \\ 0 & 2x & 3x \\ 0 & 3-x & 4-2x \end{vmatrix} = 0$

$\Rightarrow 1[2x(4 - 2x) - 3x(3 - x)] = 0$

$\Rightarrow -4x^2 + 8x - 9x + 3x^2 = 0$

$\Rightarrow -x^2 - x = 0$

$\Rightarrow x(x + 1) = 0$

$x = 0$ or $1 + x = 0 \Rightarrow x = -1$

But $x \neq 0$, So, $x = -1$

7. $\cos\theta \begin{bmatrix} \cos\theta & \sin\theta \\ -\sin\theta & \cos\theta \end{bmatrix} + \sin\theta \begin{bmatrix} \sin\theta & -\cos\theta \\ \cos\theta & \sin\theta \end{bmatrix}$

$$= \begin{bmatrix} \cos^2\theta & \sin\theta\cos\theta \\ -\sin\theta\cos\theta & \cos^2\theta \end{bmatrix} +$$

$$\begin{bmatrix} \sin^2\theta & -\cos\theta\sin\theta \\ \cos\theta\sin\theta & \sin^2\theta \end{bmatrix}$$

$$= \begin{bmatrix} \cos^2\theta + \sin^2\theta & 0 \\ 0 & \sin^2\theta + \cos^2\theta \end{bmatrix} = \begin{bmatrix} 1 & 0 \\ 0 & 1 \end{bmatrix}$$

8. Given $\Delta = \begin{vmatrix} a & b & c \\ b & c & a \\ c & a & b \end{vmatrix}$

By $R_1 \to R_1 + R_2 + R_3$

We get, $\Delta = \begin{vmatrix} a+b+c & a+b+c & a+b+c \\ b & c & a \\ c & a & b \end{vmatrix}$

$$= (a+b+c) \begin{vmatrix} 1 & 1 & 1 \\ b & c & a \\ c & a & b \end{vmatrix}$$

$[\text{By } C_2 \to C_2 - C_1 \text{ and } C_3 \to C_3 - C_1]$

$$= (a+b+c) \begin{vmatrix} 1 & 0 & 0 \\ b & c-b & a-b \\ c & a-c & b-c \end{vmatrix}$$

$$= (a+b+c)\ [(c-b)(b-c) - (a-b)(a-c)]$$
$$= (a+b+c)(-a^2 - b^2 - c^2 + ab + bc + ca)$$
$$= -(a+b+c)(a^2 + b^2 + c^2 - ab - bc - ca)$$

$$= \frac{-1}{2}(a+b+c)\ [(a-b)^2 + (b-c)^2 + (c-a)^2]$$

Which is negative.

9. Given, $\Delta = \begin{vmatrix} 1 & 1 & 1 \\ 1 & 1+\sin\theta & 1 \\ 1 & 1 & 1+\cos\theta \end{vmatrix}$

By $(R_1 \to R_2 - R_1 \text{ and } R_3 \to R_3 - R_1$

$$\Delta = \begin{vmatrix} 0 & \sin\theta & 0 \\ 1 & 1+\sin\theta & 1 \\ 0 & -\sin\theta & \cos\theta \end{vmatrix}$$

$$= 1(\sin\theta\cos\theta)$$

$$= \frac{1}{2} \times 2\sin\theta\cos\theta$$

$$= \frac{1}{2}\sin 2\theta$$

There, maximum value $= \dfrac{1}{2} \times 1 = \dfrac{1}{2}$

10. Given, $\Delta = \begin{vmatrix} a+ib & c+id \\ -(c-id) & a-ib \end{vmatrix}$

$$= (a+ib)(a-ib) + (c-id)(c+id)$$
$$= a^2 - (ib)^2 + c^2 - (id)^2$$
$$= a^2 + b^2 + c^2 + d^2$$

11. $\Delta = \begin{vmatrix} -a^2 & ab & ac \\ ba & -b^2 & bc \\ ca & cb & -c^2 \end{vmatrix}$

$$= abc \begin{vmatrix} -a & b & c \\ a & -b & c \\ a & b & -c \end{vmatrix}$$

$$= a^2 b^2 c^2 \begin{vmatrix} -1 & 1 & 1 \\ 1 & -1 & 1 \\ 1 & 1 & -1 \end{vmatrix}$$

By $c_1 \to c_1 + c_2$

$$= a^2 b^2 c^2 \begin{vmatrix} 0 & 1 & 1 \\ 0 & -1 & 1 \\ 2 & 1 & -1 \end{vmatrix}$$

$$= a^2 b^2 c^2\ [2(1+1)] = 4a^2 b^2 c^2$$

12. $\because$ A is a matrix of 3×3

$$\therefore\ A = \begin{vmatrix} a_{11} & a_{12} & a_{13} \\ a_{21} & a_{22} & a_{23} \\ a_{31} & a_{32} & a_{33} \end{vmatrix}$$

$$3A = \begin{vmatrix} 3a_{11} & 3a_{12} & 3a_{13} \\ 3a_{21} & 3a_{22} & 3a_{23} \\ 3a_{31} & 3a_{32} & 3a_{33} \end{vmatrix}$$

$\therefore\ |3A| = 3 \times 3 \times 3\ |A| = 27|A|$

Which is given as $K|A| = 27|A|$

$\therefore\ K = 27$

13. Let $\begin{vmatrix} b+c & c+a & a+b \\ y+z & z+x & x+y \\ q+r & r+p & p+q \end{vmatrix} = \Delta$

By $c_1 \to c_1 + c_2 + c_3$

We get $\Delta = \begin{vmatrix} 2(a+b+c) & c+a & a+b \\ 2(x+y+z) & z+x & x+y \\ 2(p+q+r) & r+p & p+q \end{vmatrix}$

$$= 2 \begin{vmatrix} a+b+c & -b & -c \\ x+y+z & -y & -z \\ p+q+r & -q & -r \end{vmatrix}$$

$[c_2 \to c_2 - c_1 \text{ and } c_3 \to c_3 - c_1]$

$$= 2 \begin{vmatrix} a & -b & -c \\ x & -y & -z \\ p & -q & -r \end{vmatrix}$$

$[c_1 \to c_1 + c_2 + c_3]$

$$= 2(-1)(-1) \begin{vmatrix} a & b & c \\ x & y & z \\ p & q & r \end{vmatrix} = 2 \begin{vmatrix} a & b & c \\ x & y & z \\ p & q & r \end{vmatrix}$$

Therefore, k = 2

14. Given $\Delta = \begin{vmatrix} 0 & p-q & p-r \\ q-p & 0 & q-r \\ r-p & r-p & 0 \end{vmatrix}$

By $R_1 \to R_1 - R_2$ and $R_3 \to R_3 - R_2$

We get $\Delta = \begin{vmatrix} p-q & p-q & p-q \\ q-p & 0 & q-r \\ r-q & r-q & r-q \end{vmatrix}$

$$= (p-q)(r-q) \begin{vmatrix} 1 & 1 & 1 \\ q-p & 0 & q-r \\ 1 & 1 & 1 \end{vmatrix}$$

$= 0 \; [\because R_1 \text{ and } R_3 \text{ are identical}]$

15. Given, $\Delta = \begin{vmatrix} (a-b-c) & 2b & 2c \\ 2a & (b-c-a) & 2c \\ 2a & 2b & (c-a-b) \end{vmatrix}$

By $c_1 \to c_1 + c_2 + c_3$

We get, $\Delta = \begin{vmatrix} a+b+c & 2b & 2c \\ a+b+c & b-c-a & 2c \\ a+b+c & 2b & c-a-b \end{vmatrix}$

$$= (a+b+c) \begin{vmatrix} 1 & 2b & 2c \\ 1 & b-c-a & 2c \\ 1 & 2b & c-a-b \end{vmatrix}$$

$$= (a+b+c) \begin{vmatrix} 1 & 2b & 2c \\ 0 & -(a+b+c) & 0 \\ 0 & 0 & -(a+b+c) \end{vmatrix}$$

$[R_2 \to R_2 - R_1 \text{ and } R_3 \to R_3 - R_1]$

$= (a+b+c)[(a+b+c)^2] = (a+b+c)^3$

16. Clearly, $\Delta_2 = \begin{vmatrix} 9 & 9 \\ 7 & 5 \end{vmatrix} = (45 - 63) = -18 \neq 0$

$\therefore$ Given system has no solution.

$\Rightarrow \begin{vmatrix} 9 & 4 \\ 7 & K \end{vmatrix} = 0 \Rightarrow 9K - 28 = 0$

$\Rightarrow 9K = 28$

$\therefore K = \dfrac{28}{9}$

17. We know that

A (adj A) = |A| I$_n$

$\Rightarrow |A| I_0 = \begin{bmatrix} 8 & 0 \\ 0 & 8 \end{bmatrix}$

$\Rightarrow |A| I_0 = 8 \begin{bmatrix} 1 & 0 \\ 0 & 1 \end{bmatrix}$

$\therefore$ |A| = 8

18. Let x + y + z = 2

2x + y − z = 3

and 3x + 2y + kz = 4

$\because$ The system of linear equations has unique solution, then

$\begin{vmatrix} 1 & 1 & 1 \\ 2 & 1 & -1 \\ 3 & 2 & k \end{vmatrix} \neq 0$

$\Rightarrow 1(k+2) - 1(2k+3) + 1(4-3) \neq 0$

$\Rightarrow k + 2 - 2k - 3 + 1 \neq 0$

$\Rightarrow k \neq 0$

Hence, the value of k = R − {0}

19. $\Delta = \begin{vmatrix} 1 & 1 & 1 \\ 2 & 1 & -1 \\ 3 & 2 & 0 \end{vmatrix}$

$$= \begin{vmatrix} 1 & 0 & 0 \\ 2 & -1 & -3 \\ 3 & -1 & -3 \end{vmatrix}$$

$[c_2 \to c_2 - c_1 \text{ and } c_3 \to c_3 - c_1] = 1(3-3) = 0$

Hence, non-zero solution of the system exist. Therefore, the given system has infinitely many solutions.

20. $\because$ Given system has non-zero solution.

$\therefore \begin{vmatrix} 1 & -k & -1 \\ k & -1 & -1 \\ 1 & 1 & -1 \end{vmatrix} = 0$

By $c_1 \to c_1 + c_3$ and $c_3 \to c_3 + c_2$

$$\Rightarrow \begin{vmatrix} 0 & -k & -1-k \\ k-1 & -1 & -2 \\ 0 & 1 & 0 \end{vmatrix} = 0$$

$\Rightarrow -(k-1)(1+k) = 0$

$\Rightarrow (1-k)(1+k) = 0$

$\Rightarrow 1-k^2 = 0$

$\Rightarrow k^2 = 1$

$\therefore \quad k = \pm 1$

21. $f(x) = \begin{vmatrix} 1 & x & x+1 \\ 2x & x(x-1) & x+1 \\ 3x(x-1) & x(x-1)(x-2) & x(x+1)(x-1) \end{vmatrix}$

Taking $x(x+1)$ from R_3 and x from R_2.

$$= x^2(x-1)\begin{vmatrix} 1 & x & x+1 \\ 2 & x-1 & x+1 \\ 3 & x-2 & x+1 \end{vmatrix}$$

$$= x^2(x-1)(x+1)\begin{vmatrix} 1 & x & 1 \\ 2 & x-1 & 1 \\ 3 & x-2 & 1 \end{vmatrix}$$

$(R_3 \to R_2 - R_1$ and $R_3 \to R_3 - R_1)$

$$= x^2(x^2-1)\begin{vmatrix} 1 & x & 1 \\ 1 & -1 & 0 \\ 2 & -2 & 0 \end{vmatrix}$$

$= x^2(x^2-1)[1(-2+2)] = 0$ for all x

$\therefore \quad f(10) = 0$

22. Given $A = \begin{bmatrix} 2 & 5 \\ 1 & 3 \end{bmatrix}$

$\therefore \quad |A| = 6 - 5 = 1$

$\text{adj } A = \begin{bmatrix} 3 & -5 \\ -1 & 2 \end{bmatrix}$

$\therefore \quad A^{-1} = \dfrac{1}{|A|}\text{adj }A = \dfrac{1}{1}\begin{bmatrix} 3 & -5 \\ -1 & 2 \end{bmatrix}$

$= \begin{bmatrix} 3 & -5 \\ -1 & 2 \end{bmatrix}$

23. We know that

$|AB| = |A|\,|B|$

CHAPTER 5

Continuity and Differentiability

Continuity

- **Definition of Continuity:**

  Let f is a real valued function and is a subset of real numbers and a point c lies in the domain of f, then f is continuous at c if

  $$\lim_{x \to c} f(x) = f(c)$$

  When the function f is discontinuous at c, it is called the point of discontinuity of f.

  Also, if f is defined on $[a, b]$ then continuity of a function f at a means

  $$\lim_{x \to a^+} f(x) = f(a)$$

  And continuity of the function f at b means

  $$\lim_{x \to b^-} f(x) = f(b)$$

- Every polynomial function is continuous.
- Consider two real functions f and g which are continuous at c, then sum, difference, product and quotient of the two functions will also be continuous at $x = c$.

  i.e. $(f + g)(x) = f(x) + g(x)$ is continuous at $x = c$

  $(f - g)(x) = f(x) - g(x)$ is continuous at $x = c$

  $(f \cdot g)(x) = f(x) \cdot g(x)$ is continuous at $x = c$

  Here if f is a constant function say $f(x) = \alpha$ for some real number α, then the function $(\alpha \cdot g)$ defined by $(\alpha \cdot g)(x) = \alpha \cdot g(x)$ is also continuous. If $\alpha = -1$ then continuity of f implies continuity of $-f$.

  $\left(\dfrac{f}{g}\right)(x) = \dfrac{f(x)}{g(x)}$ is continuous at $x = c$ when $g(x) \neq 0$

  Here, if f is a constant function say $f(x) = \alpha$ for some real number α, then the function $\dfrac{\alpha}{g}$ defined by

  $\dfrac{\alpha}{g}(x) = \dfrac{\alpha}{g(x)}$ is also continuous wherever $g(x) \neq 0$.

- **Here are some formulae for limits:**

  - $\lim\limits_{x \to 0} \cos x = 1$

  - $\lim\limits_{x \to 0} \dfrac{\sin x}{x} = 1$

  - $\lim\limits_{x \to 0} \dfrac{\tan x}{x} = 1$

  - $\lim\limits_{x \to 0} \dfrac{\sin^{-1} x}{x} = 1$

  - $\lim\limits_{x \to 0} \dfrac{\tan^{-1} x}{x} = 1$

  - $\lim\limits_{x \to 0} \dfrac{a^x - 1}{x} = \log_e a, \ a > 0$

  - $\lim\limits_{x \to 0} \dfrac{e^x - 1}{x} = 1$

  - $\lim\limits_{x \to 0} \dfrac{e^x - 1}{x} = 1$

  - $\lim\limits_{x \to 0} \dfrac{\log_e (1 + x)}{x} = 1$

  - $\lim\limits_{x \to a} \dfrac{x^n - a^n}{x - a} = na^{n-1}$

Differentiability

- **Differentiability:**

  Consider a real function f and a point c lies in its domain then the derivative of that function at c is defined by

  $$\lim_{h \to 0} \dfrac{f(c + h) - f(c)}{h}$$

  Provided the limit exists. It is denoted by $f'(c)$ or $\dfrac{d}{dx}\left(f(x)\right)$.

- **Some rules for algebra of derivatives:**

  - $(u + v)' = u' + v'$

  - $(u - v)' = u' - v'$

  - Product rule: $(uv)' = u'v + uv'$

  - Quotient rule: $\left(\dfrac{u}{v}\right)' = \dfrac{u'v - uv'}{v^2}, \ v \neq 0$

- A function which is differentiable at a point c is also continuous at that point but the converse is not true.

- **Chain Rule:**

  Consider a real value function f which is a composite of u and v.

  Let $t = u(x)$ and $\dfrac{dt}{dx}, \dfrac{dv}{dt}$ exists, then $\dfrac{df}{dx} = \dfrac{dv}{dt} \cdot \dfrac{dt}{dx}$

- Some important features of exponential function and logarithm function are given below

  - Domain of both the functions is set of all real numbers.
  - Range of exponential function is set of all positive real numbers and the range of log function is set of all real numbers.
  - The point $(0, 1)$ is always on the graph of exponential function and the point $(1, 0)$ is always on the graph of log function.
  - Both the functions are ever increasing.

- A relation expressed between two variable x and y in the form $x = f(t), y = g(t)$ is said to be parametric form with t as a parameter.

  By using Chain Rule we find the derivative of function in such form.

  $$\frac{dy}{dt} = \frac{dy}{dx} \cdot \frac{dx}{dt}$$

  or $\dfrac{dy}{dx} = \dfrac{\dfrac{dy}{dt}}{\dfrac{dx}{dt}}$ $\left(\text{whenever } \dfrac{dx}{dt} \neq 0\right)$

  Thus $\dfrac{dy}{dx} = \dfrac{g'(t)}{f'(t)}$

- **Second Order Derivative:**

  If $y = f(x)$

  $$\frac{dy}{dx} = f'(x)$$

  If $f'(x)$ is differentiable then $\dfrac{dy}{dx} = f'(x)$ will be differentiated again. The left side will become

  $\dfrac{d}{dx}\left(\dfrac{dy}{dx}\right)$ and is called second order derivative of y w.r.t. x.

- **Rolle's Theorem:**

  Consider a real valued function f defined on the interval $[a, b]$ such that the function is continuous on $[a, b]$, differentiable on (a, b) and $f(a) = f(b)$, then there exist a point c in (a, b) such that $f'(c) = 0$.

- **Lagrange's Mean Value Theorem:**

  Consider a real valued function f defined on the interval $[a, b]$ such that the function is continuous on $[a, b]$ and differentiable on (a, b), then there exists

  a point c in (a, b) such that $f'(c) = \dfrac{f(b) - f(a)}{b - a}$.

- Derivatives of some standard functions are listed below:

  - $\dfrac{d}{dx}(x^n) = nx^{n-1}$

  - $\dfrac{d}{dx}(k) = 0$, k is any constant

  - $\dfrac{d}{dx}(a^x) = a^x \log_e a,\ a > 0$

  - $\dfrac{d}{dx}(e^x) = e^x$

  - $\dfrac{d}{dx}(\log_a x) = \dfrac{1}{x \log_e a} = \dfrac{1}{x} \log_a e$

  - $\dfrac{d}{dx}(\log_e x) = \dfrac{1}{x}$

  - $\dfrac{d}{dx}(\sin x) = \cos x$

  - $\dfrac{d}{dx}(\cos x) = -\sin x$

  - $\dfrac{d}{dx}(\tan x) = \sec^2 x$

  - $\dfrac{d}{dx}(\sec x) = \sec x \tan x$

  - $\dfrac{d}{dx}(\cot x) = -\cosec^2 x$

  - $\dfrac{d}{dx}(\cosec x) = -\cosec x \cot x$

  - $\dfrac{d}{dx}(\sin^{-1} x) = \dfrac{1}{\sqrt{1-x^2}},\ x \in (-1, 1)$

  - $\dfrac{d}{dx}(\cos^{-1} x) = -\dfrac{1}{\sqrt{1-x^2}},\ x \in (-1, 1)$

  - $\dfrac{d}{dx}(\tan^{-1} x) = \dfrac{1}{1+x^2},\ x \in \mathbb{R}$

  - $\dfrac{d}{dx}(\cot^{-1} x) = -\dfrac{1}{1+x^2},\ x \in \mathbb{R}$

  - $\dfrac{d}{dx}(\sec^{-1} x) = \dfrac{1}{x\sqrt{x^2-1}}$, where

    $$x \in (-\infty, -1) \cup (1, \infty)$$

  - $\dfrac{d}{dx}(\cosec^{-1} x) = -\dfrac{1}{x\sqrt{x^2-1}}$, where

    $$x \in (-\infty, -1) \cup (1, \infty)$$

Exercise

1. For what value of k, the following function is continuous at $x = 1$?

$$f(x) = \begin{cases} \dfrac{x^2 - 1}{x - 1}, & x \neq 1 \\ 4k, & x = 1 \end{cases}$$

   (a) $\dfrac{1}{2}$ (b) 1

   (c) $\dfrac{1}{4}$ (d) None

2. Find the value of k for which the function

$$f(x) = \begin{cases} \dfrac{x^2 - 2x - 3}{x + 1}, & x \neq -1 \\ k, & x = -1 \end{cases}$$ is continuous at

   $x = -1$.

   (a) 4   (b) -4

   (c) 2   (d) -3

3. Find the value of k for which

$$f(x) = \begin{cases} \dfrac{3x + 4\tan x}{x}, & x \neq 0 \\ k, & x = 0 \end{cases}$$ is continuous at $x =$

   0.

   (a) 3   (b) 4

   (c) 7   (d) None

4. Let $f(x) = \begin{cases} x\sin\dfrac{1}{x}, & \text{when } x \neq 0 \\ 0, & \text{When } x = 0 \end{cases}$, then

   (a) $f(x)$ is not defined at $x = 0$

   (b) $\lim\limits_{x \to 0} f(x)$ does not exist

   (c) $f(x)$ is continuous at $x = 0$

   (d) $f(x)$ is discontinuous at $x = 0$

5. The value of k for which $f(x) = \begin{cases} \dfrac{\sin 5x}{3x}, & \text{if } x \neq 0 \\ k, & \text{if } x = 0 \end{cases}$

   is continuous at $x = 0$, is

   (a) $\dfrac{1}{3}$ (b) 0

   (c) $\dfrac{3}{5}$ (d) $\dfrac{5}{3}$

6. In order that the function $f(x) = (x + 1)^{\frac{1}{x}}$ is continuous at $x = 0$, $f(0)$ must be defined as

   (a) $f(0) = 0$ (b) $f(0) = e$

   (c) $f(0) = \dfrac{1}{e}$ (d) $f(0) = 1$

7. Let $[x]$ denotes the greatest integer less than or equal to x. If $f(x) = [x \sin \pi x]$, then $f(x)$ is

   (a) Continuous at $x = 0$

   (b) Continuous in $(-1, 0)$

   (c) Differentiable in $(-1, 1)$

   (d) All the above

8. Which of the following is not true

   (a) A polynomial function is always continuous

   (b) A continuous function is always differentiable

   (c) A differentiable function is always continuous

   (d) e^x is continuous for all x

9. Suppose $f(x)$ is differentiable at $x = 1$ and $\lim\limits_{h \to 0} \dfrac{1}{h} f(1 + h) = 5$, then $f'(1)$ equals

   (a) 5   (b) 6

   (c) 3   (d) 4

10. If $f(x) = x^2 - 2x + 4$ and $\dfrac{f(5) - f(1)}{5 - 1} = f'(c)$, then value of c will be

   (a) 0   (b) 1

   (c) 2   (d) 3

11. Let $f(x + y) = f(x) + f(y)$ and $f(x) = x^2 g(x)$ for all x, y $\in R$, where $g(x)$ is continuous function. Then $f'(x)$ is equal to

   (a) $g'(x)$

   (b) $g(0)$

   (c) $g(0) + g'(x)$

   (d) 0

12. The function which is continuous for all real values of x and differentiable at $x = 0$ is

   (a) $|x|$

   (b) $\log x$

   (c) $\sin x$

   (d) $x^{\frac{1}{2}}$

13. Which one of the following is not true always

   (a) If $f(x)$ is not continuous at $x = a$, then it is not differentiable at $x = a$

   (b) If $f(x)$ is continuous at $x = a$, then it is differentiable at $x = a$

   (c) If $f(x)$ and $g(x)$ are differentiable at $x = a$, then $f(x) + g(x)$ is also differentiable at $x = a$

   (d) If a function $f(x)$ is continuous at $x = a$, then $\lim\limits_{x \to a} f(x)$ exists.

14. Function $y = \sin^{-1}\left(\dfrac{2x}{1+x^2}\right)$ is not differentiable for

   (a) $|x| < 1$

   (b) $x = 1, -1$

   (c) $|x| > 1$

   (d) None of these

15. If $y(x) = \begin{cases} \dfrac{\log(1+2ax) - \log(1-bx)}{x}, & x \neq 0 \\ k, & x = 0 \end{cases}$ is continuous at $x = 0$, then k equals

   (a) $2a + b$ (b) $2a - b$

   (c) $b - 2a$ (d) $b + a$

16. If $f(x) = \begin{cases} x, & x < 0 \\ 1, & x = 0 \\ x^2, & x > 0 \end{cases}$, then true statement is

   (a) $\lim\limits_{x \to 0} f(x) = 1$

   (b) $\lim\limits_{x \to 0} f(x) = 0$

   (c) $f(x)$ is continuous at $x = 0$

   (d) $\lim\limits_{x \to 0} f(x)$ does not exist

17. The point of discontinuity of the function $f(x) = \dfrac{1 + \cos 5x}{1 - \cos 4x}$ is

   (a) $x = 0$

   (b) $x = \pi$

   (c) $x = \pi/2$

   (d) All of these

18. Let $f(x) = \begin{cases} \dfrac{\sin \pi x}{5x}, & x \neq 0 \\ k, & x = 0 \end{cases}$. If $f(x)$ is continuous at $x = 0$, then $k =$

   (a) $\dfrac{\pi}{5}$

   (b) $\dfrac{5}{\pi}$

   (c) 1

   (d) 0

19. If $f(x) = \begin{cases} x \sin(1/x), & x \neq 0 \\ 0, & x = 0 \end{cases}$ then at $x = 0$, the function is

   (a) Discontinuous

   (b) Continuous but not differentiable

   (c) Both continuous and differentiable

   (d) None of these

20. Let $f(xy) = f(x)f(y)$ for all $x, y \in R$. If $f'(1) = 2$ and $f(4) = 4$, then $f'(4) =$ equal to

   (a) 4

   (b) 1

   (c) $\dfrac{1}{2}$

   (d) 2

Answer Keys

1. (a)	2. (b)	3. (c)	4. (c)	5. (d)	6. (b)	7. (d)	8. (b)	9. (a)	10. (d)
11. (d)	12. (c)	13. (b)	14. (b)	15. (a)	16. (b)	17. (d)	18. (a)	19. (b)	20. (d)

Solutions

1. $\lim\limits_{x \to 1} f(x) = \lim\limits_{x \to 1} \dfrac{x^2 - 1}{x - 1}$

   $= \lim\limits_{x \to 1} \dfrac{(x-1)(x+1)}{x-1}$

   $= \lim\limits_{x \to 1} (x+1) = 1 + 1 = 2$

   $\therefore\ k = \dfrac{2}{4} = \dfrac{1}{2}$

2. $\lim\limits_{x \to -1} f(x) = \lim\limits_{x \to -1} \dfrac{x^2 - 2x - 3}{x+1}$

   $= \lim\limits_{x \to -1} \dfrac{(x-3)(x+1)}{x+1}$

   $= \lim\limits_{x \to -1} (x-3)$

   $= -1 - 3 = -4$

   $\therefore$ For continuity at $x = -1$, we have

   $\lim\limits_{x \to 1-1} f(x) = f(-1)$

   $\therefore\ f(-1) = -4$

   Hence, K = -4

3. For continuity at $x = 0$, we must have

   $\lim\limits_{x \to 0} f(x) = f(0)$

   Now, $\lim\limits_{x \to 0} f(x) = \lim\limits_{x \to 0} \dfrac{3x + 4\tan x}{x} \left[\text{form } \dfrac{0}{0} \right]$

   Applying L-hopital

   $= \lim\limits_{x \to 0} \left(3 + 4\sec^2 x \right)$

   $= 3 + 4 \sec^2(0) = 3 + 4 = 7$

   $\therefore\ f(0) = 7$ and Hence, k = 7.

4. $f(0) = 0$

   $\lim\limits_{x \to 0} f(x) = \lim\limits_{x \to 0} x \sin \dfrac{1}{x}$

   $= 0 \times$ (a finite quantity) $= 0$

   $\therefore\ f(x)$ is continuous at $x = 0$

5. For continuity at $x = 0$, we must have

   $\lim\limits_{x \to 0} f(x) = f(0)$

   Now, $\lim\limits_{x \to 0} f(x) = \lim\limits_{x \to 0} \dfrac{\sin 5x}{3x} \left[\text{from } \dfrac{0}{0} \right]$

$\lim\limits_{x \to 0} \dfrac{5 \cos 5x}{3} = \dfrac{5}{3}$

$\therefore$ We must have f(0) $= \dfrac{5}{3}$

Hence, k = $\left(\dfrac{5}{3} \right)$

6. $\lim\limits_{x \to 0} f(x) = f(0)$

   $\Rightarrow \lim\limits_{x \to 0} (1+x)^{\frac{1}{x}} = e$

   $\therefore\ f(0) = e$

7. Here, when $-1 \le x \le 1$, $0 \le x \sin \pi x < 1$

   $\Rightarrow f(x) = [x \sin \pi x] = 0$ for $-1 \le x \le 1$,

   i.e., $f(x)$ is constant function (equal to zero) in $[-1, 1]$.

   $\therefore\ f(x)$ is differentiable in $(-1, 1)$.

8. A continuous function may or may not be differentiable Therefore, option (b) is not true.

9. $f'(1) = \lim\limits_{h \to 0} \dfrac{f(1+h) - f(1)}{h}$

   $\because$ Function is differentiable.

   $\therefore$ It is continuous as it is given that

   $\lim\limits_{h \to 0} \dfrac{f(1+h)}{h} = 5$ and hence f(1) = 0

   $\therefore\ f'(1) = \lim\limits_{h \to 0} \dfrac{f(1+h)}{h} = 5$

10. $f(x) = x^2 - 2x + 4,$

    $\Rightarrow f'(x) = 2x - 2$

    At $x = c$, $f'(c) = 2c - 2$

    $f(5) = 5^2 - 2(5) + 4 = 19$

    $f(1) = 1^2 - 2(1) + 4 = 3$

    $\therefore\ \dfrac{f(5) - f(1)}{5 - 1} = f(c) \Rightarrow \dfrac{19 - 3}{5 - 1} = 2c - 2$

    $\Rightarrow \dfrac{16}{4} = 2c - 2$

    $\Rightarrow 4 = 2c - 2 \Rightarrow 2c = 6$

    $\therefore\ c = \dfrac{6}{2} = 3$

11. We have $f'(x) = \lim\limits_{h \to 0} \dfrac{f(x+h) - f(x)}{h}$

$= \lim\limits_{h \to 0} \dfrac{f(x) + f(h) - f(x)}{h}$

$[\because f(x + y) = f(x) + f(y)]$

$= \lim\limits_{h \to 0} \dfrac{f(h)}{h} = \lim\limits_{h \to 0} \dfrac{h^2 g(h)}{h} = 0 . g(0) = 0$

$[\because g$ is continuous therefore $\lim\limits_{h \to 0} g(h) = g(0)]$

12. Since $\dfrac{dy}{dx} = \cos x$ which is defined at $x = 0$ and no other differential coefficient is defined at $x = 0$

13. Every differentiable function is continuous but every continuous funcion is not differentiable. For example, $y = |x|$ is continuous at $x = 0$, but not differentiable at $x = 0$

14. $y' = \dfrac{1}{\sqrt{1 - \left(\dfrac{2x}{1+x^2}\right)^2}} \cdot \dfrac{2(1+x^2) - 4x^2}{\left(1+x^2\right)^2}$

$= \dfrac{2(1-x^2)}{\sqrt{(1-x^2)^2} \cdot (1+x^2)}$

$\Rightarrow y' = \begin{cases} \dfrac{2}{1+x^2} & \text{for } |x| < 1 \\[2mm] \dfrac{-2}{1+x^2} & \text{for } |x| > 1 \end{cases}$

Hence, for $|x| = 1$, the derivative does not exist.

15. $f(0) = \lim\limits_{x \to 0} f(0)$

$k = \lim\limits_{x \to 0} \dfrac{\log(1 + 2ax) - \log(1 - bx)}{x}$

$= \lim\limits_{x \to 0} \dfrac{\log(1 + 2ax)}{x} - \dfrac{\log(1 - bx)}{x}$

$= \lim\limits_{x \to 0} \dfrac{2a \log(1 + 2ax)}{2ax} + \dfrac{b \log(1 - bx)}{-bx}$

$= 2a + b$

16. $\lim\limits_{x \to 0^-} f(x) = 0$

$\lim\limits_{x \to 0^+} f(x) = 0$

$\therefore \lim\limits_{x \to 0} = 0$

17. $f(x) = \dfrac{1 + \cos 5x}{1 - \cos 4x}$

$1 - \cos 4x \neq 0$

$4x \neq 2n\pi$

$x \neq \dfrac{n\pi}{2}, \ n \in I$

$x \neq 0, \ \dfrac{\pi}{2}, \pi$

18. $k = \lim\limits_{x \to 0} \dfrac{\sin \pi x}{5x}$

$= \lim\limits_{x \to 0} \dfrac{\pi}{5} \dfrac{\sin \pi x}{5x} = \dfrac{\pi}{5}$

19. $\lim\limits_{x \to 0} x \sin \dfrac{1}{x} = 0 = f(0)$

therefore function is continuous but not differentiable

20. $f(xy) = f(x)f(y)$

$f'(x) = \lim\limits_{h \to 0} \dfrac{f(x+h) - f(x)}{h}$

$= \lim\limits_{h \to 0} \dfrac{f\left(x\left(1 + \dfrac{b}{x}\right)\right) - f(x)}{h}$

$= \lim\limits_{h \to 0} \dfrac{f(x) \cdot f\left(1 + \dfrac{h}{x}\right) - f(x)}{h}$

$= f(x) \lim\limits_{h \to 0} \dfrac{f\left(1 + \dfrac{h}{x}\right) - f(1)}{h}$

$= \dfrac{f(x)}{x} \lim\limits_{h \to 0} \dfrac{f\left(1 + \dfrac{h}{x}\right) - f(1)}{h/x}$

$= \dfrac{f(x)}{x} f'(1)$

$\dfrac{f'(x)}{f(x)} = \dfrac{2}{x}$

$\ln f(x) = 2 \ln x + \ln k$

$f(x) = kx^2$

$f(4) = 4$

$k = \dfrac{1}{4}$

$f(x) = \dfrac{x^2}{4}$

$f'(4) = 2$

CHAPTER 6

Application of Derivatives

Rate of Change, Increasing and Decreasing Functions and Approximations

- **Rate of Change of Bodies** representing $\dfrac{dy}{dx}$ as a rate measure:

  Let us take two variables x and y that vary with respect to another variable says, i.e. if $x = f(s)$ and $y = g(s)$, then by applying the parametric rule, we have

  $$\frac{dy}{dx} = \frac{\dfrac{dy}{ds}}{\dfrac{dx}{ds}}, \text{ if } \frac{dx}{ds} \neq 0.$$

  Thus, the rate of change of y with respect to x can be calculated using the rate of change of y and that of x both with respect to s.

- **Increasing and decreasing functions**

  - A function is said to be increasing when the y value increases as the x value increases.

    Example:

    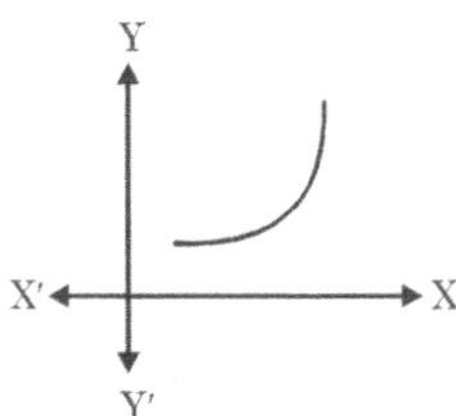

  - A function is said to be increasing when the y value decreases as the x value increases.

    Example:

    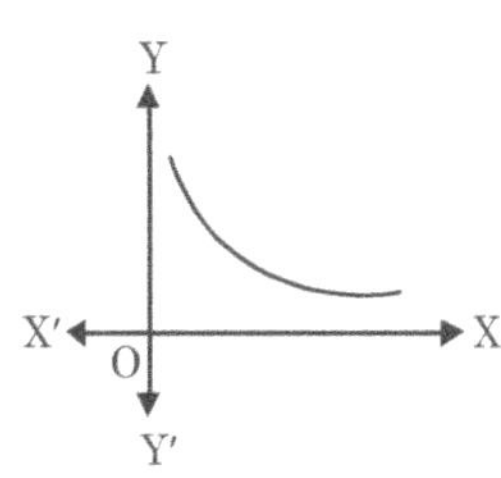

- f is strictly increasing if
  $$x_1 < x_2,$$
  $$\Rightarrow \quad f(x_1) < f(x_2).$$
  Example:

  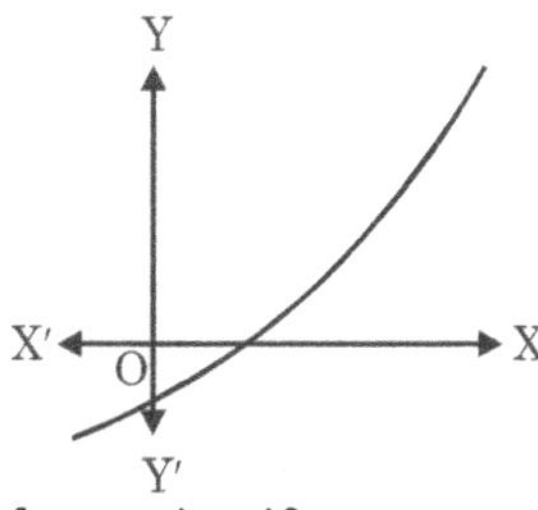

- f is strictly decreasing if $x_1 < x_2, \Rightarrow f(x_1) > f(x_2)$.
  Example:

  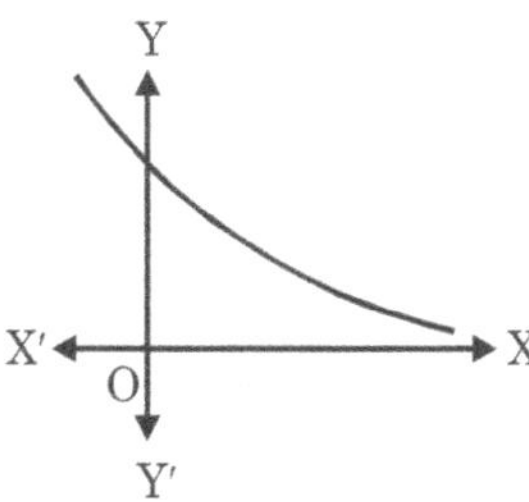

- Let f be continuous on [a, b] and differentiable on the open interval (a, b). Then:

  f is increasing in [a, b] if $f'(x) > 0$ for each $x \in (a, b)$

  f is decreasing in [a, b] if $f'(x) < 0$ for each $x \in (a, b)$

  f is a constant function in [a, b] if $f'(x) = 0$ for each $x \in (a, b)$

- **Approximations**

  - Let the given function be $y = f(x)$. Δx denotes a small increment in x.

  - The corresponding increment in y is given by $\Delta y = f(x + \Delta x) - f(x)$

  - Differential of y, denoted by dy is $dy = \left(\dfrac{dy}{dx}\right)\Delta x$

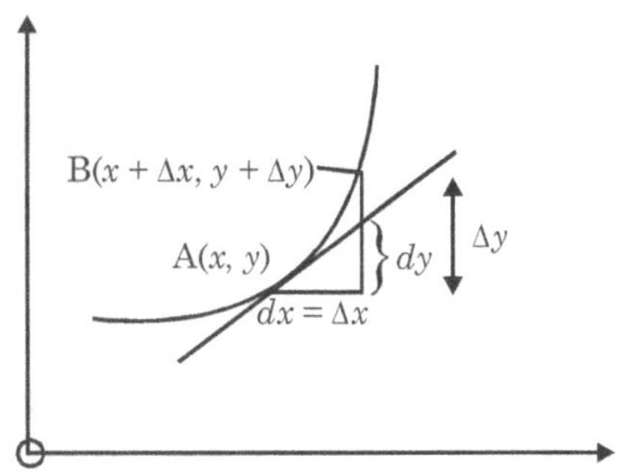

Tangents and Normals

- A tangent line is defined as a straight line that touches the given function at only one point and it represents the instantaneous rate of change of function at the point.
- A normal line to a point (x, y) on a curve is the line that goes through the point (x, y) and is perpendicular to the tangent line.

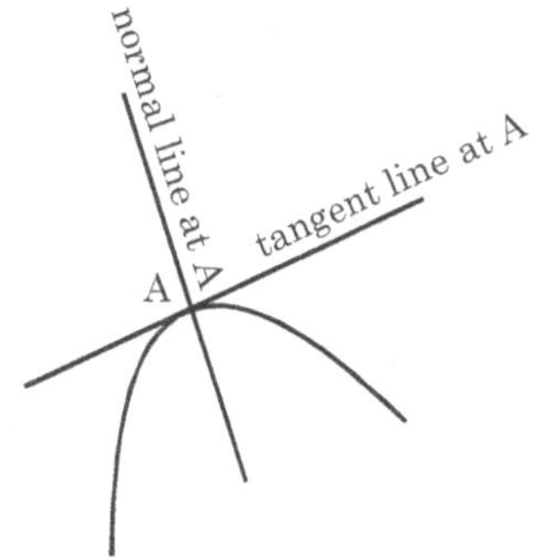

- Slope or gradient of a line: If a line makes an angle θ with the positive direction of X axis in anti-clockwise direction, then $\tan \theta$ is called the slope or gradient of the line.
- If a tangent line to the curve $y = f(x)$ makes an angle θ with x-axis in the positive direction, then

$$\text{slope of the tangent} = \tan\theta = \frac{dy}{dx}$$

- If slope of the tangent line is zero, then $\tan \theta = 0$ and so $\theta = 0$ which means the tangent line is parallel to the x-axis. In this case, the equation of the tangent at the point is given by $(y = y_0)$

- If $\theta \to \dfrac{\pi}{2}$ then $\tan \theta \to \infty$, which means the tangent line is perpendicular to the x-axis, i.e., parallel to the y-axis. In this case, the equation of the tangent at (x_0, y_0) is given by $(x = x_0)$

- Equation of tangent at (x_1, y_1) is given by $(y - y_1)$ $= m_T(x - x_1)$, where m_T is the slope of the tangent such that $m_N = \left[\dfrac{dy}{dx}\right]_{(x_1, y_1)}$

- Equation of normal at (x_1, y_1) is given by $(y - y_1) =$ $m_N(x - x_1)$, where m_N is the slope of the normal such that $m_N = \dfrac{-1}{\left[\dfrac{dy}{dx}\right]_{(x_1, y_1)}}$

- Tangent and normal are perpendicular to each other, which gives us $m_T \times m_N = -1$
- If the slope of two different curves are m_1 and m_2, then the acute angle between them is given by

$$\tan\theta = \left|\frac{m_2 - m_1}{1 + m_1 . m_2}\right|$$

- The slope intercept form of the line is $y = mx + c$, where m is the slope of the given line.

Maxima and Minima

Maxima and Minima

- The maximum value attained by a function is called maxima and the minimum value attained by the function is known as minima.
- Consider $y = f(x)$ be a well-defined function on an interval I, then
  - f is said to have a maximum value in I, if there exist a point c in I such that $f(c) > f(x)$, $\forall x \in$ I. The value corresponding to f(c) is called as maximum value of x in I and the point c is the maximum value.
  - f is said to have a minimum value in I, if there exist a point c in I such that $f(c) < f(x)$, $\forall x \in I$. The value corresponding to f(c) is called as minimum value of x in I and the point c is the minimum value.
  - f is said to have an extreme value in I, if there exist a point c in I such that f(c) is either a maximum value or a minimum value. The value corresponding to f(c) is called as extreme value of x in I and the point c is the extreme point.
- Let f be a function defined on an open interval I. Suppose c ? I be any point. If f has a local maxima or a local minima at x = c, then either f '(c) = 0 or f is not differentiable at c.

First Derivative Test

Let f be a function defined on an open interval I.
Let f be continuous at a critical point c in I. Then
- If f '(x) changes sign from positive to negative as x increases through c, i.e., if f'(x) > 0 at every point sufficiently close to and to the left of c, and f '(x) < 0 at every point sufficiently close to and to the right of c, then c is a point of local maxima.
- If f '(x) changes sign from negative to positive as x increases through c, i.e., if f '(x) < 0 at every point sufficiently close to and to the left of c,

and $f'(x) > 0$ at every point sufficiently close to and to the right of c, then c is a point of local minima.

- If $f'(x)$ does not change sign as x increases through c, then c is neither a point of local maxima nor a point of local minima. In fact, such a point is called point of inflection.

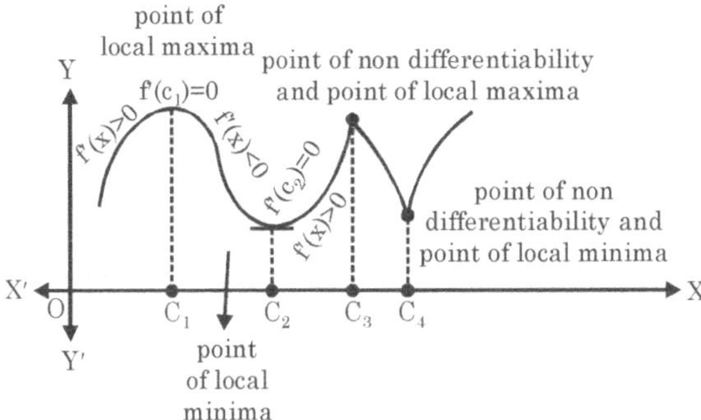

Second Derivative Test

Let f be a function defined on an interval I and $c \in I$. Let f be twice differentiable at c. Then

- $x = c$ is a point of local maxima if $f'(c) = 0$ and $f''(c) < 0$. The value $f(c)$ is local maximum value of f.
- $x = c$ is a point of local minima if $f'(c) = 0$ and $f''(c) > 0$ In this case, $f(c)$ is local minimum value of f.
- The test fails if $f'(c) = 0$ and $f''(c) = 0$. In this case, we go back to the first derivative test and find whether c is a point of local maxima, local minima or a point of inflexion.
- Maximum and Minimum values of a function in a closed interval

Let f be a continuous function on an interval $I = [a, b]$. Then f has the absolute maximum value and f attains it at least once in I. Also, f has the absolute minimum value and attains it at least once in I.

Let f be a differentiable function on a closed interval I and let c be any interior point of I. Then

- $f'(c) = 0$ if f attains its absolute maximum value at c.
- $f'(c) = 0$ if f attains its absolute minimum value at c.

In view of the above results, we have the following working rule for finding absolute maximum and/or absolute minimum values of a function in a given closed interval [a, b].

- Working Rule
  - Find all critical points of f in the interval, i.e., find points x where either $f'(x) = 0$ or f is not differentiable.
  - Take the end points of the interval.
  - At all these points (listed in Step 1 and 2), calculate the values of f
  - Identify the maximum and minimum values of f out of the values calculated in
  - This maximum value will be the absolute maximum (greatest) value off and the minimum value will be the absolute minimum (least) value of f.

Exercise

1. $f(x) = x^9 + 3x^7 + 6$ is increasing for
   (a) all positive real value of x
   (b) all negative real values of x
   (c) all non-zero real values of x
   (d) None of these

2. If $f(x) = kx^3 - 9x^2 + 9x + 3$ is increasing for every real number, then
   (a) $K < 3$　　　　(b) $K \leq 3$
   (c) $K > 3$　　　　(d) $K \geq 3$

3. For $0 < x < 1$, the function $f(x) = \dfrac{x}{\sin x}$, is
   (a) increasing
   (b) decreasing
   (c) sometimes increasing and sometimes decreasing
   (d) None of these

4. The function $f(x) = \tan x - x$
   (a) always decreases
   (b) never decreases
   (c) sometimes increases and sometimes decreases
   (d) None of these

5. If $f(x) = \dfrac{a \sin x + 2 \cos x}{\sin x + \cos x}$ is increasing for all values of x, then
   (a) $a < 1$　　　　(b) $a < 2$
   (c) $a > 1$　　　　(d) $a > 2$

6. The value of k for which $f(x) = \sin x - kx$ is decreasing for all $x \in R$, is
   (a) $K < 1$　　　　(b) $K > 1$
   (c) $K \leq 1$　　　　(d) $K \geq 1$

7. $f(x) = \sin x$ is increasing in
   (c) $\left]\dfrac{\pi}{2}, \pi\right[$　　　(b) $\left]\pi, \dfrac{3\pi}{2}\right[$
   (c) $]0, \pi[$　　　　(d) None of these

8. $f(x) = \dfrac{2x}{\log x}$ increasing in
   (a) $]0,1[$　　　　(b) $]1, e[$
   (c) $]e, \infty[$　　　(d) $]-\infty, e[$

9. If $x > 0$ and $x + y = 18$, the maximum value of xy is
   (a) 144　　　　(b) 81
   (c) 80　　　　(d) 77

10. If $y = a \log x + bx^2 + x$ has its extremum values at $x = -1$ and $x = 2$, then
    (a) $a = -\dfrac{1}{2}, b = 2$　　　(b) $a = 2, b = -1$
    (c) $a = 2, b = -\dfrac{1}{2}$　　　(d) $a = -2, b = -\dfrac{1}{2}$

11. The minimum value of $f(x) = |x + 2|$ is
    (a) -2　　　　(b) 2
    (c) 0　　　　(d) None

12. The points of maxima of $f(x) = \cos x$ are given by
    (a) $x = n\pi$　　　　(b) $x = 2n\pi$
    (c) $x = \dfrac{1}{2}n\pi$　　　(d) $x = (2n + 1)\pi$

13. $f(x) = \tan x$ has
    (a) no point of maxima
    (b) no point of minima
    (c) neither point of maxima nor point of minima
    (d) None of these

14. The least and greatest values of $f(x) = \dfrac{x-1}{x+1}$ in $[0, 4]$ are
    (a) $\dfrac{3}{5}, 1$　　　(b) $-1, \dfrac{3}{5}$
    (c) $-1, \dfrac{-3}{5}$　　　(d) None

15. The maximum value of $f(x) = (x - 2)(x - 3)^2$ is
    (a) 0　　　　(b) $\dfrac{4}{27}$
    (c) $\dfrac{7}{3}$　　　(d) 3

16. The least value of $f(x) = e^x + e^{-x}$, is
    (a) -2　　　　(b) 0
    (c) 2　　　　(d) None of these

17. The maximum area of a rectangle of perimeter 176 cm, is
    (a) 1854 cm^2　　　(b) 1936 cm^2
    (c) 2110 cm^2　　　(d) None of these

18. The sum of two positive numbers is 12. If their product is minimum, then the numbers are
    (a) 8, 4　　　　(b) 6, 6
    (c) 7, 5　　　　(d) None of these

19. If $x = t^2$ and $y = 2t$, then equation of the normal at $t = 1$ is

   (a) $x + y - 3 = 0$

   (b) $x + y - 1 = 0$

   (c) $x + y + 1 = 0$

   (d) $x + y + 3 = 0$

20. The equation of tangent to the curve $y = 2\cos x$ at $x = \dfrac{\pi}{4}$ is

   (a) $y - \sqrt{2} = 2\sqrt{2}\left(x - \dfrac{\pi}{4}\right)$ (b) $y + \sqrt{2} = \sqrt{2}\left(x + \dfrac{\pi}{4}\right)$

   (c) $y - \sqrt{2} = -\sqrt{2}\left(x - \dfrac{\pi}{4}\right)$ (d) $y - \sqrt{2} = \sqrt{2}\left(x - \dfrac{\pi}{4}\right)$

Answer Keys

1. (c)	2. (c)	3. (a)	4. (b)	5. (d)	6. (b)	7. (d)	8. (c)	9. (b)	10. (c)
11. (c)	12. (b)	13. (c)	14. (d)	15. (b)	16. (c)	17. (b)	18. (b)	19. (a)	20. (c)

Solutions

1. $f(x) = x^9 + 3x^7 + 6$

  $\Rightarrow f'(x) = 9x^8 + 21x^6$

  Clearly, $f'(x) > 0$ for all non-zero real values of x.

  $\therefore$ $f(x)$ is increasing for all non-zero real values of x.

2. $f(x) = kx^3 - 9x^2 + 9x + 3$

  $\Rightarrow f'(x) = 3kx^2 - 18x + 9$

  $= 3(kx^2 - 6x + 3)$

  This is positive when k is positive and

  $36 - 12k < 0$

  i.e. $k > \dfrac{36}{12}$

  $\therefore$ $k > 3$

3. $f(x) = \dfrac{x}{\sin x}$

  $f'(x) = \dfrac{\sin x - x\cos x}{\sin^2 x} = \dfrac{\cos x(\tan x - x)}{\sin^2 x}$

  $0 < x < 1 \Rightarrow \tan x > x$ and $\cos x > 0$

  $\Rightarrow (\tan x - x) > 0$ and $\cos x > 0$

  $\therefore$ $f'(x) > 0$

  Hence, $f(x)$ is increasing.

4. $f(x) = \tan x - x$

  $\Rightarrow f'(x) = \sec^2 x - 1$

  $\Rightarrow f'(x) \geq 0$ for all x.

  $\therefore$ $f(x)$ never decrease.

5. $f(x) = \dfrac{a\sin x + 2\cos x}{\sin x + \cos x}$

  $\Rightarrow f'(x) = \dfrac{(a - 2)}{(\sin x + \cos x)^2}$

  $\Rightarrow f'(x) > 0 \Rightarrow a - 2 > 0 \Rightarrow a > 2$

6. $f(x) = \sin x - kx$

  $\Rightarrow f'(x) = \cos x - k$

  $\therefore$ $f(x)$ is decreasing

  $\Rightarrow f'(x) < 0$

  $\Rightarrow \cos x - k < 0$

  $\Rightarrow \cos x < k$

  $\Rightarrow k > 1\,[\because \cos x \leq 1]$

7. $f(x) = \sin x$

  $\Rightarrow f'(x) = \cos x > 0$ in $\left]-\dfrac{\pi}{2}, \dfrac{\pi}{2}\right[$

  $\therefore$ $f(x)$ is increasing in $\left]-\dfrac{\pi}{2}, \dfrac{\pi}{2}\right[$

8. $f(x) = \dfrac{2x}{\log x}$

  $\Rightarrow f'(x) = \dfrac{(\log x).2 - 2x.\dfrac{1}{x}}{(\log x)^2} = \dfrac{2(\log x - 1)}{(\log x)^2}$

  $\Rightarrow f'(x) > 0 \Rightarrow \log x - 1 > 0$

  $\Rightarrow \log x > 1$

  $\Rightarrow x > e$

  $\therefore$ $f(x)$ is increasing in $]e, \infty[$

9. $x + y = 18 \Rightarrow y = 18 - x$

Let $M = xy = x(18 - x)$

$$\Rightarrow \frac{dM}{dx} = (18 - 2x) \ \& \ \frac{d^2M}{dx^2} = -2$$

$$\frac{dM}{dx} = 0 \Rightarrow 18 - 2x = 0 \Rightarrow x = \frac{18}{2} = 9$$

Also, $\dfrac{d^2M}{dx^2} < 0$

$\therefore \ x = 9$ is a point of maxima.

Maximum value of $M = 9 \times (18 - 9) = 81$

10. $y = a\log x + bx^2 + x$

$$\Rightarrow \frac{dy}{dx} = \frac{a}{x} + 2bx + 1$$

$$\frac{dy}{dx} = 0 \Rightarrow \frac{a}{x} + 2bx + 1 = 0 \dots\dots\dots(i)$$

$\therefore \ x = -1$ and $x = 2$ must satisfy (i)

$-a - 2b + 1 = 0 \qquad \dots(ii)$

and $a + 8b + 2 = 0 \qquad \dots(iii)$

On solving equation (ii) & (iii), we get

$b = -\dfrac{1}{2}$ and $a = 2$

11. $f(x) = |x + 2|$ is non-negative for all $x \in R$.

The least value of $|x + 2|$ is 0.

12. $f(x) = \cos x$

$\Rightarrow \ f'(x) = -\sin x, \ f'(x) = -\cos x.$

for points of maxima, we must have $f'(x) = 0$ and $f''(x) < 0$.

This happens at $x = 2n\pi$

13. $f(x) = \tan x \Rightarrow f'(x) = \sec^2 x \neq 0$

$\therefore \ f(x)$ has neither a point of maxima nor a point of minima.

14. $f(x) = \dfrac{x-1}{x+1}$

$$\therefore \ f'(x) = \frac{(x+1) - (x-1)}{(x+1)^2} = \frac{2}{(x+1)^2}$$

$\Rightarrow \ f'(x) \neq 0$

Hence, $f(x)$ has neither maxima nor minima.

15. $f(x) = (x - 2)(x - 3)^2$

$\therefore \ f'(x) = (x - 2) \, 2 \, (x - 3) + (x - 3)^2$

$= (x - 3) \, [2x - 4 + x - 3]$

$= (x - 3)(3x - 7)$

and $f''(x) = 3(x - 3) + (3x - 7) = (6x - 16)$

$f'(x) = 0 \Rightarrow (x - 3)(3x - 7) = 0$

$$\therefore x = 3 \ \text{ or } \ x = \frac{7}{3}$$

$f''(3) = (18 - 16) = 2 > 0$

$$f''\left(\frac{7}{3}\right) = \left(6 \times \frac{7}{3} - 16\right) = -2 < 0$$

$\therefore \ x = \dfrac{7}{3}$ is a point of maxima.

Hence, maximum value $= \left(\dfrac{7}{3} - 2\right)\left(\dfrac{7}{3} - 3\right)^2 = \dfrac{4}{27}$

16. $f(x) = e^x + e^{-x}$

$\Rightarrow \ f'(x) = e^x - e^{-x}$ and $f''(x) = e^x + e^{-x}$

$f'(x) = 0 \Rightarrow e^x - e^{-x} = 0 \Rightarrow e^x = e^{-x} \Rightarrow e^{2x} = 1$

$\Rightarrow \ x = 0$

$$f''(0) = \left(e^0 + \frac{1}{e^0}\right) = 2 > 0$$

$\therefore \ x = 0$ is a point of minima.

Hence, least value of $f(x) = f(0) = 2$

17. Semi - perimeter = 88 cm

Let length = x cm, then

breadth = $(88 - x)$ cm

$\therefore \ A = x(88 - x) = 88x - x^2$

$$\Rightarrow \frac{dA}{dx} = 88 - 2x \text{ and } \frac{d^2A}{dx^2} = -2 < 0$$

$$\frac{dA}{dx} = 0 \Rightarrow x = 44$$

$\therefore \ x = 44$ is a point of maxima.

Hence, maximum area $= (44 \times 44)$

$= 1936 \ \text{cm}^2$

18. Let $x + y = 12$, $x > 0$ and $y > 0$

and $P = xy = x(12 - x) = 12x - x^2$

$$\therefore \frac{dP}{dx} = 12 - 2x \text{ and } \frac{d^2P}{dx^2} = -2 < 0$$

$$\frac{dP}{dx} = 0 \Rightarrow 12 - 2x = 0 \Rightarrow x = 6$$

$\therefore$ x = 6 is a point of maxima

Hence, x = y = 6

19. $x = t^2$, y = 2 t

at t = 1, x = 1, y = 2

$$\frac{dy}{dx} = \frac{dy/dt}{dx/dt}$$

$$= \frac{2}{2t} = \frac{1}{t}$$

Slope of tangent at t = 1, = 1

Slope of normal = –1

Equation of normal y – 2 = –(x – 1)

x + y – 3 = 0

20. y = 2 cos x

$$\frac{dy}{dx} = -2 \sin x$$

$$m = \left(\frac{dy}{dx}\right)_{x=\pi/4}$$

$$= -2\left(\sin\frac{\pi}{4}\right)$$

$$= \frac{-2}{\sqrt{2}} = -\sqrt{2}$$

at $x = \frac{\pi}{4}$, $y = 2\cos\frac{\pi}{4} = \sqrt{2}$

Equation of tangent

$$y - \sqrt{2} = -\sqrt{2}\left(x - \frac{\pi}{4}\right)$$

CHAPTER 7

Integrals

Indefinite Integrals

- Integration is the inverse of differentiation. Instead of differentiating a function, we will be given the derivative of a function and we would be asked to find its primitive function. Such a process is called integration or anti differentiation.

  If $\dfrac{d}{dx}F(x) = f(x)$. Then we write $\int f(x)dx = F(x) + C$.

  These integrals are called indefinite integrals or general integrals and C is called the constant of integration.

- The integral of a function are unique upto an additive constant, i.e. any two integrals of a function differ by a constant.

- When a polynomial function P is integrated, the result is a polynomial whose degree is one more than that of P.

- Geometrically, the indefinite integral of a function represents a family of curves placed parallel to each other having parallel tangents at the points of intersection of the curves of the family with the lines perpendicular to the axisrepresenting the variable of integration.

- Two indefinite integrals with the same derivative lead to the same family of curves and so they are equivalent.

- Some properties of indefinite integral are as follows:

  $\quad\triangleright\ \int [f(x) + g(x)]dx = \int f(x)dx + \int g(x)dx$

  $\quad\triangleright$ For any real number a, $\int af(x)dx = a\int f(x)dx$

  $\quad\triangleright$ Properties (i) and (ii) can be generalised to a finite number of functions $f_1, f_2, f_3,...f_n$ and the real numbers, $a_1, a_2, a_3,...a_n$ giving

  $\quad \int a_1 f_1(x)dx + a_2 f_2(x)dx + ... + a_n f_n(x)dx$

  $\qquad = a_1\int f_1(x)dx + a_2\int f_2(x)dx + ... a_n\int f_n(x)dx$.

- Some basic integrals are as follows:

  $\quad\triangleright\ \int x^n dx = \dfrac{x^{n+1}}{n+1} + C \quad ,n \neq -1$

  $\triangleright\ \int dx = x + C$

  $\triangleright\ \int \cos x\,dx = \sin x + C$

  $\triangleright\ \int \sin x\,dx = -\cos x + C$

  $\triangleright\ \int \sec^2 x\,dx = \tan x + C$

  $\triangleright\ \int \mathrm{cosec}^2 x\,dx = -\cot x + C$

  $\triangleright\ \int \sec x \tan x\,dx = \sec x + C$

  $\triangleright\ \int \mathrm{cosec}\,x \cot x\,dx = -\mathrm{cosec}\,x + C$

  $\triangleright\ \int \dfrac{dx}{\sqrt{1-x^2}} = \sin^{-1} x + C$

  $\triangleright\ \int \dfrac{dx}{\sqrt{1-x^2}} = -\cos^{-1} x + C$

  $\triangleright\ \int \dfrac{dx}{1+x^2} = \tan^{-1} x + C$

  $\triangleright\ \int \dfrac{dx}{1+x^2} = -\cot^{-1} x + C$

  $\triangleright\ \int \dfrac{dx}{x\sqrt{x^2-1}} = \sec^{-1} x + C$

  $\triangleright\ \int \dfrac{dx}{x\sqrt{x^2-1}} = -\mathrm{cosec}^{-1} x + C$

  $\triangleright\ \int e^x dx = e^x + C$

  $\triangleright\ \int \dfrac{1}{x}dx = \log|x| + C$

  $\triangleright\ \int a^x dx = \dfrac{a^x}{\log a} + C$

- **Integration by substitution:**

  The method in which we change the variable to some other variable is called the method of substitution. It often reduces an integral to one of the fundamental integrals.

  The integral $\int f(x)dx$ can be substituted into another form by changing the independent variable x to t by substituting $x = g(t)$.

Consider, $A = \int f(x)dx$

Put $x = g(t)$, therefore $\dfrac{dx}{dt} = g'(t)$.

$\Rightarrow dx = g'(t)dt$

Thus, $A = \int f(x)dx = \int f(g(t))g'(t)dt$

Using substitution method we obtain the following standard integrals.

➤ $\int \tan x\,dx = \log|\sec x| + C$

➤ $\int \cot x\,dx = \log|\sin x| + C$

➤ $\int \sec x\,dx = \log|\sec x + \tan x| + C$

➤ $\int \cosec x\,dx = \log|\cosec x - \cot x| + C$

- **Integrals of some particular functions are as follows:**

➤ $\int \dfrac{dx}{x^2 - a^2} = \dfrac{1}{2a}\log\left|\dfrac{x-a}{x+a}\right| + C$

➤ $\int \dfrac{dx}{a^2 - x^2} = \dfrac{1}{2a}\log\left|\dfrac{a+x}{a-x}\right| + C$

➤ $\int \dfrac{dx}{x^2 + a^2} = \dfrac{1}{a}\tan^{-1}\dfrac{x}{a} + C$

➤ $\int \dfrac{dx}{\sqrt{x^2 - a^2}} = \log\left|x + \sqrt{x^2 - a^2}\right| + C$

➤ $\int \dfrac{dx}{\sqrt{a^2 - x^2}} = \sin^{-1}\dfrac{x}{a} + C$

➤ $\int \dfrac{dx}{\sqrt{x^2 + a^2}} = \log\left|x + \sqrt{x^2 + a^2}\right| + C$

- **Integration by Partial Fractions:**
A rational function is defined as the ratio of two polynomials in the form $\dfrac{P(x)}{Q(x)}$, where $P(x)$ and $Q(x)$ are polynomials in x and $Q(x) \neq 0$. If $\dfrac{P(x)}{Q(x)}$ is improper, then $\dfrac{P(x)}{Q(x)} = T(x) + \dfrac{P_1(x)}{Q(x)}$ where T(x) is a polynomial in x and $\dfrac{P_1(x)}{Q(x)}$ is a proper rational function. Assume we want to evaluate $\int \dfrac{P(x)}{Q(x)}dx$, where $\dfrac{P(x)}{Q(x)}$ is a proper rational function. It is possible to write the integrand as a sum of simpler rational functions by partial fraction decomposition as follows:

➤ $\dfrac{px + q}{(x-a)(x-b)} = \dfrac{A}{x-a} + \dfrac{B}{x-b}, a \neq b$

➤ $\dfrac{px+q}{(x-a)^2} = \dfrac{A}{x-a} + \dfrac{B}{(x-a)^2}$

➤ $\dfrac{px^2 + qx + r}{(x-a)(x-b)(x-c)} = \dfrac{A}{x-a} + \dfrac{B}{x-b} + \dfrac{C}{x-c}$

➤ $\dfrac{px^2 + qx + r}{(x-a)^2(x-b)} = \dfrac{A}{(x-a)} + \dfrac{B}{(x-a)^2} + \dfrac{C}{(x-b)}$

➤ $\dfrac{px^2 + qx + r}{(x-a)(x^2 + bx + c)} = \dfrac{A}{x-a} + \dfrac{Bx + C}{x^2 + bx + c}$, where $x^2 + bx + c$ cannot be factorized further.

- **Integration by parts:**
If $f(x)$ and $g(x)$ are the two functions then,

$\int f(x)g(x)dx = f(x)\int g(x)dx - \int\left[f'(x)\int g(x)dx\right]dx$,

where $f(x)$ is the first function and $g(x)$ is the second function. It can be stated as follows: "The integration of the product of two functions = (First function) x (integral of the second function) – Integral of [(differential coefficient of the first function) x (integral of the second function)]"

- Integral of the type $\int e^x\left[f(x) + f'(x)\right]dx = e^x f(x) + C$

- Some special types of integrals are as follows:

➤ $\int \sqrt{x^2 - a^2}\,dx = \dfrac{x}{2}\sqrt{x^2 - a^2} - \dfrac{a^2}{2}\log\left|x + \sqrt{x^2 - a^2}\right| + C$

➤ $\int \sqrt{x^2 + a^2}\,dx = \dfrac{x}{2}\sqrt{x^2 + a^2} + \dfrac{a^2}{2}\log\left|x + \sqrt{x^2 + a^2}\right| + C$

➤ $\int \sqrt{a^2 - x^2}\,dx = \dfrac{x}{2}\sqrt{a^2 - x^2} + \dfrac{a^2}{2}\sin^{-1}\dfrac{x}{a} + C$

➤ Integrals of the types $\int \dfrac{dx}{ax^2 + bx + c}$ or $\int \dfrac{dx}{\sqrt{ax^2 + bx + c}}$ can be transformed into standard form by expressing $ax^2 + bx + c$

$= a\left[x^2 + \dfrac{b}{a}x + \dfrac{c}{a}\right] = a\left[\left(x + \dfrac{b}{2a}\right)^2 + \left(\dfrac{c}{a} - \dfrac{b^2}{4a^2}\right)\right]$

➤ Integrals of the types $\int \dfrac{px + q\,dx}{ax^2 + bx + c}$ or $\int \dfrac{(px+q)\,dx}{\sqrt{ax^2 + bx + c}}$ can be transformed into standard form by expressing $px + q$

$= A\dfrac{d}{dx}\left(ax^2 + bx + c\right) + B\ = A(2ax + b) + B$,

where A and B are determined by comparing coefficients on both sides.

Properties of a Definite Integrals and Limit of a sum

- **Definite Integrals:**

A definite integral is denoted by $\int_a^b f(x)dx$, where a is called the lower limit of the integral and b is called the upper limit of the integral.

- **Definite integral as the limit of a sum:**

The definite integral $\int_a^b f(x)dx$ is the area bounded by the curve $y = f(x)$, the ordinates $x = a$, $x = b$ and the x-axis. This can be mathematically defined as following:

$$\int_a^b f(x)dx = (b-a)\lim_{h \to 0}\frac{1}{n}\left[f(a) + f(a+h)\right.$$
$$\left. +...+ f(a+(n-1)h)\right]$$

Where, $h = \dfrac{b-a}{n} \to 0$ as $n \to \infty$ $\int_a^b f(x)dx$ is defined as the area function where the area of the region is bounded by the curve $y = f(x)$, $a \leq x \leq b$, the $x - axis$ and the ordinates $x = a$ and $x = b$. Let x be

a given point in $[a, b]$. Then $\int_a^x f(x)dx$ represents the **Area function $A(x)$**.

- **First fundamental theorem of integral calculus:**

Let f be a continuous function on the closed interval $[a, b]$ and let $A(x) = \int_a^b f(x)dx$ for all $x \geq a$ be the area function. Then $A'(x) = f(x)$, for all $x \in [a, b]$.

- **Second fundamental theorem of integral calculus:**

Let f be continuous function defined on the closed interval $[a, b]$ and F be an anti derivative of f. Then

$$\int_a^b f(x)dx = \left[F(x)\right]_a^b = F(b) - F(a).$$

- **Properties of Definite Integrals** are as follows:

➤ $P_0 : \int_a^b f(x)dx = \int_a^b f(t)dt$

➤ $P_1 = \int_a^b f(x)dx = -\int_b^a f(x)dx.$

In particular $\int_a^a f(x)dx = 0$

➤ $P_2 : \int_a^b f(x)dx = \int_a^c f(x)dx + \int_c^b f(x)dx$

➤ $P_3 : \int_a^b f(x)dx = \int_a^b f(a+b-x)dx$

➤ $P_4 : \int_0^a f(x)dx = \int_0^a f(a-x)dx$

➤ $P_5 : \int_0^{2a} f(x)dx = \int_0^a f(x)dx + \int_0^a f(2a-x)dx$

➤ $P_6 : \int_0^{2a} f(x)dx = 2\int_0^a f(x)dx$, if $(2a-x) = f(x)$

and 0, if $(2a-x) = -f(x)$.

➤ $P_7 : \int_{-a}^a f(x)dx = \begin{cases} 2\int_0^a f(x)dx, \text{ if } f \text{ is an even function,} \\ \quad \text{i.e., } f(-x) = f(x)(2a-x) = f(x) \\ \\ 0, \text{ if } f \text{ is an odd function,} \\ \quad \text{i.e., if } f(-x) = -f(x) \end{cases}$

Exercise

1. $\int \log x\, dx = ?$

   (a) $\dfrac{1}{x} + C$ (b) $\dfrac{1}{2}(\log x)^2 + C$

   (c) $x(\log x + 1) + C$ (d) None of these

2. $\int (\log x)^2\, dx = ?$

   (a) $\dfrac{2\log x}{x} + C$

   (b) $\dfrac{1}{2}(\log x)^3 + C$

   (c) $x(\log x)^2 - 2x \log x + 2x + C$
   (d) $x(\log x)^2 + 2x \log x - 2x + C$

3. $\int \sin^{-1} x\, dx = ?$

   (a) $-\cos^{-1} x$

   (b) $\dfrac{1}{\sqrt{1-x^2}} + C$

   (c) $x\sin^{-1} x - \sqrt{\;-\;^2} + C$

   (d) $x\sin^{-1} x + \sqrt{\;-\;^2} + C$

4. $\int \tan^2 x\, dx = ?$

   (a) $\dfrac{1}{3}\tan^3 x + C$ (b) $2\tan x \sec^2 x + C$

   (c) $\tan x - x + C$ (d) $\tan x + x + C$

5. $\int \sin^2 x\, dx = ?$

   (a) $\dfrac{1}{2}\sin 2x + C$ (b) $\dfrac{1}{3}\sin^3 x + C$

   (c) $\dfrac{1}{2}x - \dfrac{1}{4}\,\;+ C$ (d) $x - \dfrac{1}{2}\,\;+ C$

6. $\int \dfrac{(1-x^2)}{(1+x^2)}\, dx = ?$

   (a) $2\tan^{-1} x + C$
   (b) $-x + \tan^{-1} x + C$
   (c) $-x + 2\tan^{-1} x + C$
   (d) $x - 2\tan^{-1} x + C$

7. $\int \sqrt{ax+b}\, dx = ?$

   (a) $\dfrac{2}{3}a(ax+b)^{\frac{3}{2}} + C$ (b) $\dfrac{3}{2}a(ax+b)^{\frac{3}{2}} + C$

   (c) $\dfrac{2}{3a}(ax+b)^{\frac{3}{2}} + C$ (d) $\dfrac{3}{2a}(ax+b)^{\frac{3}{2}} + C$

8. $\int \dfrac{dx}{(e^x - 1)} = ?$

   (a) $\log|e^x - 1| + C$ (b) $\log |1 - e^{-x}| + C$

   (c) $x + \log |e^x - 1| + C$ (d) None of these

9. $\int \dfrac{(1+\cos x)}{(1-\cos x)}\, dx = ?$

   (a) $\tan\left(\dfrac{x}{2}\right) - x + C$ (b) $-2\cot\left(\dfrac{x}{2}\right) - x + C$

   (c) $-2\cot\left(\dfrac{x}{2}\right) + x + C$ (d) $-2\tan\left(\dfrac{x}{2}\right) - x + C$

10. $\int \dfrac{1}{(1-\cos x)}\, dx = ?$

    (a) $\dfrac{1}{(x - \sin x)} + C$ (b) $\log |x - \sin x| + C$

    (c) $\log \left|\tan\left(\dfrac{x}{2}\right)\right| + C$ (d) $-\cot\dfrac{x}{2} + C$

11. $\int \dfrac{\sin x}{(1+\sin x)}\, dx = ?$

    (a) $x + \tan x - \sec x + C$
    (b) $x - \tan x + \sec x + C$
    (c) $x - \tan x - \sec x + C$
    (d) None of these

12. $\int \dfrac{\sin^2 x}{(1-\cos x)}\, dx = ?$

    (a) $x - \sin x + C$ (b) $x + \sin x + C$

    (c) $\dfrac{x^2}{2} - \dfrac{1}{2}\,\;+ C$ (d) None of these

13. $\int \dfrac{(\cos 2x - \;\alpha)}{(\;-\;\alpha)}\, dx = ?$

    (a) $2\sin x + 2x \cos \alpha = C$
    (b) $2x \sin x + 2 \cos \alpha \cos x + C$
    (c) $2\sin x - 2x \sin \alpha + C$
    (d) None of these

14. $\int \cos^2 nx\,dx = ?$

(a) $\dfrac{x}{2} + \dfrac{1}{4n}\sin 2nx + C$ (b) $\dfrac{nx}{2} + \dfrac{1}{4n}\cos 2nx + C$

(c) $nx + \dfrac{1}{2n}\sin 2nx + C$ (d) None of these

15. $\int \sin 3x \sin 2x\,dx = ?$

(a) $-\dfrac{1}{5}\cos 5x + C$

(b) $\dfrac{1}{2}\sin x + \dfrac{1}{10}\sin 5x + C$

(c) $\dfrac{1}{2}\sin x - \dfrac{1}{10}\sin 5x + C$

(d) $-\dfrac{1}{3}\sin 3x - \dfrac{1}{2}\sin 2x + C$

16. $\int_a^4 x\sqrt{x}\,dx = ?$

(a) 8.4 (b) 8.8

(c) 12.4 (d) 7

17. $\int_0^7 \dfrac{1}{\sqrt{3x+4}}\,dx = ?$

(a) 10 (b) 2.5

(c) 0.4 (d) 2

18. $\int_0^{\frac{\pi}{4}} \tan^2 x\,dx = ?$

(a) $\left(1 + \dfrac{\pi}{4}\right)$ (b) $\left(1 - \dfrac{\pi}{4}\right)$

(c) $\left(1 + \dfrac{\pi}{2}\right)$ (d) $\left(1 - \dfrac{\pi}{2}\right)$

19. $\int_0^1 \dfrac{1}{\left(1+x^2\right)}\,dx = ?$

(a) $\dfrac{\pi}{2}$ (b) $\dfrac{\pi}{3}$

(c) $\dfrac{\pi}{4}$ (d) None

20. $\int_0^2 \dfrac{1}{\sqrt{4-x^2}}\,dx = ?$

(a) 1 (b) $\sin^{-1}\dfrac{1}{2}$

(c) $\dfrac{\pi}{4}$ (d) None

21. $\int_0^a \left(\dfrac{a-x}{a+x}\right)dx = ?$

(a) $a(1 - 2\log 2)$ (b) $a(2\log 2 - 1)$

(c) $a\left(1 - \dfrac{1}{2}\log 2\right)$ (d) None

22. $\int_{-a}^a x|x|\,dx = ?$

(a) 0 (b) $\dfrac{2a^3}{3}$

(c) $2a$ (d) None

23. $\int_{\pi}^{2\pi} |\sin x|\,dx = ?$

(a) 0 (b) 1

(c) 2 (d) None

24. Let $f(x) = \begin{cases} 2x+1, & \text{when } 1 \le x \le 2 \\ x^2 + 1, & \text{when } 2 \le x \le 3 \end{cases}$ then,

$\int_1^3 f(x)\,dx = ?$

(a) $\dfrac{17}{6}$ (b) $\dfrac{34}{3}$

(c) $\dfrac{16}{3}$ (d) None

25. $\int_0^{2a} f(x)\,dx - \int_0^a f(2a-x)\,dx = ?$

(a) $\int_0^a f(x)\,dx$ (b) $\int_0^a f(a+x)\,dx$

(c) $\int_a^{2a} f(x)\,dx$ (d) $\int_a^{2a} f(a+x)\,dx$

26. $\int_0^a \{f(x) + f(-x)\}\,dx = ?$

(a) 0 (b) $\int_0^a f(x)\,dx = ?$

(c) $\int_{-a}^a f(x)\,dx$ (d) $-\int_{-a}^a f(-x)\,dx$

27. $\int_a^b \dfrac{f(x)}{f(x) + f(a+b-x)}\,dx = ?$

(a) $(b-a)$ (b) $\dfrac{1}{2}(a+b)$

(c) $\dfrac{1}{2}(b-a)$ (d) None of these

28. $\int_3^5 \dfrac{x^2}{\left(x^2-4\right)}\,dx = ?$

   (a) $2 - \log 15 + \log 7$

   (b) $2 + \log 15 - \log 7$

   (c) $2 + 4\log 3 - 4\log 7 + 4\log 5$

   (d) $2 - \tan^{-1}\left(\dfrac{15}{7}\right)$

29. $\int_1^2 \dfrac{\log x}{x^2}\,dx = ?$

   (a) $2(\log 2 - 1)$ (b) $\dfrac{1}{2}\left(1 - \log 2\right)$

   (c) $\dfrac{1}{2}\log 2 - 1$ (d) None

30. $\int_0^1 \left(\dfrac{1-x}{1+x}\right)dx = ?$

   (a) $\dfrac{1}{2}\log 2$ (b) $2\log 2$

   (c) $(2\log 2 - 1)$ (d) None

Answer Keys

1. (d)	2. (c)	3. (d)	4. (c)	5. (c)	6. (c)	7. (c)	8. (b)	9. (b)	10. (d)
11. (b)	12. (b)	13. (a)	14. (a)	15. (c)	16. (c)	17. (d)	18. (b)	19. (c)	20. (d)
21. (b)	22. (a)	23. (c)	24. (b)	25. (a)	26. (c)	27. (c)	28. (b)	29. (b)	30. (c)

Solutions

1. $I = \int \left\{ \underset{I}{(\log x)}.\underset{II}{1} \right\} dx$

  $= (\log x)x - \int \dfrac{1}{x}.x\,dx$

  $= x\log x - x + C$

  $= x(\log x - 1) + C$

2. $I = \int \left\{ \underset{I}{(\log x)^2}.\underset{II}{1} \right\} dx$

  $= (\log x)^2.x - \int \dfrac{2\log x}{x}.x\,dx$

  $= x(\log x)^2 - 2\int \log x\,dx$

  $= x(\log x)^2 - 2[x(\log x - 1)] + C$

3. $I = \int \left\{ \underset{I}{(\sin^{-1} x)}.\underset{II}{1} \right\} dx$

  $= (\sin^{-1} x)x - \int \dfrac{1}{\sqrt{1-x^2}}.x\,dx$

  $= x\sin^{-1} x + \dfrac{1}{2}\int \dfrac{(-2x)}{\sqrt{1-x^2}}\,dx$

  $= x\sin^{-1} x + \dfrac{1}{2}\int \dfrac{dt}{\sqrt{t}}$, where $(1-x^2) = t$

  $= x\sin^{-1} x + \sqrt{t} + C$

  $= x\sin^{-1} x + \sqrt{1-x^2} + C$

4. $I = \int \tan^2 x\,dx = \int \left(\sec^2 x - 1\right)dx$

  $= \int \sec^2 x\,dx - \int dx$

  $= \tan x - x + C$

5. $I = \dfrac{1}{2}\int 2\sin^2 x\,dx$

  $= \dfrac{1}{2}\int (1 - \cos 2x)\,dx$

  $= \dfrac{1}{2}\left[x - \dfrac{1}{2}\sin 2x \right] + C$

  $= \dfrac{1}{2}x - \dfrac{1}{4}\sin 2x + C$

6. On dividing $(-x^2 + 1)$ by $(x^2 + 1)$, we get

  $I = \int \left\{ -1 + \dfrac{2}{\left(1+x^2\right)} \right\} dx$

  $= -x + 2\tan^{-1}x + C$

7. Putting $ax + b = t$ and $dx = \dfrac{1}{a}dt$, we get

$$I = \frac{1}{a}\int \sqrt{t}\ dt = \frac{1}{a}\cdot\frac{2}{3}t^{\frac{3}{2}} + C$$

$$= \frac{2}{3a}(ax + b)^{\frac{3}{2}} + C$$

8. $I = \int \dfrac{dx}{e^x\left(1 - e^{-x}\right)} = \int \dfrac{e^{-x}}{\left(1 - e^{-x}\right)}dx$

On putting $(1 - e^{-x}) = t$ and $e^{-x}\ dx = dt$, we get

$$I = \int \frac{1}{t}dt = \log\ |t| + C = \log\ |1 - e^{-x}| + C$$

9. $I = \int \dfrac{2\cos^2\left(\dfrac{x}{2}\right)}{2\sin^2\left(\dfrac{x}{2}\right)}dx$

$$= \int \cot^2\left(\frac{x}{2}\right)\ dx$$

$$= \int \left[\cos ec^2\left(\frac{x}{2}\right) - 1\right]\ dx$$

$$= -2\cot\left(\frac{x}{2}\right) - x + C$$

10. $I = \int \dfrac{1}{2\sin^2\left(\dfrac{x}{2}\right)}\ dx$

$$= \frac{1}{2}\int \cos ec^2\left(\frac{x}{2}\right)dx$$

$$= \frac{1}{2}\times 2\times\left(-\cot\frac{x}{2}\right) + C$$

$$= -\cot\frac{x}{2} + C$$

11. $I = \int \dfrac{(1 + \sin x) - 1}{(1 + \sin x)}dx$

$$= \int\left\{1 - \frac{1}{(1 + \sin x)}\right\}dx$$

$$= \int dx - \int \frac{dx}{(1 + \sin x)}$$

$$= x - (\tan x - \sec x) + C$$

$$= x - \tan x + \sec x + C$$

12. $I = \int \dfrac{\left(1 - \cos^2 x\right)}{(1 - \cos x)}dx$

$$= \int(1 + \cos x)dx$$

$$= x + \sin x + C$$

13. $I = \int \dfrac{\left(2\cos^2 x - 1\right) - \left(2\cos^2 \alpha - 1\right)}{(\cos x - \cos \alpha)}dx$

$$= 2\int \frac{\left(\cos^2 x - \cos^2 \alpha\right)}{(\cos x - \cos \alpha)}dx$$

$$= 2\int(\cos x + \cos \alpha)dx$$

$$= 2\sin x + 2 x\cos \alpha + C$$

14. $I = \dfrac{1}{2}\int 2\cos^2 nx\ dx$

$$I = \frac{1}{2}\int(1 + \cos 2nx)\ dx$$

$$= \frac{1}{2}\left[x + \frac{\sin 2nx}{2n}\right] + C = \frac{x}{2} + \frac{\sin 2nx}{4n} + C$$

15. $I = \dfrac{1}{2}\int 2\sin 3x\cdot\sin 2x\ dx$

$$= \frac{1}{2}\int(\cos x - \cos 5x)dx$$

$$= \frac{1}{2}\sin x - \frac{1}{10}\sin 5x + C$$

16. $I = \int_1^4 x^{\frac{3}{2}}dx = \left[\dfrac{2}{5}x^{\frac{5}{2}}\right]_1^4$

$$= \left(\frac{64}{5} - \frac{2}{5}\right) = \frac{62}{5} = 12.4 \qquad \text{[1]}$$

17. $I = \int_0^7 (3x + 4)^{\frac{-1}{2}}dx$

$$= \left[\frac{(3x + 4)^{\frac{1}{2}}}{\frac{1}{2}}\cdot\frac{1}{3}\right]_0^7$$

$$= \frac{2}{3}\left[\sqrt{3x + 4}\right]_0^7 = \frac{2}{3}(5 - 2) = \frac{2}{3}\times 3 = 2$$

18. $I = \int_0^{\frac{\pi}{4}}\left(\sec^2 x - 1\right)dx = \left[\tan x - x\right]_0^{\frac{\pi}{4}}$

$$= \left(\tan\frac{\pi}{4} - \frac{\pi}{4}\right) - 0 = \left(1 - \frac{\pi}{4}\right)$$

19. $I = \int_0^1 \dfrac{1}{1+x^2}\,dx$

$ = \left[\tan^{-1}x\right]_0^1 = \left[\tan^{-1}(1) - \tan^{-1}(0)\right]$

$ = \dfrac{\pi}{4}$

20. $I = \int_0^2 \dfrac{1}{\sqrt{4-x^2}}\,dx$

$ = \left[\sin^{-1}\left(\dfrac{x}{2}\right)\right]_0^2$

$ = [\sin^{-1}(1) - \sin^{-1}(0)]$

$ = \dfrac{\pi}{2}$

21. On dividing $(-x + a)$ by $(x + a)$, we get

$I = \int_0^a \left(-1 + \dfrac{2a}{x+a}\right)dx$

$ = \left[-x + 2a\log|x+a|\right]_0^a$

$ = (-a + 2a\log 2) = a(2\log 2 - 1)$

22. Let $f(x) = x\,|x|$., then

$f(-x) = -x\,|-x| = -x\,|x| = -f(x)$

$\therefore\ \ f(x)$ is an odd function.

Hence, $\int_{-a}^{a} f(x)\,dx = 0$

23. $\pi \le x \le 2\pi \Rightarrow \sin x < 0$

$\Rightarrow\ |\sin x| = -\sin x$

$\therefore I = \int_{\pi}^{2\pi}|\sin x|\,dx$

$ = \int_{\pi}^{2\pi} -\sin x\,dx = \left[\cos x\right]_{\pi}^{2\pi} = 2$

24. $I = \int_1^2 f(x)\,dx + \int_2^3 f(x)\,dx$

$ = \int_1^2 (2x+1)\,dx + \int_2^3 \left(x^2 + 1\right)dx$

$ = \left[x^2 + x\right]_1^2 + \left[\dfrac{x^3}{3} + x\right]_2^3$

$ = (4+2) - 2 + (9+3) - \left(\dfrac{8}{3} + 2\right)$

$ = 16 - \dfrac{8}{3} - 2 = \dfrac{42-8}{3} = \dfrac{34}{3}$

25. $\int_a^{2a} f(x)\,dx = \int_0^a \{f(x) + f(2a - x)\}\,dx$

$\Rightarrow \int_a^{2a} f(x)\,dx - \int_0^a f(2a - x)\,dx = \int_0^a f(x)\,dx$

26. We know that

$\int_{-a}^{a} f(x)\,dx = \int_0^a \left[f(x) + f(-x)\right]dx$

27. $I = \int_a^b \dfrac{f(x)}{f(x) + f(a+b-x)}\,dx$ ...(i)

$\Rightarrow I = \int_a^b \dfrac{f(a+b-x)}{f(a+b-x) + f(x)}\,dx$ ...(ii)

from equation (i) + (ii), we get

$2I = \int_a^b dx = \left[x\right]_a^b = (b-a)$

$\therefore\ I = \dfrac{1}{2}(b-a)$

28. $I = \int_3^5 \left(1 + \dfrac{4}{x^2 - 4}\right)dx$

$ = \int_3^5 dx + 4\int_3^5 \dfrac{1}{x^2 - 4}\,dx$

$ = \left[x\right]_3^5 + 4 \times \dfrac{1}{4}\left[\log\left|\dfrac{x-2}{x+2}\right|\right]_3^5$

$ = 2 + \log\dfrac{15}{7} = 2 + \log 15 - \log 7$

29. $I = \int_1^2 \left\{(\log x)\cdot\dfrac{1}{x^2}\right\}dx$

$ = \left[(\log x)\left(-\dfrac{1}{x}\right)\right]_1^2 - \int_1^2 \left(-\dfrac{1}{x}\right)\cdot\dfrac{1}{x}\,dx$

$ = \left(-\dfrac{1}{2}\log 2\right) - \left[\dfrac{1}{x}\right]_1^2 = \dfrac{1}{2}(1 - \log 2)$

30. On dividing $(-x + 1)$ by $(x + 1)$, we get

$I = \int_0^1 \left(-1 + \dfrac{2}{x+1}\right)dx$

$ = \left[-x + 2\log(x+1)\right]_0^1$

$ = 2\log 2 - 1$

CHAPTER 8

Application of Integrals

Summary

- **Area under simple curves**
  - Consider that a curve y = f(x), the line x = a, x = b and x-axis collectively acquires an area and the area under the curve is considered as composed of large number of vertical thin strips. Now assume that there is an arbitrary strip with height y and width dx.

    Then dA which represents area of elementary strip = ydx, where y = f(x).

    Total area A of the region between the curve y = f(x), x = a, x = b and x-axis is equal to the sum of areas of all elementary vertical thin strips across the region PQRS.

    which is given by, $A = \int_a^b y\,dx = \int_a^b f(x)\,dx$

    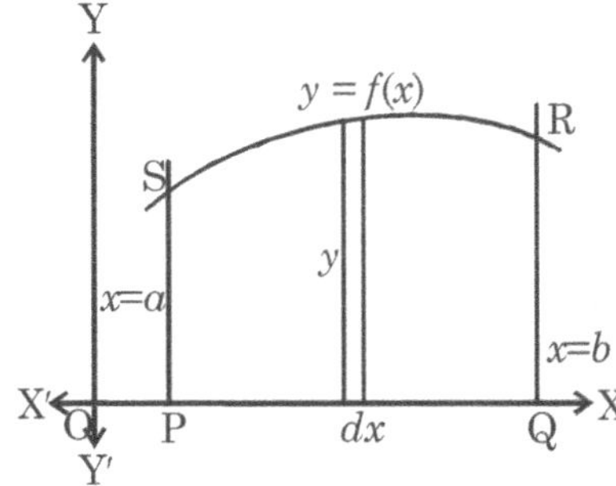

    Elementary Area: The area which is located at an arbitrary position within the region which is specified by some value of x between a and b
  - Now consider the area A of the region which is bounded by the curve x = g(y), the lines y = c, y = d and y-axis.

    Total area A of the region between the curve x = g(y), y = c, y = d and y-axis is equal to the sum of areas of all elementary horizontal thin strips.

    In this case the area A is given by

    $$A = \int_c^d x\,dy = \int_c^d g(y)\,dy$$

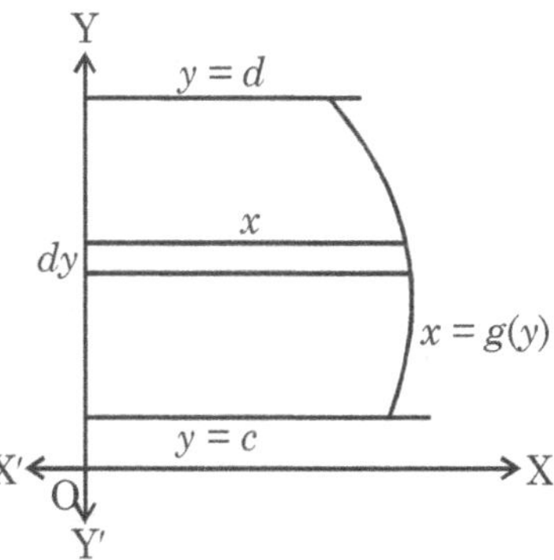

- If the curve is positioned below x-axis, which is f(x) < 0 from x = a to x = b, then the numerical value of the area which is bounded by the curve y = f(x), x-axis and the ordinates x = a, x = b will come out to be negative. But, if the numerical value of the area is to be taken into consideration, then is given by:

$$A = \left| \int_a^b f(x)\,dx \right|$$

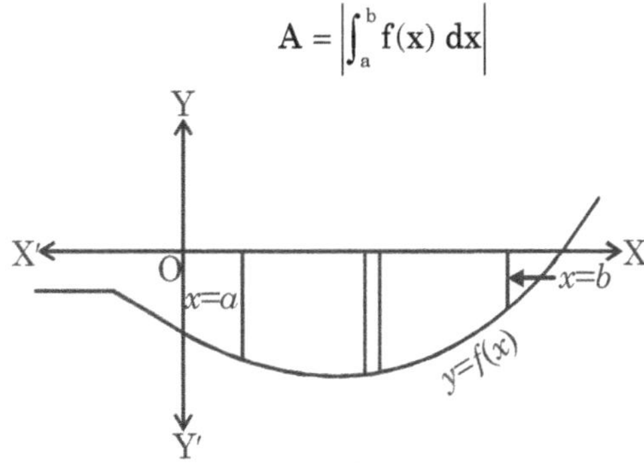

- There is a possibility that some portion of the curve is located above x-axis and some portion of it is located below x-axis.

  Let suppose A_1 is the area below x-axis and A_2 is the area above x-axis. Now, the area of the region which is bounded by the curve y = f(x), x = a, x = b and x-axis can be given by $A = |A_1| + |A_2|$.

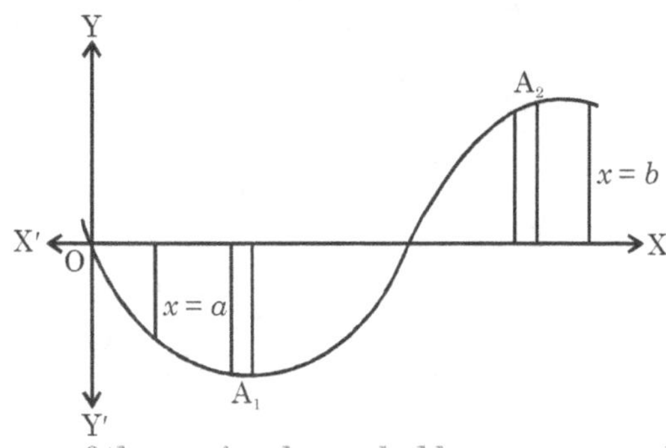

- **Area of the region bounded by a curve and a line**
  - ➢ Area of the region bounded by a line and a curve is used to find the area bounded by a line and a parabola, a line and an ellipse, a line and a circle etc. The standard equation will be used for these mentioned curves.
  - ➢ Area of the region can be calculated by taking the sum of the area of either horizontal or vertical elementary strips but vertical strips are mostly preferred.
- **Area between two curves**
  - ➢ Assume that there are two curves, $y = f(x)$ and $y = g(x)$, where $f(x) \geq g(x)$ in $[a, b]$. The ordinates $x = a$ and $x = b$ give the point of intersection of these two curves. Suppose that these curves intersect at $f(x)$ with width dx.

    Consider an elementary vertical strip of height y, where $y = f(x)$.

    $\therefore \qquad dA = y\, dx$

    Now the area is given by,

    $$A = \int_a^b \left[f(x) - g(x) \right] dx = \int_a^b f(x)\, dx - \int_a^b g(x) dx$$

which can be stated as,

A = Area bounded by the curve $\{y = f(x)\}$

$\qquad$ – Area bounded by the curve $\{y = g(x)\}$

where $f(x) > g(x)$.

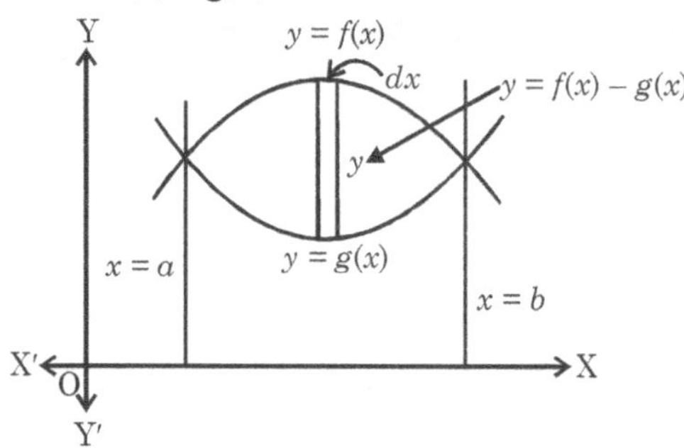

- ➢ In other case if the two curves $y = f(x)$ and $y = g(x)$ where $f(x) \geq g(x)$ in $[a, c]$ and $f(x) \leq g(x)$ in $[c, b]$ with a condition that $a < c < b$, intersect at $x = a$, $x = c$ and $x = b$, then the area bounded by the curves is given by:

$$A = \int_a^c \left| f(x) - g(x) \right| dx + \int_c^b \left| g(x) - f(x) \right| dx$$

which is stated as:

Total area = Area of the region ACBDA

$\qquad\qquad$ + Area of the region BPRQB

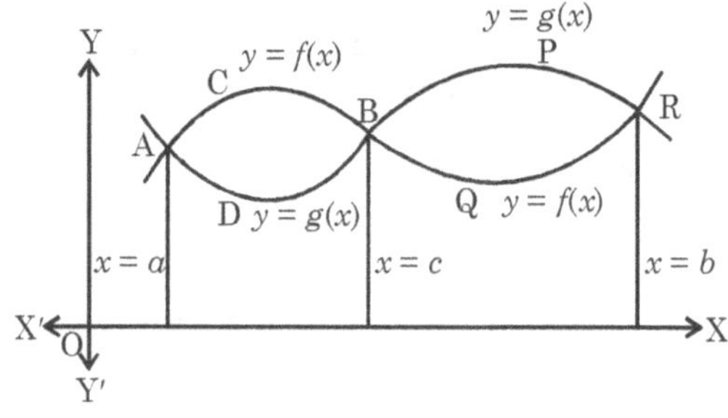

Exercise

1. The area bounded by the curve, $y = x^3$, x – axis and the two ordinates $x = 1$, $x = 2$ is

   (a) $\dfrac{15}{2}$ (b) $\dfrac{15}{4}$

   (c) $\dfrac{17}{2}$ (d) $\dfrac{17}{4}$

2. The area bounded by the curves $y = \sin^4 x$, $x = 0$, $x = \dfrac{\pi}{2}$ and $y = 0$, is

   (a) $\dfrac{3}{8}$ (b) $\dfrac{3}{16}$

   (c) $\dfrac{3\pi}{18}$ (d) $\dfrac{3\pi}{16}$

3. The area bounded by the curves $xy = 1$, $x = 1$, $x = 3$ and $y = 0$, is

   (a) log 2 (b) log 3
   (c) log 4 (d) None

4. The area of the loop between the curve $y = a$ sin x and x – axis, is

   (a) a (b) 2a
   (c) 3a (d) 4a

5. If A is the area lying between the curve $y = \sin x$ and x – axis, between $x = 0$ and $x = \dfrac{\pi}{2}$, then area of the region between the curve $y = \sin 2x$ and x – axis, in the same interval, is

   (a) A (b) 2A

   (c) $\dfrac{A}{2}$ (d) $\dfrac{3A}{4}$

6. The area bounded by the curve $y = f(x)$, the x – axis and the ordinates x $= 1$ and $x = b$ is $(b – 1)$ cos $(3b + 4)$. Then, $f(x) = ?$

   (a) $(x – 1) \sin(3x + 4)$
   (b) $3(x – 1) \sin(3x + 4) + \cos(3x + 4)$
   (c) $\cos(3x + 4) – 3(x – 1)\sin(3x + 4)$
   (d) None of these

7. Area bounded by curve $xy = c$, x-axis between $x = 1$ and $x = 4$, is

   (a) c log 3 sq. units
   (b) 2 log c sq. units
   (c) 2c log 2 sq. units
   (d) 2c log5 sq. units

8. If area bounded by the curves $y^2 = 4ax$ and $y = mx$ is $\dfrac{a^2}{3}$, then the value of m is

   (a) 2 (b) – 2
   (c) 1/2 (d) None of these

9. Area bounded by the curve $y = k \sin x$ between $x = \pi$ and $x = 2\pi$, is

   (a) 2K sq. units (b) 0

   (c) $\dfrac{K^2}{2}$ sq. units (d) K sq. units

10. The area of the region bounded by the curves $y = |x – 2|$, $x = 1$, $x = 3$ and the x-axis is

    (a) 4 (b) 2
    (c) 3 (d) 1

11. The area enclosed by the parabola $y^2 = 4ax$ and the straight line $y = 2ax$, is

    (a) $\dfrac{a^2}{3}$ sq. units (b) $\dfrac{1}{3a^2}$ sq. units

    (c) $\dfrac{1}{3a}$ sq. units (b) $\dfrac{2}{3a}$ sq. units

12. Area of the region bounded by the curve $y = \tan x$, tangent drawn to the curve at $x = \dfrac{\pi}{4}$ and the x-axis is

    (a) $\dfrac{1}{4}$ (b) $\log \sqrt{2} - \dfrac{1}{4}$

    (c) $\log \sqrt{2} + \dfrac{1}{4}$ (d) None of the above

13. The area of the region bounded by $y = |x – 1|$ and $y = 1$ is

    (a) 2 (b) 1
    (c) 1/2 (d) None of these

14. Area bounded by the parabola $y^2 = 4ax$ and its latus rectum is

    (a) $\dfrac{2}{3}a^2$ sq. units (b) $\dfrac{4}{3}a^2$ sq. units

    (c) $\dfrac{8}{3}a^2$ sq. units (d) $\dfrac{3}{8}a^2$ sq. units

15. The area of region $\{(x, y) : x^2 + y^2 \le 1 \le x + y\}$ is

    (a) $\dfrac{\pi^2}{5}$ (b) $\dfrac{\pi^2}{2}$

    (c) $\dfrac{\pi^2}{3}$ (d) $\dfrac{\pi}{4} - \dfrac{1}{2}$

16. The area bounded by the curves $y^2 - x = 0$ and $y - x^2 = 0$ is

    (a) $\dfrac{7}{3}$ (b) $\dfrac{1}{3}$

    (c) $\dfrac{5}{3}$ (d) 1

17. The area of the upper half of the circle whose equation is $(x - 1)^2 + y^2 = 1$ is given by

    (a) $\displaystyle\int_0^2 \sqrt{2x - x^2}\,dx$

    (b) $\displaystyle\int_0^1 \sqrt{2x - x^2}\,dx$

    (c) $\displaystyle\int_1^2 \sqrt{2x - x^2}\,dx$

    (d) $\dfrac{\pi}{4}$

18. The area bounded by the circle $x^2 + y^2 = 4$, line $x = \sqrt{3}y$ and x-axis lying in the first quadrant, is

    (a) $\dfrac{\pi}{2}$ (b) $\dfrac{\pi}{4}$

    (c) $\dfrac{\pi}{3}$ (d) π

19. The area bounded by curves $y = \cos x$ and $y = \sin x$ and ordinates $x = 0$ and $x = \dfrac{\pi}{4}$ is

    (a) $\sqrt{2}$ (b) $\sqrt{2} + 1$

    (c) $\sqrt{2} - 1$ (d) $\sqrt{2}(\sqrt{2} - 1)$

20. For which of the following values of m, the area of the region bounded by the curve $y = x - x^2$ and the line $y = mx$ equals $\dfrac{9}{2}$

    $(a) -4$ $(b) -2$

    $(c)\ 2$ $(d)\ 4$

Answer Keys

1. (b)	2. (d)	3. (b)	4. (b)	5. (a)	6. (c)	7. (c)	8. (a)	9. (a)	10. (d)
11. (c)	12. (b)	13. (b)	14. (c)	15. (d)	16. (b)	17. (a)	18. (c)	19. (c)	20. (b)

Solutions

1. Given curve is $y = x^3$

   $y > 0$ for $1 < x < 2$

   and it does not intersect x-axis at any point between $x = 1$ and $x = 2$

   $\therefore \text{Area}(A) = \displaystyle\int_1^2 x^3 dx = \left[\dfrac{x^4}{4}\right]_1^2 = \dfrac{15}{4}$ sq – units

2. Required area is between the curve, x-axis and the ordinates $x = 0$, $x = \dfrac{\pi}{2}$

   $\therefore \text{Area}(A) = \displaystyle\int_0^{\frac{\pi}{2}} \sin^4 x\ dx$

   $= \dfrac{3.1}{4.2} \times \dfrac{\pi}{2} = \dfrac{3\pi}{16}$ sq – units

3. The required area is the area between the curve $xy = 1$ and x – axis between the ordinates $x = 1$ and $x = 3$.

   $\therefore \text{Area}(A) = \displaystyle\int_1^3 y\ dx = \displaystyle\int_1^2 \dfrac{1}{x}dx$

   $= \left[\log x\right]_1^3 = \log 3$ sq – units

4. The curve $y = a\sin x$ interacts x-axis at $x = 0$ and $x = \pi$.

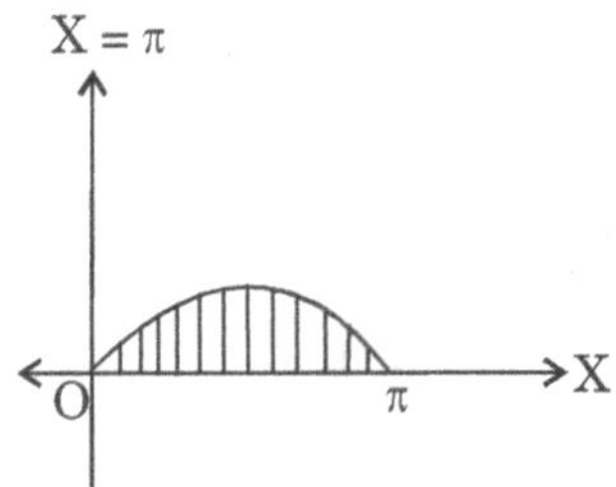

   $\therefore \text{Area}(A) = \displaystyle\int_0^{\pi} a\sin x\,dx$

   $= \left[-a\cos x\right]_0^{\pi}$

   $= 2a$ sq-units

5. $A = \int_0^{\frac{\pi}{2}} \sin x \, dx$

$= \left[-\cos x \right]_0^{\frac{\pi}{2}} = 1 \text{ sq} - \text{unit}$

and $A_1 = \int_0^{\frac{\pi}{2}} \sin 2x \, dx$

$= \int_0^{\frac{\pi}{2}} 2 \sin x . \cos x \, dx$

$= \left[\sin^2 x \right]_0^{\frac{\pi}{2}} = 1$

$\therefore \quad A_1 = A$

6. $\int_1^b f(x) \, dx = (b-1) \cos(3b+4)$

On differentiating both sides w.r.t. b, we get,

$f(b) = -3(b-1) \sin(3b+4) + \cos(3b+4)$

$\Rightarrow \quad f(x) = \cos(3x+4) - 3(x-1) \sin(3x+4).$

7. Area $= \int_1^4 y \, dx = \int_1^4 \frac{C}{x} \, dx$

$= C \left[\log x \right]_1^4$

$= C \left[\log 4 - \log 1 \right] = C \log 4$

$= C \left[\log 2^2 \right] = 2C \log 2$

8.

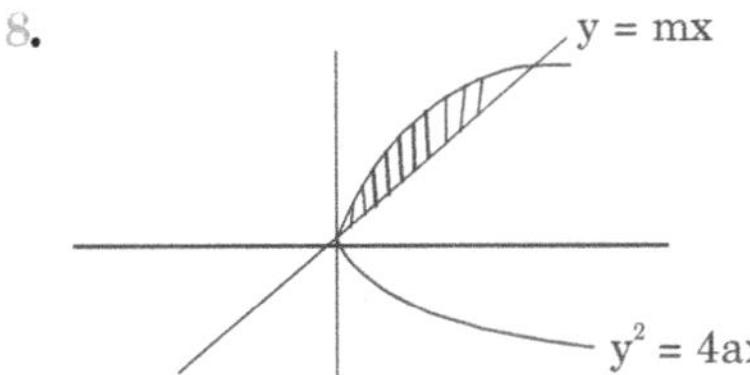

$(mx)^2 = 4ax$

$x = \frac{4a}{m^2}, \ 0$

Area $= \int_0^{\frac{4a}{m^2}} (y_1 - y_2) \, dx = \int_0^{\frac{4a}{m^2}} \left(\sqrt{4ax} - mx \right) dx$

$\frac{a^2}{3} = \left[\frac{2\sqrt{4a}\, x^{3/2}}{3} - m \frac{x^2}{2} \right]_0^{\frac{4a}{m^2}}$

$\frac{a^2}{3} = \left[\frac{4}{3} \sqrt{a} \left(\frac{4a}{m^2} \right)^{3/2} - \frac{m}{2} \left(\frac{4a}{m^2} \right)^2 \right]$

$\frac{1}{3} = \left(\frac{4}{3} \frac{8}{m^3} - \frac{8}{m^3} \right)$

$m^3 = 8, \ m = 2$

9. Area $= \int_\pi^{2\pi} |y| \, dx$

$= \int_\pi^{2\pi} k |\sin x| \, dx$

$= -k \int_\pi^{2\pi} \sin x \, dx$

$= k \left[\cos x \right]_\pi^{2\pi}$

$= 2k$

10.

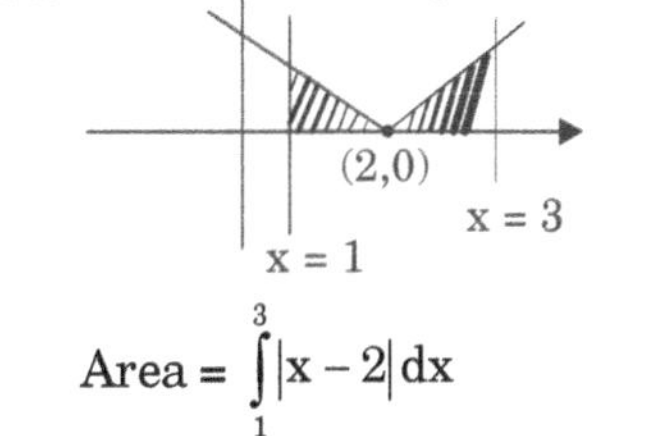

Area $= \int_1^3 |x-2| \, dx$

$= \int_1^2 (2-x) \, dx + \int_2^3 (x-2) \, dx$

$= \left[2x - \frac{x^2}{2} \right]_1^2 + \left[\frac{x^2}{2} - 2x \right]_2^3$

$= 1$

11. $y^2 = 4ax$

$y = 2ax$

$(2ax)^2 = 4ax$

$x = 0, \ \frac{1}{a}$

Area $= \int_0^{1/a} (y_1 - y_2) \, dx$

$= \int_0^{1/a} \sqrt{4ax} - 2ax \, dx$

$= \left[2\sqrt{a} \cdot \frac{2}{3} x^{3/2} - ax^2 \right]_0^{1/a}$

$= \frac{4}{3} \frac{1}{a} - \frac{1}{a}$

$= \frac{1}{a} \left(\frac{4}{3} - 1 \right) = \frac{1}{3a}$

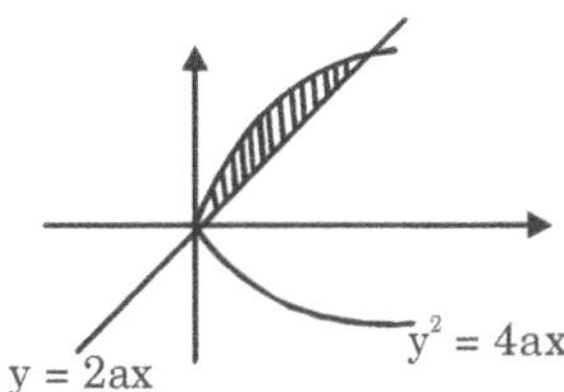

12.

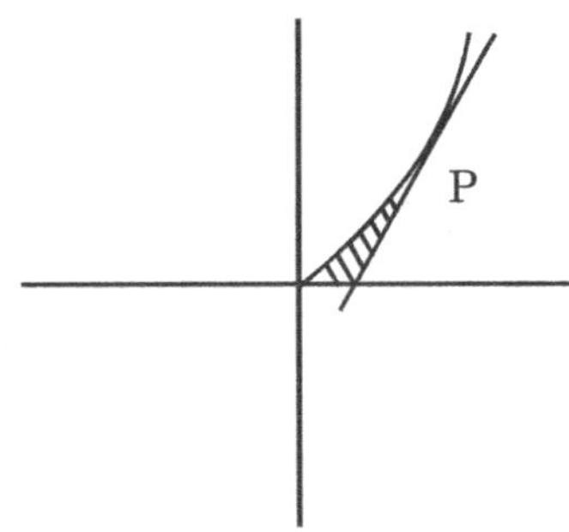

$y = \tan x,\ x = \tan^{-1} y$

at $x = \dfrac{\pi}{4}, y = \tan\dfrac{\pi}{4} = 1$

$P\left(\dfrac{\pi}{4}, 1\right)$

$\dfrac{dy}{dx} = \sec^2 x$

$m = \sec^2\dfrac{\pi}{4} = 2$

Equation of tangent $y - 1 = 2\left(x - \dfrac{\pi}{4}\right)$

$y = 2x - \dfrac{\pi}{2} + 1$

$x = \dfrac{y}{2} + \dfrac{\pi}{4} - \dfrac{1}{2}$

$\text{Area} = \int_0^1 (x_2 - x_1)\,dy$

$= \int_0^1 \left(\dfrac{y}{2} + \dfrac{\pi}{4} - \dfrac{1}{2} - \tan^{-1} y\right)dy$

$= \left[\dfrac{y^2}{4} + \left(\dfrac{\pi}{4} - \dfrac{1}{2}\right)y - y\tan^{-1}y + \dfrac{1}{2}\ln(1+y^2)\right]_0^1$

$= \dfrac{1}{4} + \dfrac{\pi}{4} - \dfrac{1}{2} - \dfrac{\pi}{4} + \dfrac{1}{2}\ln 2$

$= \ln\sqrt{2} - \dfrac{1}{4}$

13.

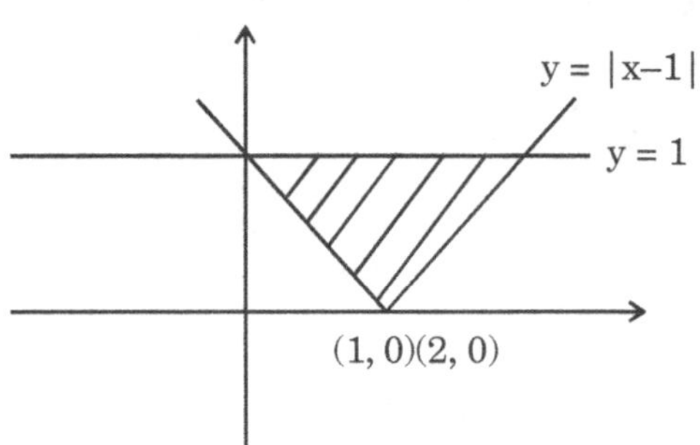

$\text{Area} = \int_0^2 (1 - |x-1|)\,dx$

$= [x]_0^2 + \int_0^1 (x-1)\,dx - \int_1^2 (x-1)dx$

$= 2 + \left[\dfrac{x^2}{2} - x\right]_0^1 - \left[\dfrac{x^2}{2} - x\right]_1^2 = 1$

14.

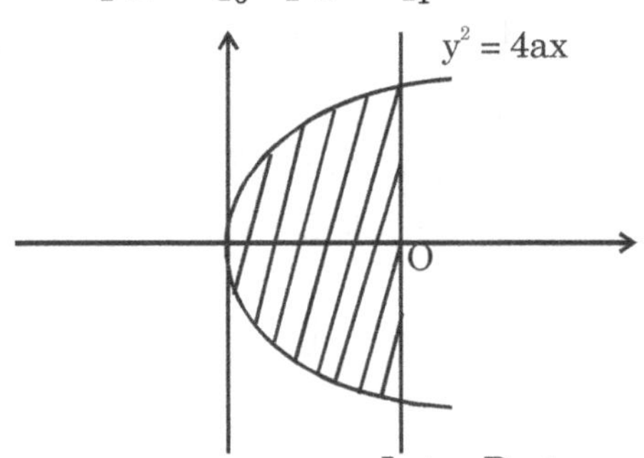

$y = \sqrt{4ax}$

$\text{Area} = 2\int_0^a \sqrt{4ax}\,dx$

$= 2\left[2\sqrt{a}\,\dfrac{2x^{3/2}}{3}\right]_0^a$

$= \dfrac{8}{3}a^2$

15.

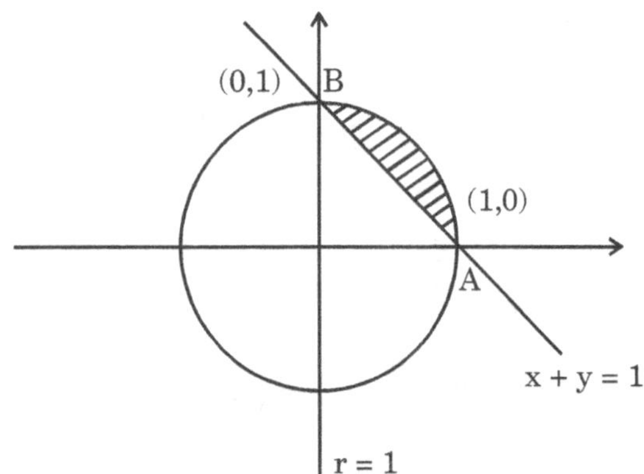

$$\text{Area} = \frac{\pi r^2}{4} - \text{Area of } \triangle OAB$$

$$= \frac{\pi}{4} - \frac{1}{2} \times 1 \times 1$$

$$= \frac{\pi}{4} - \frac{1}{2}$$

16.

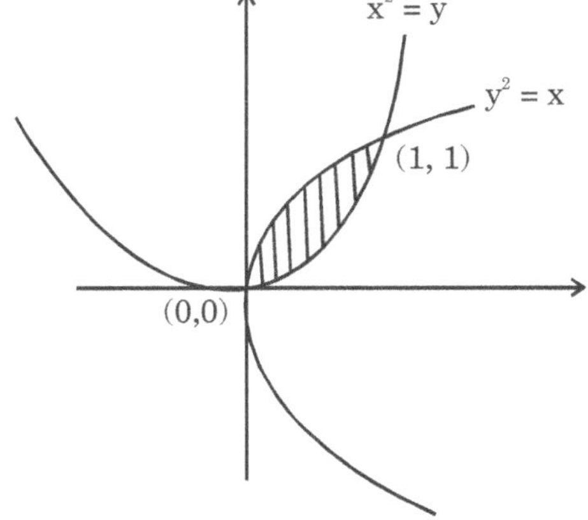

$$\text{Area} = \int_0^1 (y_1 - y_2)$$

$$= \int_0^1 (\sqrt{x} - x^2)dx$$

$$= \left[\frac{2}{3}x^{3/2} - \frac{x^3}{3}\right]_0^1 = \frac{2}{3} - \frac{1}{3} = \frac{1}{3}$$

17.

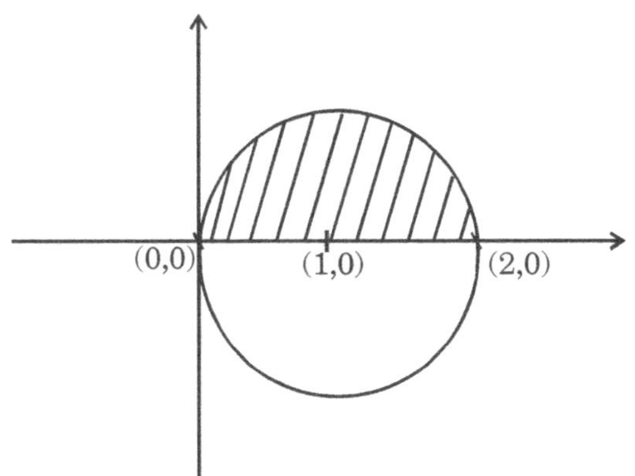

$$(x - 1)^2 + y^2 = 1$$

$$y = \pm\sqrt{1 - (x-1)^2}$$

$$= \pm\sqrt{2x - x^2}$$

$$\text{Area} = \int_0^2 \sqrt{2x - x^2}\,dx$$

18.

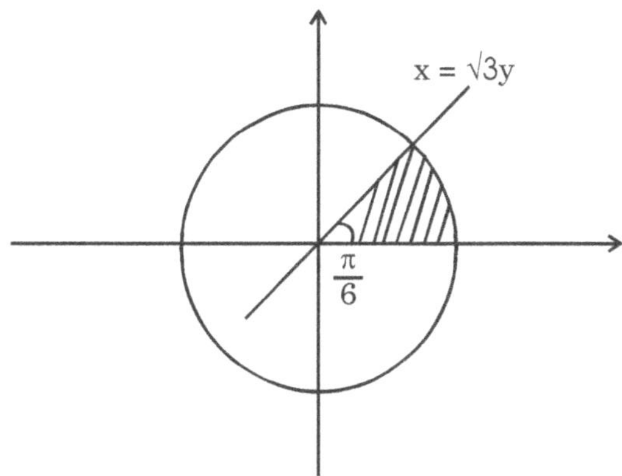

$$x^2 + y^2 = 4, \ r = 2$$

$$x = \sqrt{3}y$$

$$y = \frac{1}{\sqrt{3}}x$$

$$m = \tan\theta = \frac{1}{\sqrt{3}}$$

$$\theta = \frac{\pi}{6}$$

$$\text{Area} = \theta.\frac{r^2}{2} = \frac{\pi}{6} \times \frac{(2)^2}{2}$$

$$= \frac{\pi}{3}$$

19.

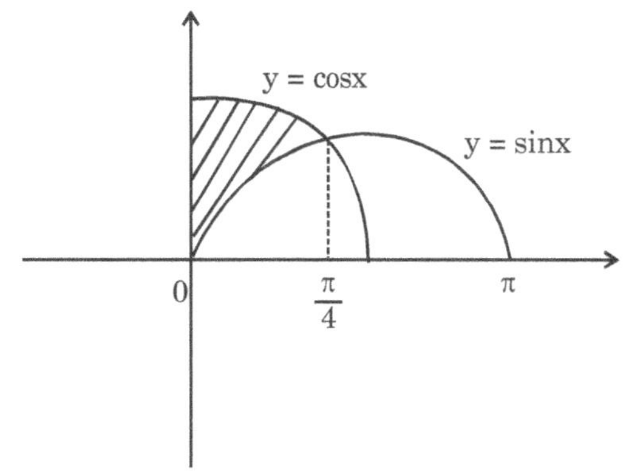

Area $\int_0^{\pi/4}(\cos x - \sin x)dx$

$= [\sin x + \cos x]_0^{\pi/4}$

$= \dfrac{1}{\sqrt{2}} + \dfrac{1}{\sqrt{2}} - 1$

$= \sqrt{2} - 1$

20.

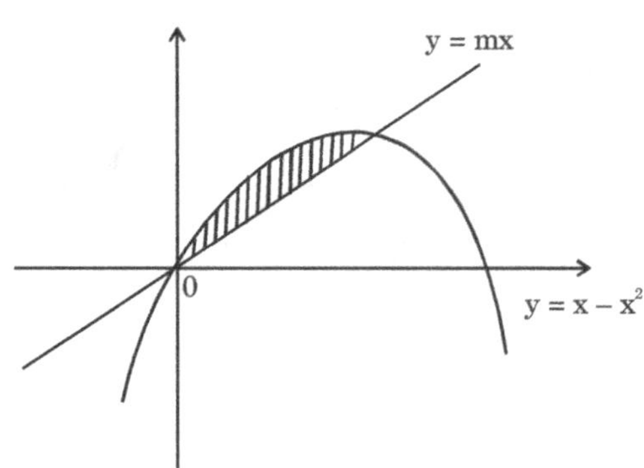

$y = x - x^2$

$y = mx$

$mx = x - x^2$

$x = 0,\ x = 1 - m$

Area $= \displaystyle\int_0^{1-m}(x - x^2 - mx)dx$

$\dfrac{9}{2} = \dfrac{(1-m)^2}{2} - \dfrac{(1-m)^3}{3} - \dfrac{m(1-m)^2}{2}$

$(1-m)^3 = 27,\ \ 1 - m = 3$

$m = -2$

CHAPTER 9

Differential Equations

Formation of Differential Equations

- **Differential Equation:** Differential equation is an equation which involves derivative of the dependent variable with respect to independent variable. Here $x\dfrac{dy}{dx} + y = 0$ is the example of differential equation.

- General notations for derivatives are:

$$\frac{dy}{dx} = y', \frac{d^2y}{dx^2} = y'', \frac{d^3y}{dx^3} = y'''$$

or $\dfrac{d^n y}{dx^n} = y_n$

- **Order of a differential equation:** The order of the highest order derivative in any given differential equation is called the order of the differential equation.

  Example: $\dfrac{dy}{dx} - \sin x = 0$ has the order 1.

- **Degree of a differential equation:** If a differential equation involves a polynomial equation in its derivative, then its degree can be defined as the highest power of the highest order derivative in it.

  Example: $\dfrac{dy}{dx} - \sin x = 0$ has the degree 1.

  Degree (if defined) and order are always positive.

Solution of Different Types of Differential Equations

- **Solution of a differential equation:** Solution of a differential equation is a function satisfying that differential equation.

  - **General Solution:** The solution having the arbitrary constants (equal to the order of the differential equation) is called a general or primitive solution of the differential equation.

  - **Particular Solution:** The solution which does not have the arbitrary constants is called a particular solution. It is acquired by substituting the particular values in the arbitrary constants.

- If the general solution of any differential equation is given, then the function is to be differentiated successively (as many times as the total number of arbitrary constants) in order to form the differential equation and then the arbitrary constants are eliminated.

- A differential equation which can be separated completely such that the terms which contains x can be written with dx and that of containing y with dy, can be solved with the help of variable separable method. The solution of such equations are of the form $\int f(x)dx = \int g(x)dx + C$, where C is an arbitrary constant.

- **Homogeneous Differential Equation:** A differential equation of the form $\dfrac{dy}{dx} = f(x,y)$ is called as homogeneous differential equation if f (x, y) is a homogeneous function of degree 0.

- To solve a homogeneous equation of the form $\dfrac{dy}{dx} = f(x,y) = g\left(\dfrac{y}{x}\right)$, substitutions are made as $\dfrac{y}{x} = v$ or y = vx and then general solution is found out by solving $\dfrac{dy}{dx} = v + x\dfrac{dv}{dx}$.

- To solve a homogeneous equation of the form $\dfrac{dx}{dy} = f(x,y)$, substitutions are made as $\dfrac{x}{y} = v$ or x = vy and then general solution is found out by writing $\dfrac{dx}{dy} = v + y\dfrac{dv}{dy}$.

- **Linear Differential Equation:** A differential equation which can be expressed as $\dfrac{dy}{dx} + Py = Q$, where P and Q are the constants or functions of x only, is called a linear differential equations of first order.
- To solve a linear differential equation, it is first written as $\dfrac{dy}{dx} + Py = Q$, then the integrating factor is found as I.F. $= e^{\int Pdx}$. After that, the solution is given by $y(\text{I.F.}) = \int (Q \times \text{I.F.})dx + C$.
- If the linear differential equation is of the form $\dfrac{dx}{dy} + Px = Q$ (P and Q are constants or functions of y only), then I.F. $= e^{\int Pdy}$ and the solution is given by $x(\text{I.F.}) = \int (Q \times \text{I.F.})dy + C$.

Exercise

1. The order and degree of the D. E.

$$\dfrac{d^2y}{dx^2} = \left[1 + \left(\dfrac{dy}{dx}\right)^2\right]^{\frac{3}{2}}$$ are respectively.

   (a) 2, 1　　　　　　(b) 1, 6

   (c) 1, 3　　　　　　(d) 2, 2

2. The D.E. for the family of the curves $y = Ae^{Bx}$, where A and B are parameters, is given by

   (a) $\dfrac{d^2y}{dx^2} = y\dfrac{dy}{dx}$　　　　(b) $\dfrac{d^2y}{dx^2} = y\dfrac{dx}{dy}$

   (c) $y\dfrac{d^2y}{dx^2} = \left(\dfrac{dy}{dx}\right)^2$　　　(d) $y\dfrac{d^2y}{dx^2} + \left(\dfrac{dx}{dy}\right) = 0$

3. The solution of a differential equation of degree 2 and order 3 contains, how many arbitrary constants?

   (a) 2　　　　　　(b) 3

   (c) 1　　　　　　(d) 5

4. The D.E. of the family of straight lines $y = mx + \dfrac{a}{m}$, where m is the parameter, is

   (a) $(x - y)\dfrac{dy}{dx} = a$

   (b) $x\dfrac{dy}{dx} = a$

   (c) $x\left(\dfrac{dy}{dx}\right)^2 - y\dfrac{dy}{dx} + a = 0$

   (d) $x\left(\dfrac{dy}{dx}\right)^2 - y\dfrac{dy}{dx} = a$

5. The differential equation $y\dfrac{dy}{dx} + x = a$ represents

   (a) a set of circles whose centres are on x-axis
   (b) a set of circles whose centres are on y-axis
   (c) a set of parabolas
   (d) a set of ellipses

6. The order of the D.E. of all conics whose centres lie at the origin, is

   (a) 2　　　　　　(b) 3

   (c) 4　　　　　　(d) 1

7. The differential equation of all parabolas with y-axis as their axes of symmetry, is

   (a) $x\dfrac{d^2x}{dy^2} + \left(\dfrac{dx}{dy}\right)^2 = 0$　　(b) $x\dfrac{d^2x}{dy^2} + 2\dfrac{dx}{dy} = 0$

   (c) $y\dfrac{d^2y}{dx^2} + \left(\dfrac{dy}{dx}\right)^2 = 0$　　(d) None of these

8. The family of curves represented by the D.E. $x\dfrac{dy}{dx} = \cot y$, is

   (a) $y \cos x = C$　　　　(b) $x \cos y = C$

   (c) $\log(x \cos y) = C$　　(d) None of these

9. The D.E. whose solution is $y = (x + c)e^x$, is

   (a) $\dfrac{dy}{dx} = e^x y$　　　　(b) $\dfrac{dy}{dx} = e^x + y$

   (c) $\dfrac{dy}{dx} = e^x - y$　　　　(d) $\dfrac{dy}{dx} = \dfrac{e^x}{y}$

10. The general solution of the D.E.

$$\sqrt{1+x^2}\,dy + \sqrt{1+y^2}\,dx = 0 \text{ is}$$

(a) $\sin^{-1} x + \sin^{-1} y = C$

(b) $\tan^{-1} x + \tan^{-1} y = C$

(c) $\left(x + \sqrt{1+x^2}\right)\left(y + \sqrt{1+y^2}\right) = k$

(d) None of these

11. The differential equation whose solution is $\tan^{-1} x + \tan^{-1} y = C$, is

(a) $(1 + x^2)\,y_1 = (1 + y^2)$

(b) $(1 + x^2)\,y_1 + (1 + y^2) = 0$

(c) $(1 + y^2)\,y_1 = (1 + x^2)$

(d) None of these

12. The solution of the differential equation

$$\left(x + y\right)^2 \frac{dy}{dx} = a^2, \text{ is}$$

(a) $x(x - y) = y + (a + C)$

(b) $x + y = a \tan\left(\dfrac{y - C}{a}\right)$

(c) $y(x - y) = a + C$

(d) None of these

13. The general solution of the D.E. $\dfrac{dy}{dx} + \dfrac{\tan y}{\tan x} = 0$ is

(a) $\cos x \cos y = C$

(b) $\sin x \sin y = C$

(c) $\cos x + \cos y = C$

(d) $\sin x + \sin y = C$

14. The general solution of the D.E.

$$\frac{dy}{dx} + \sqrt{\frac{1-y^2}{1-x^2}} = 0, \text{ is}$$

(a) $\sin h^{-1} x + \sin h^{-1} y = C$

(b) $\sin^{-1} x + \sin^{-1} y = C$

(c) $\cos h^{-1} x + \cosh^{-1} y = C$

(d) None of these

15. The general solution of the D.E. $\dfrac{dy}{dx} = xy + x + y + 1$, is

(a) $\log y = x + y + C$

(b) $\log (y + 1) = \dfrac{1}{2}x^2 + x + C$

(c) $\log (x + 1) = \dfrac{1}{2}y^2 + y + C$

(d) None of these

16. The integrating factors of the D.E.

$$\sin x \frac{dy}{dx} + y \cos x = \sin 2x, \text{ is}$$

(a) $\cos x$ \qquad\qquad (b) $\sin x$

(c) $-\sin x$ \qquad\qquad (d) $-\cos x$

17. The integrating factor of the D.E.

$$\frac{dy}{dx} + \frac{2xy}{\left(1 - x^2\right)} = \frac{x}{\sqrt{1 - x^2}}, \text{ is}$$

(a) $(1 - x^2)$ \qquad\qquad (b) $\dfrac{1}{\left(1 - x^2\right)}$

(c) $\dfrac{x}{\left(1 - x^2\right)}$ \qquad\qquad (d) $\dfrac{x}{\sqrt{1 - x^2}}$

18. The general solution of the D.E. $\dfrac{dy}{dx} + 1 = \sec(x + y)$ is

(a) $\sin(x + y) = x + C$

(b) $\cos(x + y) = C$

(c) $\sin(x + y) + x = C$

(d) None of these

19. The solution of $(x + 2y^3)\dfrac{dy}{dx} = y$ is

(a) $\dfrac{x}{y} = y^2 + c$ \qquad\qquad (b) $xy = y + c$

(c) $\dfrac{y}{x} = x + c$ \qquad\qquad (d) None of these

20. The solution of the differential equation $x\,dy + y\,dx - \sqrt{1 - x^2 y^2}\,dx = 0$ is

(a) $\sin^{-1} xy = C - x$ \qquad (b) $xy = \sin(x + C)$

(c) $\log(1 - x^2 y^2) = x + C$ \qquad (d) $y = x \sin x + C$

Answer Keys

1. (d) \quad 2. (c) \quad 3. (b) \quad 4. (c) \quad 5. (a) \quad 6. (b) \quad 7. (a) \quad 8. (b) \quad 9. (b) \quad 10. (c)

11. (b) \quad 12. (b) \quad 13. (b) \quad 14. (b) \quad 15. (b) \quad 16. (b) \quad 17. (b) \quad 18. (a) \quad 19. (a) \quad 20. (b)

Solutions

1. On squaring both sides of given D.E., we get

$$\left(\frac{d^2y}{dx^2}\right)^2 = \left[1+\left(\frac{dy}{dx}\right)^2\right]^3$$

This highest order derivative is of order 2 whose power is 2.

∴ Given D.E. has order = 2, Degree = 2

2. Given equation is $y = Ae^{Bx}$ ...(i)

This equation has two parameters. So, we differentiate it two times and eliminate A and B from these three equations.

∴ $\dfrac{dy}{dx} = ABe^{Bx} \Rightarrow \dfrac{1}{y}\cdot\dfrac{dy}{dx} = B$

$$\frac{1}{y}\frac{d^2y}{dx^2} - \frac{1}{y^2}\left(\frac{dy}{dx}\right)^2 = 0$$

$$\Rightarrow y\frac{d^2y}{dx^2} = \left(\frac{dy}{dx}\right)^2$$

3. The solution of a D.E. of order 3 will contain 3 arbitrary constants.

4. $y = mx + \dfrac{a}{m}$ ...(i)

$\Rightarrow y_1 = m$ ...(ii)

Substituting $m = y_1$ in equation (i), we get

$$y = xy_1 + \frac{a}{y_1} \Rightarrow xy_1^2 - yy_1 + a = 0$$

i.e. $x\left(\dfrac{dy}{dx}\right)^2 - y\dfrac{dy}{dx} + a = 0$

5. $y\dfrac{dy}{dx} + x = a$

$\Rightarrow y\,dy + (x-a)\,dx = 0$

$\Rightarrow \int y\,dy + \int (x-a)\,dx = $ constant

$\Rightarrow y^2 + (x-a)^2 = c^2$

This represents the family of circles with centres on x-axis.

6. The general equation of all conics with centre at the origin is $ax^2 + 2hxy + by^2 = 0$, where a, b and h are parameters.

Since this equation contains three arbitrary constants, so its D.E. is of order 3.

7. The general equation of a parabola with y-axis as the axis of symmetry, is $x^2 = 4a(y-k)$, where a and k are parameters.

$\Rightarrow 2x\dfrac{dx}{dy} = 4a$, i.e. $x\dfrac{dx}{dy} = 2a$

$$\Rightarrow x\frac{d^2x}{dy^2} + \left(\frac{dx}{dy}\right)^2 = 0$$

8. $x\dfrac{dy}{dx} = \cot y$

$\Rightarrow \tan y\,dy = \dfrac{1}{x}\,dx$

$\Rightarrow \int \dfrac{1}{x}dx = \int \tan y\,dy$

$\Rightarrow \log x = \log \sec y + \log C$

$\Rightarrow x = C \sec y$

$\Rightarrow x \cos y = C$

9. Given equation is $y = (x+C)e^x$ ...(i)

It has one parameter C. So, we differentiate it only once and eliminate C.

Now $\dfrac{dy}{dx} = (x+C)e^x + e^x$ ...(ii)

$\Rightarrow \dfrac{dy}{dx} = y + e^x$ [using (i) in (ii)]

10. $\sqrt{1+x^2}\;dy + \sqrt{1+y^2}\;dx = 0$

$$\Rightarrow \frac{1}{\sqrt{1+y^2}}dy + \frac{1}{\sqrt{1+x^2}}dx = 0$$

$$\Rightarrow \int \frac{dy}{\sqrt{1+y^2}} + \int \frac{dx}{\sqrt{1+x^2}} = C$$

$$\ln\left(y + \sqrt{1+y^2}\right) + \ln\left(x + \sqrt{1+x^2}\right) = \ln k$$

$$\left(x + \sqrt{1+x^2}\right)\left(y + \sqrt{1+y^2}\right) = k$$

11. $\tan^{-1}x + \tan^{-1}y = C$

On differentiating (i), we get

$$\frac{1}{\left(1+x^2\right)} + \frac{1}{\left(1+y^2\right)}\cdot y_1 = 0$$

$$\Rightarrow (1+x^2)\,y_1 + (1+y^2) = 0$$

12. On putting $x + y = v$ and $1 + \dfrac{dy}{dx} = \dfrac{dv}{dx}$, we get

$$v^2\left(\dfrac{dv}{dx} - 1\right) = a^2$$

$$\Rightarrow \dfrac{dv}{dx} = \dfrac{a^2}{v^2} + 1 \Rightarrow \dfrac{dv}{dx} = \dfrac{a^2 + v^2}{v^2}$$

$$\Rightarrow \int \dfrac{v^2}{\left(v^2 + a^2\right)}dv = \int dx \Rightarrow \int \left\{1 - \dfrac{a^2}{v^2 + a^2}\right\}dv$$

$$= x + C$$

$$\Rightarrow v - \dfrac{a^2}{a}\tan^{-1}\dfrac{v}{a} = x + C \Rightarrow v - a\tan^{-1}\dfrac{v}{a} = x + C$$

$$\Rightarrow (x + y) - a\tan^{-1}\left(\dfrac{x + y}{a}\right) = x + C$$

$$\Rightarrow a\tan^{-1}\left(\dfrac{x + y}{a}\right) = y - c$$

$$\Rightarrow x + y = a\tan\left(\dfrac{y - C}{a}\right)$$

13. $\dfrac{dy}{dx} + \dfrac{\tan y}{\tan x} = 0$

$$\Rightarrow \int \cot y\, dy + \int \cot x\, dx = \text{constant}$$

$\Rightarrow \log \sin y + \log \sin x = \log C$

$\Rightarrow \log (\sin x.\ \sin y) = \log C$

$\Rightarrow \sin x.\ \sin y = C$

14. Given D.E. is $\dfrac{dy}{dx} + \dfrac{\sqrt{1 - y^2}}{\sqrt{1 - x^2}} = 0$

$$\Rightarrow \dfrac{dy}{\sqrt{1 - y^2}} + \dfrac{dx}{\sqrt{1 - x^2}} = 0$$

$$\Rightarrow \int \dfrac{dy}{\sqrt{1 - y^2}} + \int \dfrac{dx}{\sqrt{1 - x^2}} = \text{constant}$$

$\Rightarrow \sin^{-1} y + \sin^{-1} x = C$

15. Given D.E. is

$$\dfrac{dy}{dx} = (x + 1)(y + 1)$$

$$\Rightarrow \int \dfrac{dy}{y + 1} = \int (x + 1)dx$$

$$\Rightarrow \log(y + 1) = \dfrac{x^2}{2} + x + C$$

16. $(\sin x)\dfrac{dy}{dx} + y\cos x = \sin 2x$

$$\Rightarrow \dfrac{dy}{dx} + y\cot x = 2\cos x$$

$$\therefore \text{ I.F.} = e^{\int \cot x\, dx} = e^{\log \sin x} = \sin x$$

17. $\text{I.F.} = e^{\int \frac{2x}{\left(1 - x^2\right)}dx}$

$$= e^{-\int \frac{(-2x)}{\left(1 - x^2\right)}dx} = e^{-\log\left(1 - x^2\right)} = e^{\log\left\{\frac{1}{\left(1 - x^2\right)}\right\}}$$

$$= \dfrac{1}{1 - x^2}$$

18. On putting $x + y = v$ and $1 + \dfrac{dy}{dx} = \dfrac{dx}{dx}$, we get

$$\dfrac{dv}{dx} = \sec v$$

$$\Rightarrow \int \cos v\, dv = \int dx$$

$\Rightarrow \sin v = x + C$

$\Rightarrow \sin (x + y) = x + C$

19. $\left(x + 2y^3\right)\dfrac{dy}{dx} = y$

$$\dfrac{dy}{dx} = \dfrac{x}{y} + 2y^2$$

$$\dfrac{dx}{dy} - \dfrac{x}{y} = 2y^2$$

$$\text{I.F.} = e^{\int -\frac{1}{y}dy} = e^{-\ln y} = e^{\ln \frac{1}{y}} = \dfrac{1}{y}$$

Now,

$$x \cdot \dfrac{1}{y} = \int (2y)^2 \dfrac{1}{y}\, dy$$

$$\dfrac{x}{y} = y^2 + c$$

20. $x\,dy + y\,dx = \sqrt{1 - x^2 y^2}\ dx$

$$\int \dfrac{d(xy)}{\sqrt{1 - x^2 y^2}} = \int dx$$

$\sin^{-1}(xy) = x + C$

$xy = \sin(x + C)$

CHAPTER 10

Vector Algebra

Algebra of Vectors

- A vector quantity has both magnitude and direction where the magnitude is a distance between the initial and terminal point of the vector. Let's assume a vector starts at a point A and ends at a point B. Therefore the magnitude of the vector is denoted by $\left|\overrightarrow{AB}\right|$.

- $\overrightarrow{OA} = \vec{r} = x\hat{i} + y\hat{j} + z\hat{k}$ is the position vector of any point $A(x, y, z)$ having a magnitude equal to $\sqrt{x^2 + y^2 + z^2}$. Where O is the origin $(0, 0, 0)$ and P is any point in the space.

- The angles α, β, γ are known as the direction angles which are made by the position vector and the positive x, y, z – axes respectively and their cosine values $(\cos\alpha, \cos\beta, \cos\gamma)$ are known as direction cosines, denoted by l, m, n respectively.

- The projections of a vector along the respective axes are represented by the direction ratios which are the scalar components of the vector. They are denoted by a, b, c respectively.

- The direction cosines, direction ratios, and magnitude of a vector are related as:

$$l = \frac{a}{r}, m = \frac{b}{r}, n = \frac{c}{r}$$

- In general, $l^2 + m^2 + n^2 = 1$ but $a^2 + b^2 + c^2 \neq 1$.

- Zero vector (also known as a null vector) is symbolized by $\vec{0}$. Its initial and terminal points coincide.

- A unit vector has a magnitude equal to 1 and is denoted by $\hat{a}$.

- If two or more than two vectors have the same initial points, they are called as co-initial vectors.

- The vectors which are parallel to the same line are known as collinear vectors.

- The vectors having equal magnitude and same direction are called equal vectors.

- A vector having the same magnitude as the given vector but opposite direction is known as the negative of the given vector.

- **Triangle law of vector addition:** Let's say that $A, B,$ and C are the vertices of a triangle then

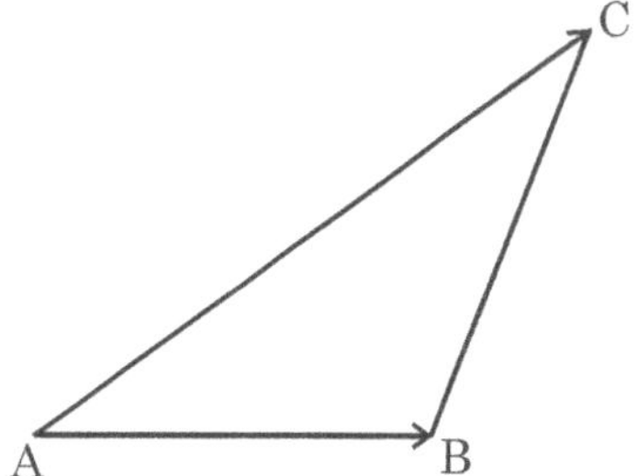

$$\overrightarrow{AC} = \overrightarrow{AB} + \overrightarrow{BC}$$

- **Parallelogram law of vector addition:** If two vectors are represented by the two adjacent sides of a parallelogram, then their sum is represented by the diagonal of that parallelogram through their common point. For example, the

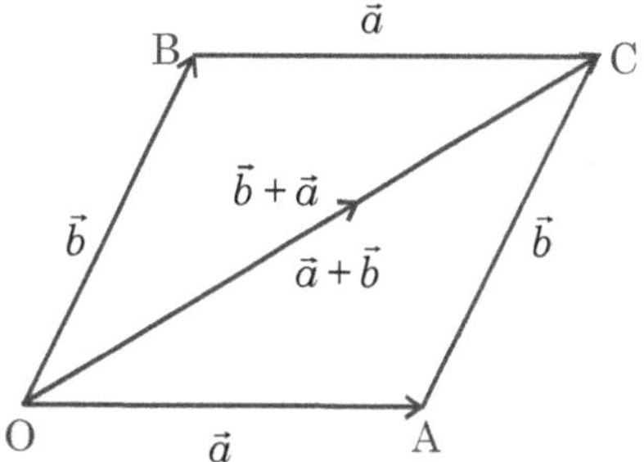

$$\overrightarrow{OC} = \overrightarrow{OA} + \overrightarrow{OB}$$

$$\Rightarrow \overrightarrow{OC} = \vec{a} + \vec{b}$$

- Vector addition is commutative as well as associative in nature and also has zero vector as an additive identity.

- The multiplication of any vector $\vec{a}$ by a scalar λ is denoted by $\lambda\vec{a}$ and has the same direction as the original vector if λ is positive and opposite direction if λ is negative. Its magnitude is $\left|\lambda\vec{a}\right| = |\lambda|\left|\vec{a}\right|$.

- The unit vector of any vector $\vec{a}$ in its direction is

written as $\hat{a} = \dfrac{1}{|\vec{a}|}\vec{a}$

- The unit vectors along the positive x, y, z axes are denoted by $\hat{i}, \hat{j}, \hat{k}$ respectively.

- **Component form of a vector:** The component form of any vector is $\vec{r} = x\hat{i} + y\hat{j} + z\hat{k}$ where x, y, z are called as the scalar components and $x\hat{i}, y\hat{j}, z\hat{k}$ as the vector components of $\vec{r}$. x, y, z is also called the rectangular components.

- If two vectors are in their component form as $\vec{a} = a_1\hat{i} + a_2\hat{j} + a_3\hat{k}$ and $\vec{b} = b_1\hat{i} + b_2\hat{j} + b_3\hat{k}$, then

  - The sum of the vectors $\vec{a}$ and $\vec{b}$ is given by

    $\vec{a} + \vec{b} = (a_1 + b_1)\hat{i} + (a_2 + b_2)\hat{j} + (a_3 + b_3)\hat{k}$.

  - The difference of the vectors $\vec{a}$ and $\vec{b}$ is given by $\vec{a} - \vec{b} = (a_1 - b_1)\hat{i} + (a_2 - b_2)\hat{j} + (a_3 - b_3)\hat{k}$

  - The vectors $\vec{a}$ and $\vec{b}$ are equal if $a_1 = b_1, a_2 = b_2$ and $a_3 = b_3$.

  - The multiplication of a vector $\vec{a}$ by scalar λ is given by $\lambda\vec{a} = (\lambda a_1)\hat{i} + (\lambda a_2)\hat{j} + (\lambda a_3)\hat{k}$.

- **Vector joining two points:** The magnitude of a vector $\overrightarrow{A_1 A_2}$ joining two points $\overrightarrow{A_1}(x_1, y_1, z_1)$ and $\overrightarrow{A_2}(x_2, y_2, z_2)$ is

  $\overrightarrow{A_1 A_2} = \sqrt{(x_2 - x_1)^2 + (y_2 - y_1)^2 + (z_2 - z_1)^2}$

- **Section Formula:** The position vector of a point C dividing the line segment joining two points A and B (having position vectors $\vec{a}, \vec{b}$ respectively) in the ratio of $m : n$

  - Internally: $\vec{r} = \dfrac{m\vec{b} + n\vec{a}}{m + n}$

  - Externally: $\vec{r} = \dfrac{m\vec{b} - n\vec{a}}{m - n}$

  - If C is the midpoint of A and B, then $\vec{r} = \dfrac{\vec{a} + \vec{b}}{2}$

Product of Two Vectors, Scalar Triple Product

- **Scalar (or dot) product of two vectors $\vec{a}$ and $\vec{b}$:** The scalar product of two vectors having an angle θ between them is denoted by $\vec{a} \cdot \vec{b}$ and is defined by

  $\vec{a} \cdot \vec{b} = |\vec{a}||\vec{b}|\cos\theta$

  $\Rightarrow \cos\theta = \dfrac{\vec{a} \cdot \vec{b}}{|\vec{a}||\vec{b}|}$

  or $\theta = \cos^{-1}\left(\dfrac{\vec{a} \cdot \vec{b}}{|\vec{a}||\vec{b}|}\right)$

- If $\vec{a} \cdot \vec{b} = 0 \Leftrightarrow \vec{a} \perp \vec{b}$

- Properties of scalar product:

  - Let $\vec{a}, \vec{b}$ and $\vec{c}$ be any three vectors then

    $\vec{a} \cdot (\vec{b} + \vec{c}) = \vec{a} \cdot \vec{b} + \vec{a} \cdot \vec{c}$

  - Let $\vec{a}$ and $\vec{b}$ be any two vectors, and λ be any scalar. Then $(\lambda\vec{a}) \cdot \vec{b} = \lambda(\vec{a} \cdot \vec{b}) = \vec{a} \cdot (\lambda\vec{b})$

- Projection of a vector $\vec{a}$ on another vector $\vec{b}$ is given as $\left(\dfrac{\vec{a} \cdot \vec{b}}{|\vec{a}|}\right)$.

- Projection of a vector $\vec{b}$ on another vector $\vec{a}$ is given as $\left(\dfrac{\vec{a} \cdot \vec{b}}{|\vec{b}|}\right)$.

- **Vector (or cross) product of two vectors $\vec{a}$ and $\vec{b}$:** The vector product of two vectors having an angle θ between them is denoted by $\vec{a} \times \vec{b}$ and is defined by:

  $\vec{a} \times \vec{b} = |\vec{a}||\vec{b}|\sin\theta\, \hat{n}$

  $\sin\theta = \dfrac{|\vec{a} \times \vec{b}|}{|\vec{a}||\vec{b}|}$

- If $\vec{a} \times \vec{b} = \vec{0} \Leftrightarrow \vec{a} \parallel \vec{b}$

- If the vectors are in their component form as $\vec{a} = a_1\hat{i} + a_2\hat{j} + a_3\hat{k}$ and $\vec{b} = b_1\hat{i} + b_2\hat{j} + b_3\hat{k}$, then their cross product is given by

$$\vec{a} \times \vec{b} = \begin{vmatrix} \hat{i} & \hat{j} & \hat{k} \\ a_1 & a_2 & a_3 \\ b_1 & b_2 & b_3 \end{vmatrix}$$

The dot product is given by

$$\vec{a} \cdot \vec{b} = a_1 b_1 + a_2 b_2 + a_3 b_3$$

- Properties of vector product:

  ➢ Let $\vec{a}, \vec{b}$ and $\vec{c}$ be any three vectors then

  $\vec{a} \times \left(\vec{b} + \vec{c}\right) = \vec{a} \times \vec{b} + \vec{a} \times \vec{c}$.

➢ Let $\vec{a}$ and $\vec{b}$ be any two vectors, and λ be any scalar. Then $\left(\lambda \vec{a}\right) \times \vec{b} = \lambda \left(\vec{a} \times \vec{b}\right) = \vec{a} \times \left(\lambda \vec{b}\right)$

- Scalar triple product of three vectors $[A, B, C]$ is given by $\vec{A} \cdot \left(\vec{B} \times \vec{C}\right)$ which is the volume of a parallelepiped whose sides are given by vectors $\vec{A}, \vec{B}$ and $\vec{C}$.

Exercise

1. The value of m for which the vectors $\vec{a} = \hat{i} - \hat{j}$ and $\vec{b} = -2\hat{i} + m\hat{j}$ are collinear, is

   (a) $\dfrac{1}{2}$

   (b) 2

   (c) 3

   (d) –3

2. If the position vectors of A and B are $\left(3\hat{i} - 8\hat{j}\right)$ and $\left(-6\hat{i} + 4\hat{j}\right)$, then a unit vector in the direction of $\overline{AB}$ is

   (a) $-\dfrac{1}{5}\left(3\hat{i} + 4\hat{j}\right)$

   (b) $\dfrac{1}{5}\left(-3\hat{i} + 4\hat{j}\right)$

   (c) $\dfrac{1}{15}\left(3\hat{i} - 4\hat{j}\right)$

   (d) None of these

3. The unit vector parallel to the resultant of the vectors $\left(2\hat{i} + 4\hat{j} - 5\hat{k}\right)$ and $\left(\hat{i} + 2\hat{j} + 3\hat{k}\right)$ is.

   (a) $\dfrac{\left(\hat{i} + 2\hat{j} - 8\hat{k}\right)}{49}$

   (b) $\dfrac{\left(3\hat{i} + 6\hat{j} - 2\hat{k}\right)}{49}$

   (c) $\dfrac{\left(\hat{i} + 2\hat{j} - 8\hat{k}\right)}{7}$

   (d) $\dfrac{\left(3\hat{i} + 6\hat{j} - 2\hat{k}\right)}{7}$

4. If θ is the angle between the vectors $\vec{a} = \left(\hat{i} + 2\hat{j} + 3\hat{k}\right)$ and $\vec{b} = \left(-3\hat{i} + 2\hat{j} + \hat{k}\right)$, then cos θ = ?

   (a) $\dfrac{2}{5}$

   (b) $\dfrac{3}{7}$

   (c) $\dfrac{2}{7}$

   (d) $\dfrac{3}{5}$

5. If $\vec{a} = \left(\hat{i} + \hat{j}\right), \vec{b} = \left(\hat{j} + \hat{k}\right)$ and $\vec{c} = \left(\hat{i} + \hat{k}\right)$, then a unit vector in the direction of $\left(\vec{a} - 2\vec{b} + 3\vec{c}\right)$ is

   (a) $\dfrac{1}{3\sqrt{2}}\left(4\hat{i} + \hat{j} - \hat{k}\right)$

   (b) $\dfrac{1}{3\sqrt{2}}\left(4\hat{i} - \hat{j} + \hat{k}\right)$

   (c) $\dfrac{1}{\sqrt{2}}\left(4\hat{i} - \hat{j} + \hat{k}\right)$

   (d) None of these

6. If $\left(2\hat{i} - 3\hat{j} + \hat{k}\right)$ and $\left(\hat{i} - \hat{j} - \hat{k}\right)$ are the position vectors of the points A and B respectively, then the unit vector along $\overline{AB}$ is

   (a) $\dfrac{\left(\hat{i} - 2\hat{j} + 2\hat{k}\right)}{3}$

   (b) $\dfrac{\left(-\hat{i} + 2\hat{j} - 2\hat{k}\right)}{3}$

   (c) $\dfrac{\left(-\hat{i} + 2\hat{j} - 2\hat{k}\right)}{9}$

   (d) None of these

7. If $\vec{a} = 4\hat{i} - \hat{j} + \hat{k}$ and $\vec{b} = 4\hat{i} - 2\hat{j} + \hat{k}$, then find a unit vector parallel to the vector $\vec{a} + \vec{b}$.

   (a) $\dfrac{6\hat{i} - 3\hat{j} + 2\hat{k}}{7}$

   (b) $\dfrac{8\hat{i} - 3\hat{j} + 2\hat{k}}{\sqrt{77}}$

   (c) $\dfrac{8\hat{i} - 3\hat{j} + 2\hat{k}}{9}$

   (d) None of these

8. Find the sum of three vectors $\vec{a} = \hat{i} - 3\hat{j} + 4\hat{k}$, $\vec{b} = 2\hat{i} + \hat{j} - \hat{k}$ and $\vec{c} = 3\hat{i} - 6\hat{j} + 3\hat{k}$ is

   (a) $2\hat{i} + 5\hat{j} - 8\hat{k}$

   (b) $5\hat{i} - 8\hat{j} - 6\hat{k}$

   (c) $6\hat{i} - 8\hat{j} - 6\hat{k}$

   (d) None of these

9. If a line has direction ratios 3, –2, –4 then what are its direction?

(a) $\dfrac{1}{\sqrt{29}}, \dfrac{-3}{\sqrt{29}}, \dfrac{-2}{\sqrt{29}}$

(b) $\dfrac{3}{\sqrt{29}}, \dfrac{-2}{\sqrt{29}}, \dfrac{-4}{\sqrt{29}}$

(c) $\dfrac{2}{3}, \dfrac{-1}{3}, \dfrac{-2}{3}$

(d) None of these

10. What is the positive vector of the mid-point of vector joining the points P(3, 8, 4) and Q(5, 2, –2) ?

(a) $4\hat{i} + 5\hat{j} + \hat{k}$

(b) $3\hat{i} + 5\hat{j} + \hat{k}$

(c) $2\hat{i} + \hat{j} + 5\hat{k}$

(d) None of these

11. The angle between the vectors $\left(\hat{i} + 3\hat{j} + 2\hat{k}\right)$ and $\left(2\hat{i} - 4\hat{j} - \hat{k}\right)$ is

(a) $\sin^{-1}\left(\dfrac{5}{7}\right)$

(b) $\sin^{-1}\left(\dfrac{6}{7}\right)$

(c) $\sin^{-1}\left(\dfrac{3}{5}\right)$

(d) $\sin^{-1}\left(\dfrac{4}{7}\right)$

12. If θ is acute and the vector $(\sin\theta)\hat{i} + (\cos\theta)\hat{j}$ is perpendicular to the vector $\left(\hat{i} - \sqrt{3}\hat{j}\right)$ then θ = ?

(a) $\dfrac{\pi}{6}$

(d) $\dfrac{\pi}{5}$

(c) $\dfrac{\pi}{4}$

(d) $\dfrac{\pi}{3}$

13. The projection of $\vec{a} = \left(2\hat{i} + 3\hat{j} + 3\hat{k}\right)$ on $\vec{b} = \left(\hat{i} - 2\hat{j} + \hat{k}\right)$ is

(a) $\hat{i} - 2\hat{j} + \hat{k}$

(b) $-\hat{i} + 2\hat{j} - \hat{k}$

(c) $\dfrac{1}{\sqrt{6}}\left(-\hat{i} + 2\hat{j} - \hat{k}\right)$

(d) $\dfrac{1}{6}\left(-\hat{i} + 2\hat{j} - \hat{k}\right)$

14. If $\left|\vec{a} \times \vec{b}\right|^2 + \left(\vec{a} \cdot \vec{b}\right)^2 = 144$ and $|\vec{a}| = 4$, then $|\vec{b}|$ = ?

(a) 16

(b) 8

(c) 12

(d) 3

15. If $\left|\vec{a} \times \vec{b}\right| = \vec{a} \cdot \vec{b}$, then the angle between $\vec{a}$ and $\vec{b}$ is

(a) $\dfrac{\pi}{6}$

(b) $\dfrac{\pi}{4}$

(c) $\dfrac{\pi}{3}$

(d) $\dfrac{\pi}{2}$

16. The length of projection of the vector $\vec{a} = \left(7\hat{i} + \hat{j} - 4\hat{k}\right)$ on the vector $\vec{b} = \left(2\hat{i} + 6\hat{j} + 3\hat{k}\right)$ is

(a) $\dfrac{6}{7}$

(b) 1

(c) $\dfrac{8}{7}$

(d) None

17. The value of λ for which the vectors $\vec{a} = 2\hat{i} - 3\hat{j} + \hat{k}$, $\vec{b} = \hat{i} + 2\hat{j} - 3\hat{k}$ and $\vec{c} = \hat{j} + \lambda\hat{k}$ are coplanar, is

(a) 1

(b) –1

(c) 2

(d) –3

18. If $\vec{a}, \vec{b}$ and $\vec{c}$ be any three vectors, then $\vec{a} \times \left(\vec{b} + \vec{c}\right)$ = ?

(a) $\vec{a} \times \vec{b} + \vec{a} \times \vec{c}$

(b) $\vec{a} \cdot \vec{b} + \vec{a} \cdot \vec{c}$

(c) $\vec{a} \times \vec{b} + \vec{a} \cdot \vec{c}$

(d) None

19. If $\vec{a} = 2\hat{i} + 3\hat{j} + 3\hat{k}, \vec{b} = -4\hat{i} + 2\hat{j} + \hat{k}$ and $\vec{c} = 3\hat{i} + \hat{j} + 4\hat{k}$, then find $\vec{a} \cdot \left(\vec{b} \times \vec{c}\right)$

(a) 33

(b) 39

(c) 41

(d) None of these

20. The vector of magnitude 3 and perpendicular to each one of the vectors $\left(4\hat{i} - \hat{j} + 3\hat{k}\right)$ and $\left(-2\hat{i} + \hat{j} - 2\hat{k}\right)$ is

(a) $\left(\hat{i} - 2\hat{j} + 2\hat{k}\right)$

(b) $\left(-\hat{i} + 2\hat{j} + 2\hat{k}\right)$

(c) $\dfrac{\left(-3\hat{i} + 6\hat{j} + 6\hat{k}\right)}{\sqrt{3}}$

(d) None of these

Answer Keys

1. (b)	2. (b)	3. (d)	4. (c)	5. (b)	6. (b)	7. (b)	8. (d)	9. (b)	10. (a)
11. (a)	12. (d)	13. (d)	14. (d)	15. (b)	16. (c)	17. (b)	18. (a)	19. (c)	20. (b)

Solutions

1. Since $\vec{a}$ and $\vec{b}$ are collinear, we have $\vec{a} = t\vec{b}$ for some scalar t.

$$\Rightarrow \hat{i} - \hat{j} = \hat{t}\left(-2\hat{i} + m\hat{j}\right)$$

$$\Rightarrow (-2t)\hat{i} + (mt)\hat{j} = \left(\hat{i} - \hat{j}\right)$$

$$\Rightarrow -2t = 1,\ mt = -1$$

$$\therefore\ t = -\frac{1}{2}\ \text{and}\ m = \frac{-1}{\left(\frac{-1}{2}\right)} = 2$$

2. $\overline{AB}$ = position vector of B − positive vector of A

$$= \left(-6\hat{i} + 4\hat{j}\right) - \left(3\hat{i} - 8\hat{j}\right)$$

$$= -6\hat{i} + 4\hat{j} - 3\hat{i} + 8\hat{j}$$

$$= -9\hat{i} + 12\hat{j}$$

$$\left|\overline{AB}\right| = \sqrt{(-9)^2 + (12)^2} = \sqrt{81 + 144} = \sqrt{225} = 15$$

$$\therefore\ \text{Required vector} = \frac{-9\hat{i} + 12\hat{i}}{15} = \frac{-3\hat{i} + 4\hat{j}}{5}$$

$$= \frac{1}{5}\left(-3\hat{i} + 4\hat{j}\right)$$

3. Let $\vec{a} = 2\hat{i} + 4\hat{j} - 5\hat{k}$ and $\vec{b} = \hat{i} + 2\hat{j} - 3\hat{k}$

$$\text{Resultant} = \left(\vec{a} + \vec{b}\right) = \left(3\hat{i} + 6\hat{j} - 2\hat{k}\right)$$

$$\left|\vec{a} + \vec{b}\right| = \sqrt{3^2 + 6^2 + (-2)^2}$$

$$= \sqrt{9 + 36 + 4} = \sqrt{49} = 7$$

$$\therefore\ \text{Required vector} = \frac{\left(3\hat{i} + 6\hat{j} - 2\hat{k}\right)}{7}$$

4. $\left|\vec{a}\right| = \sqrt{1^2 + 2^2 + 3^2} = \sqrt{1 + 4 + 9} = \sqrt{14}$

and $\left|\vec{b}\right| = \sqrt{(-3)^2 + 2^2 + 1^2} = \sqrt{9 + 4 + 1} = \sqrt{14}$

$$\vec{a} \cdot \vec{b} = \left(\hat{i} + 2\hat{j} + 3\hat{k}\right) \cdot \left(-3\hat{i} + 2\hat{j} + \hat{k}\right)$$

$$= [1 \cdot (-3) + 2 \cdot 2 + 3 \cdot 1] = [-3 + 4 + 3] = 4$$

$$\therefore\ \cos\theta = \frac{\vec{a} \cdot \vec{b}}{\left|\vec{a}\right|\left|\vec{b}\right|} = \frac{4}{\sqrt{14}\sqrt{14}} = \frac{2}{7}$$

5. $\left(\vec{a} - 2\vec{b} + 3\vec{c}\right) = \left(\hat{i} + \hat{j}\right) - 2\left(\hat{j} + \hat{k}\right) + 3\left(\hat{i} + \hat{k}\right)$

$$= 4\hat{i} - \hat{j} + \hat{k}$$

and $\left|\vec{a} - 2\vec{b} + 3\vec{c}\right| = \sqrt{(4)^2 + (-1)^2 + (1)^2}$

$$= \sqrt{16 + 1 + 1} = \sqrt{18} = 3\sqrt{2}$$

$$\therefore\ \text{Required vector} = \frac{\left(4\hat{i} - \hat{j} + \hat{k}\right)}{3\sqrt{2}}$$

6. $\overrightarrow{AB}$ = Position vector of B − position vector of A

$$= \left(\hat{i} - \hat{j} - \hat{k}\right) - \left(2\hat{i} - 3\hat{j} + \hat{k}\right)$$

$$= \left(-\hat{i} + 2\hat{j} - 2\hat{k}\right)$$

$$\therefore\ \left|\overrightarrow{AB}\right| = \sqrt{(-1)^2 + 2^2 + (-2)^2}$$

$$= \sqrt{1 + 4 + 4} = \sqrt{9} = 3$$

$$\therefore\ \text{Required vector} = \frac{\left(-\hat{i} + 2\hat{j} - 2\hat{k}\right)}{3}$$

7. $\vec{a} + \vec{b} = 4\hat{i} - \hat{j} + \hat{k} + 4\hat{i} - 2\hat{j} + \hat{k}$

$$= 8\hat{i} - 3\hat{j} + 2\hat{k}$$

and $\left|\vec{a} + \vec{b}\right| = \sqrt{(8)^2 + (-3)^2 + (2)^2}$

$$= \sqrt{64 + 9 + 4} = \sqrt{77}$$

$\therefore$ Unit vector parallel to

$$\left(\vec{a} + \vec{b}\right) = \frac{8\hat{i} - 3\hat{j} + 2\hat{k}}{\sqrt{77}}$$

8. Given, $\vec{a} = \hat{i} - 3\hat{j} + 4\hat{k}$

$$\vec{b} = 2\hat{i} + \hat{j} - \hat{k}\ \text{and}\ \vec{c} = 3\hat{i} - 6\hat{j} + 3\hat{k}$$

$$\therefore\ \left(\vec{a} + \vec{b} + \vec{c}\right) = \left(\hat{i} - 3\hat{j} + 4\hat{k}\right) + \left(2\hat{i} + \hat{j} - \hat{k}\right) +$$

$$\left(3\hat{i} - 6\hat{j} + 3\hat{k}\right) = 6\hat{i} - 8\hat{j} + 6\hat{k}$$

9. Given a = 3, b = −2 and c = −4

$$\therefore\ \sqrt{a^2 + b^2 + c^2} = \sqrt{(3)^2 + (-2)^2 + \left(-4^2\right)}$$

$$= \sqrt{9 + 4 + 16} = \sqrt{29}$$

$\therefore$ Direction cosines are

$$l = \frac{3}{\sqrt{29}},\ m = \frac{-2}{\sqrt{29}},\ n = \frac{-4}{\sqrt{29}}$$

10. Given P = (3, 8, 4) and Q = (5, 2, −2)

$$\therefore\ \overrightarrow{OR} = \frac{\left(3\hat{i} + 8\hat{j} + 4\hat{k}\right) + \left(5\hat{i} + 2\hat{j} - 2\hat{k}\right)}{2}$$

$$= \frac{8\hat{i} + 10\hat{j} + 2\hat{k}}{2} = 4\hat{i} + 5\hat{j} + \hat{k}$$

11. Let $\vec{a} = \hat{i} + 3\hat{j} + 2\hat{k}$ and $\vec{b} = 2\hat{i} - 4\hat{j} - \hat{k}$

$$\therefore \ \vec{a} \times \vec{b} = \begin{vmatrix} \hat{i} & \hat{j} & \hat{k} \\ 1 & 3 & 2 \\ 2 & -4 & -1 \end{vmatrix} = 5\hat{i} + 5\hat{j} - 10\hat{k}$$

$$\therefore \ \left|\vec{a} \times \vec{b}\right| = \sqrt{5^2 + 5^2 + (-10)^2} = \sqrt{25 + 25 + 100}$$

$$= \sqrt{150} = 5\sqrt{6}$$

Also, $\left|\vec{a}\right| = \sqrt{1^2 + 3^2 + 2^2} = \sqrt{1 + 9 + 4} = \sqrt{14}$

and $\left|\vec{b}\right| = \sqrt{2^2 + \left(-4^2\right) + (-1)^2} = \sqrt{4 + 16 + 1} = \sqrt{21}$

$$\therefore \ \sin\theta = \frac{\left|\vec{a} \times \vec{b}\right|}{\left|\vec{a}\right|\left|\hat{b}\right|} = \frac{5\sqrt{6}}{\sqrt{14}\sqrt{21}} = \frac{5}{7}$$

$$\therefore \ \theta = \sin^{-1}\left(\frac{5}{7}\right)$$

12. Let $\vec{a} = (\sin\theta)\hat{i} + (\cos\theta)\hat{j}$ and $\vec{b} = \hat{i} - \sqrt{3}\hat{j}$, then

$\because \vec{a} \perp \vec{b} \Rightarrow \vec{a}.\vec{b} = 0$

$$\Rightarrow \left[(\sin\theta)\hat{i} + (\cos\theta)\hat{j}\right].\left(\hat{i} - \sqrt{3}\hat{j}\right) = 0$$

$$\Rightarrow \sin\theta - \sqrt{3}\cos\theta = 0$$

$$\Rightarrow \sin\theta - \sqrt{3}\cos\theta \Rightarrow \tan\theta = \sqrt{3}$$

$$\Rightarrow \tan\theta = \tan\frac{\pi}{3}$$

$$\therefore \ \theta = \frac{\pi}{3}$$

13. $\vec{a}.\vec{b} = \left(2\hat{i} + 3\hat{j} + 3\hat{k}\right).\left(\hat{i} - 2\hat{j} + \hat{k}\right) = 2 - 6 + 3 = -1$

$\left|\vec{b}\right|^2 = (1)^2 + (-2)^2 + (1)^2 = 1 + 4 + 1 = 6$

$$\therefore \ \text{Projection of } \vec{a} \text{ on } \vec{b} = \frac{(\vec{a}.\vec{b})\,\vec{b}}{\left|\vec{b}\right|^2}$$

$$= \frac{-1}{6}\left(\hat{i} - 2\hat{j} + \hat{k}\right) = \frac{1}{6}\left(-\hat{i} + 2\hat{j} - \hat{k}\right)$$

14. $\left|\vec{a} \times \vec{b}\right|^2 + \left(\vec{a}.\vec{b}\right)^2 = \left|\vec{a}\right|^2\left|\vec{b}\right|^2$ (We know)

$$\Rightarrow \left|\vec{a}\right|^2\left|\vec{b}\right|^2 = 144$$

$$\Rightarrow (4)^2\left|\vec{b}\right|^2 = 144$$

$$\Rightarrow \left|\vec{b}\right|^2 = \frac{144}{16} = 9$$

$$\therefore \ \left|\vec{b}\right| = \sqrt{9} = 3$$

15. $\because \left|\vec{a} \times \vec{b}\right| = \vec{a}.\vec{b} \Rightarrow ab\sin\theta = ab\cos\theta$

$$\Rightarrow \frac{\sin\theta}{\cos\theta} = 1$$

$$\Rightarrow \tan\theta = 1 \Rightarrow \tan\theta = \tan\frac{\pi}{4}$$

16. $\vec{a}.\vec{b} = \left(7\hat{i} + \hat{j} - 4\hat{k}\right).\left(2\hat{i} + 6\hat{j} + 3\hat{k}\right)$

$$= 14 + 6 - 12 = 8$$

and $\left|\vec{b}\right| = \sqrt{(2)^2 + (6)^2 + (3)^2} = \sqrt{4 + 36 + 9} = \sqrt{49} = 7$

$$\therefore \ \text{Length of projection of } \vec{a} \text{ on } \vec{b} = \frac{\vec{a}.\vec{b}}{\left|\vec{b}\right|} = \frac{8}{7}$$

17. $\because \vec{a}, \vec{b}$ and $\vec{c}$ are coplanar.

$$\therefore \ \begin{vmatrix} 2 & -3 & 1 \\ 1 & 2 & -3 \\ 0 & 1 & \lambda \end{vmatrix} = 0$$

$$\Rightarrow 2(2\lambda + 3) + 3\lambda + 1 = 0$$

$$\Rightarrow 4\lambda + 6 + 3\lambda + 1 = 0$$

$$\Rightarrow 7\lambda + 7 = 0 \Rightarrow 7\lambda = -7$$

$$\therefore \ \lambda = \frac{-7}{7} = -1$$

18. $\vec{a} \times \left(\vec{b} + \vec{c}\right) = \vec{a} \times \vec{b} + \vec{a} \times \vec{c}$.

19. $\vec{a}.\left(\vec{b} + \vec{c}\right) = \begin{vmatrix} 2 & 3 & 3 \\ -4 & 2 & 1 \\ 3 & 1 & 4 \end{vmatrix}$

On expanding along R_1,
$= 2(8 - 1) - 3(-16 - 3) + 3(-4 - 6)$
$= 2 \times 7 - 3 \times (-19) + 3 \times (-10)$
$= 14 + 57 - 30 = 14 + 27 = 41$

20. Let $\vec{a} = 4\hat{i} - \hat{j} + 3\hat{k}$ and $\vec{b} = -2\hat{i} + \hat{j} - 2\hat{k}$, then a

vector perpendicular to both $\vec{a}$ and $\vec{b}$ is $\left(\vec{a} \times \vec{b}\right)$

$$\therefore \ \left(\vec{a} \times \vec{b}\right) \begin{vmatrix} \hat{i} & \hat{j} & \hat{k} \\ 4 & -1 & 3 \\ -2 & 1 & -2 \end{vmatrix} = \left(-\hat{i} + 2\hat{j} + 2\hat{k}\right)$$

and $\left|\vec{a} \times \vec{b}\right| = \sqrt{(-1)^2 + 2^2 + 2^2} = \sqrt{1 + 4 + 4} = \sqrt{9} = 3$

$\therefore$ Unit vector perpendicular to $\vec{a}$ and $\vec{b}$

$$= \frac{\left(-\hat{i} + 2\hat{j} + 2\hat{k}\right)}{3}$$

$\therefore$ Required vector

$$= \frac{3\left(-\hat{i} + 2\hat{j} + 2\hat{k}\right)}{3} = \left(-\hat{i} + 2\hat{j} + 2\hat{k}\right)$$

CHAPTER 11

Three Dimensional Geometry

Direction Cosines and Lines

- **Direction Cosines:**

These are the cosines of the angles made by the line with the positive directions of the coordinate axes.

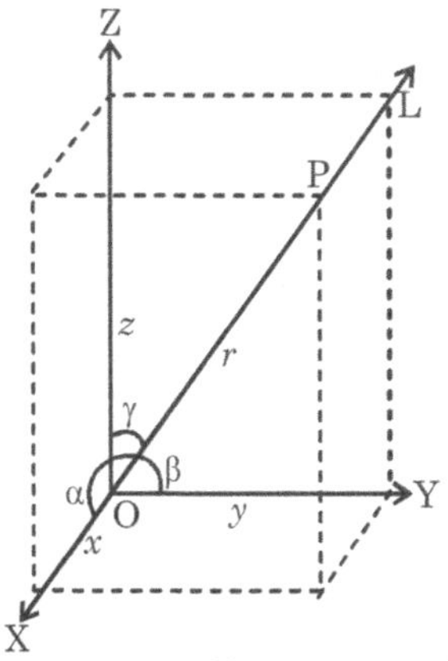

The direction cosines of line joining the points $A(x_1, y_1, z_1)$ and $B(x_2, y_2, z_2)$ are

$$\pm\frac{x_2 - x_1}{AB}, \pm\frac{y_2 - y_1}{AB}, \pm\frac{z_2 - z_1}{AB} \text{ where}$$

$$AB = \sqrt{(x_2 - x_1)^2 + (y_2 - y_1)^2 + (z_2 - z_1)^2}$$

Assume the direction cosines of the line are l, m and n and that the line is passing through the point $A(x_1, y_1, z_1)$, then the equation of the line is

$$\frac{x - x_1}{l} = \frac{y - y_1}{m} = \frac{z - z_1}{n}$$

Also, $l^2 + m^2 + n^2 = 1$

- **Direction Cosines:**

Direction ratios are any three numbers which are proportional to the direction cosines.

Let the direction ratios be a, b and c, then

$$l = \pm\frac{a}{\sqrt{a^2 + b^2 + c^2}}, m = \pm\frac{b}{\sqrt{a^2 + b^2 + c^2}} \text{ and}$$

$$n = \pm\frac{c}{\sqrt{a^2 + b^2 + c^2}}$$

- **Lines:**

➤ Equation of the line which passes through two given points:

Assume that the position vectors of $A(x_1, y_1, z_1)$ and $B(x_2, y_2, z_2)$ are $\vec{a}$ and $\vec{b}$ respectively.

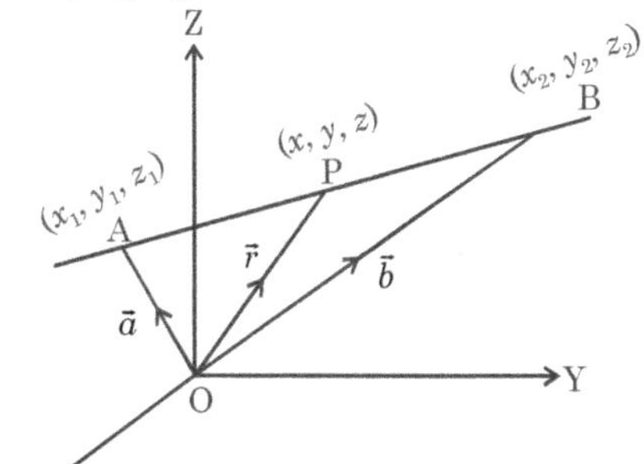

Then, the vector equation of the line is

$$\vec{r} = \vec{a} + k\left(\vec{b} - \vec{a}\right), k \in \mathbb{R}$$

The equation of the line in Cartesian form is

$$\frac{x - x_1}{x_2 - x_1} = \frac{y - y_1}{y_2 - y_1} = \frac{z - z_1}{z_2 - z_1}$$

➤ Equation of the line which passes through a given point having a given direction

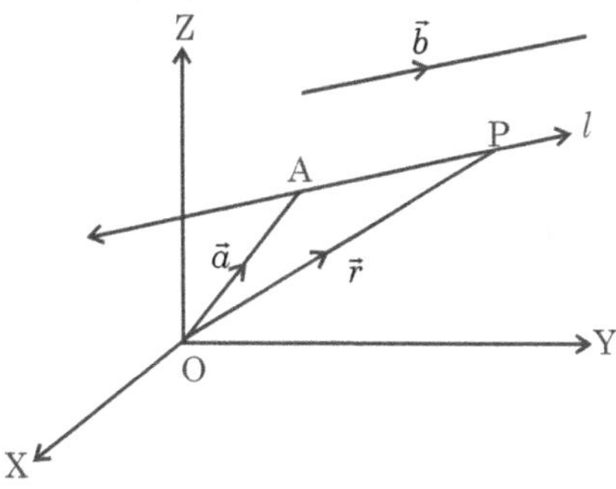

The vector equation of the line is $\vec{r} = \vec{a} + \lambda \vec{b}$

The equation of the line in Cartesian form when it passes through $A(x_1, y_1, z_1)$ is

$$\frac{x - x_1}{a} = \frac{y - y_1}{b} = \frac{z - z_1}{c}$$ where the direction ratios are a, b and c.

The angle between the lines $\vec{r} = a_1\hat{i} + b_1\hat{j} + c_1\hat{k}$ and $\vec{r} = a_2\hat{i} + b_2\hat{j} + c_2\hat{k}$ is given by

$$\cos\theta = \left| \frac{a_1a_2 + b_1b_2 + c_1c_2}{\sqrt{a_1{}^2 + b_1{}^2 + c_1{}^2}\ \sqrt{a_2{}^2 + b_2{}^2 + c_2{}^2}} \right|$$

The shortest distance between the lines $\vec{r} = \vec{a_1} + \lambda\vec{b_1}$ and $\vec{r} = \vec{a_2} + \mu\vec{b_2}$ is given by

$$\left| \frac{\left(\vec{b_1} \times \vec{b_2}\right) \cdot \left(\vec{a_2} - \vec{a_1}\right)}{\left|\vec{b_1} \times \vec{b_2}\right|} \right|$$

The shortest distance between the lines $\dfrac{x - x_1}{a_1} = \dfrac{y - y_1}{b_1} = \dfrac{z - z_1}{c_1}$ and

$\dfrac{x - x_2}{a_2} = \dfrac{y - y_2}{b_2} = \dfrac{z - z_2}{c_2}$ is given by

$$\left| \frac{\begin{vmatrix} x_2 - x_1 & y_2 - y_1 & z_2 - z_1 \\ a_1 & b_1 & c_1 \\ a_2 & b_2 & c_2 \end{vmatrix}}{\sqrt{\left(b_1c_2 - b_2c_1\right)^2 + \left(c_1a_2 - c_2a_1\right)^2 + \left(a_1b_2 - a_2b_1\right)^2}} \right|$$

Plane

- **Plane**

A surface so that when the two points are taken on it, the line segment lies joining the two points lies on the surface is called a plane.

The equation of the plane is $\vec{r} \cdot \hat{n} = d$ where $\hat{n}$ is the unit vector normal to plane of origin. The equation of the plane in normal form is $lx + my + nz = d$ where l, m, n are direction cosines.

- **Equation of a plane perpendicular to a given vector**

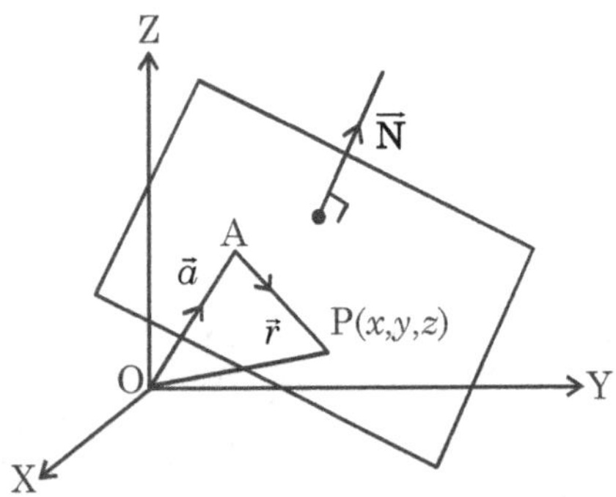

The equation of a plane through a point whose position vector is $\vec{a}$ and perpendicular to the vector $\vec{N}$ is $\left(\vec{r} - \vec{a}\right) \cdot \vec{N} = 0$

Equation of a plane perpendicular to a given vector and passing through a given point is $A(x - x_1) + B(y - y_1) + C(z - z_1) = 0$

- **Equation of a plane passing through three non collinear points**

Let the non collinear points be $R(x_1, y_1, z_1)$, $S(x_1, y_2, z_2)$, $T(x_3, y_3, z_3)$ and $\vec{r}$ be the position vector.

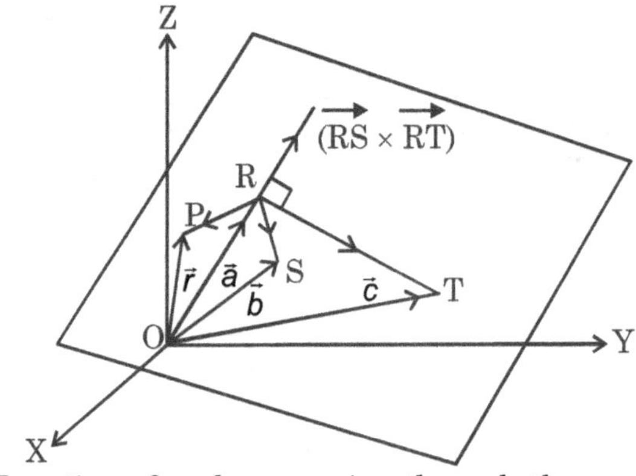

Equation of a plane passing through three non collinear points is

$$\left(\vec{r} - \vec{a}\right) \cdot \left[\left(\vec{b} - \vec{a}\right) \times \left(\vec{c} - \vec{a}\right)\right] = 0$$

In Cartesian plane,

$$\begin{vmatrix} x - x_1 & y - y_1 & z - z_1 \\ x_2 - x_1 & y_2 - y_1 & z_2 - z_1 \\ x_3 - x_1 & y_3 - y_1 & z_3 - z_1 \end{vmatrix} = 0$$

The equation of the plane in the intercept form is $\dfrac{x}{a} + \dfrac{y}{b} + \dfrac{z}{c} = 1$ where a, b, c are x, y, z intercepts respectively.

- **The plane passing through intersection of two given lines**

It has the equation

$$\vec{r} \cdot \left(\vec{n_1} + \lambda\vec{n_2}\right) = d_1 + \lambda d_2$$

In Cartesian system,

$$(A_1x + B_1y + C_1z - d_1) + l(A_2x + B_2y + C_2z - d_2) = 0$$

- **Angle between two planes**

The angle between the planes is given by the angle between their normals.

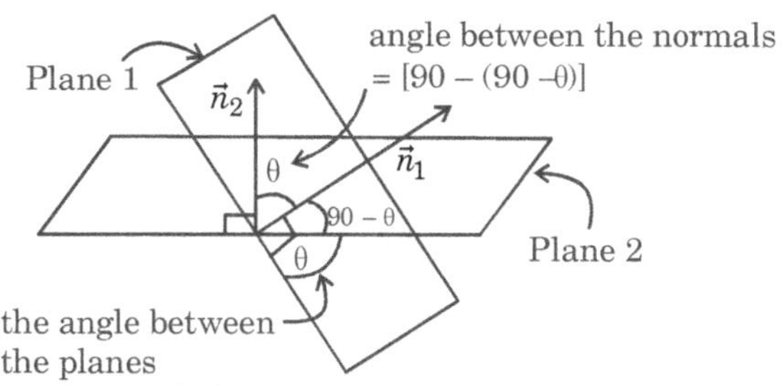

Let the angle between the planes be θ.

$$\cos\theta = \left| \frac{\vec{n}_1 \cdot \vec{n}_2}{\left\|\vec{n}_1\right\|\left\|\vec{n}_2\right\|} \right|$$ where $\vec{n}_1, \vec{n}_2$ are normal to the planes.

In Cartesian form, $A_1x + B_1y + C_1z + D_1 = 0$ and $A_2x + B_2y + C_2z + D_2 = 0$

$$\cos\theta = \left| \frac{A_1 A_2 + B_1 B_2 + C_1 C_2}{\sqrt{A_1{}^2 + B_1{}^2 + C_1{}^2}\sqrt{A_2{}^2 + B_2{}^2 + C_2{}^2}} \right|$$

The distance between a plane $Ax + By + Cz + D$ and the point (x_1, y_1, z_1) is given by

$$\left| \frac{A_1 x + B_1 y + C_1 z + D_1}{\sqrt{A^2 + B^2 + C^2}} \right|$$

The angle between the line $\vec{r} = \vec{a} + \lambda \vec{b}$ and the plane $\vec{r} \cdot \hat{n} = d$ is $\sin\varphi = \left| \dfrac{\vec{b} \cdot \hat{n}}{\left\|\vec{b}\right\|\left\|\hat{n}\right\|} \right|$

Exercise

1. The distance between the points A(1, −1, 3) and B(2, 3, −5) is

   (a) 13 units

   (b) $\sqrt{13}$ units

   (c) 9 units

   (d) None

2. The distance of the point P(−8, 5, −6) from the origin is

   (a) 19 units

   (b) $\sqrt{19}$ units

   (c) $5\sqrt{5}$ units

   (d) None

3. The coordinates of the point which divides the join of the points A(5, 4, 2) and B(−1, −2, 4) in the ratio 2 : 3 is

   (a) (13, 8, 14)

   (b) $\left(\dfrac{13}{2}, 4, 7\right)$

   (c) $\left(\dfrac{13}{5}, \dfrac{8}{5}, \dfrac{14}{5}\right)$

   (d) None of these

4. The ratio in which the point R(5, 4, −6) divides the joint of the points P(3, 2, −4) and Q(9, 8, −10) is

   (a) 2 : 3

   (b) 3 : 4

   (c) 1 : 3

   (d) 1 : 2

5. The direction cosines of y-axis are

   (a) (1, 0, 1)

   (b) (0, 1, 0)

   (c) $\left(\dfrac{1}{\sqrt{2}}, 0, \dfrac{1}{\sqrt{2}}\right)$

   (d) None of these

6. If a line make angles α, β, γ with x - axis, y - axis and z - axis respectively, then $\sin^2\alpha + \sin^2\beta + \sin^2\gamma$ = ?

   (a) 1

   (b) 3

   (c) 2

   (d) None of these

7. The direction ratios of a line are 6, 2, −3. Its direction cosines are

   (a) $\left(\dfrac{6}{5}, \dfrac{2}{5}, \dfrac{-3}{5}\right)$

   (b) $\left(\dfrac{6}{11}, \dfrac{2}{11}, \dfrac{-3}{11}\right)$

   (c) $\left(\dfrac{6}{7}, \dfrac{2}{7}, \dfrac{-3}{7}\right)$

   (d) None of these

8. The direction cosines of the vector $\vec{r} = 2\hat{i} + 3\hat{j} - 2\hat{k}$ are

   (a) $\left(\dfrac{2}{\sqrt{17}}, \dfrac{3}{\sqrt{17}}, \dfrac{-2}{\sqrt{17}}\right)$

   (b) $\left(\dfrac{2}{3}, 1, \dfrac{-2}{3}\right)$

   (c) $\left(\dfrac{2}{\sqrt{7}}, \dfrac{3}{\sqrt{7}}, \dfrac{-2}{\sqrt{7}}\right)$

   (d) None of these

9. The direction cosines of the line segment joining the points A(7, −5, 9) and B(5, −3, 8) are

   (a) (−2, 2, −1)

   (b) $\left(-\dfrac{1}{2}, \dfrac{1}{2}, -1\right)$

   (c) $\left(-\dfrac{2}{3}, \dfrac{2}{3}, \dfrac{-1}{3}\right)$

   (d) None of these

10. The angle between the lines whose direction ratios are $(3, 4, 5)$ and $(4, -3, 5)$ is
    (a) $30°$ (b) $45°$
    (c) $60°$ (d) $90°$

11. The direction cosines of the line which is perpendicular to the lines having direction ratios $(1, -1, 2)$ and $(2, 1, -1)$ respectively, are
    (a) $\left(\dfrac{-1}{5}, 1, \dfrac{3}{5}\right)$ (b) $\left(\dfrac{-2}{\sqrt{35}}, \dfrac{3}{\sqrt{35}}, \dfrac{5}{\sqrt{35}}\right)$
    (c) $\left(\dfrac{-1}{\sqrt{35}}, \dfrac{5}{\sqrt{35}}, \dfrac{3}{\sqrt{35}}\right)$ (d) None of these

12. If (a_1, b_1, c_1) and (a_2, b_2, c_2) are the direction ratios of two parallel lines, then
    (a) $a_1 a_2 + b_1 b_2 + c_1 c_2 = 0$
    (b) $a_1^2 + b_1^2 + c_1^2 = a_2^2 + b_2^2 + c_2^2$
    (c) $a_1 = a_2, b_1 = b_2, c_1 = c_2$
    (d) $\dfrac{a_1}{a_2} = \dfrac{b_1}{b_2} = \dfrac{c_1}{c_2}$

13. The angle between the planes $3x + 4y + 5z = 16$ and $4x - 3y + 5z = 9$ is
    (a) $\dfrac{\pi}{2}$ (b) $\dfrac{\pi}{6}$
    (c) $\dfrac{\pi}{3}$ (d) $\dfrac{\pi}{4}$

14. The distance of the point $(2, 3, -1)$ from the plane $2x - 3y + 4z = 10$ is
    (a) $\dfrac{19}{\sqrt{29}}$ (b) $\dfrac{\sqrt{19}}{29}$
    (c) $\dfrac{19}{29}$ (d) None of these

15. Equation of xz-plane is
    (a) $x = 0, z = 0$ (b) $y = 0$
    (c) $x = z \neq 0$ (d) None of these

16. Equation of a plane parallel to yz-plane and at a distance a from it, is
    (a) $y = z = a$ (b) $x = a$
    (c) $y = z \neq a$ (d) None of these

17. The length of perpendicular drawn from origin to the plane $6x - 3y + 2z - 14 = 0$ is
    (a) 14 units   (b) 5 units
    (c) 2 units   (d) 7 units

18. The point where the plane $ax + by + cz + d = 0$, meets the y-axis, is
    (a) $\left(0, -\dfrac{d}{b}, 0\right)$ (b) $\left(-\dfrac{d}{a}, 0, \dfrac{-d}{c}\right)$
    (c) $\left(0, \dfrac{d}{b}, 0\right)$ (d) $\left(\dfrac{d}{a}, 0, \dfrac{d}{c}\right)$

19. Equation to the plane which makes intercepts 2, 3, 4 on co-ordinates axes, is
    (a) $x + y + z = \sqrt{29}$ (b) $2x + 3y + 4z = 1$
    (c) $\dfrac{x}{2} + \dfrac{y}{3} + \dfrac{z}{4} = 1$ (d) None of these

20. The intercepts made by the plane $2x - 4y + 3x = 12$ on the coordinate axes are
    (a) $2, -4, 3$ (b) $\dfrac{1}{6}, \dfrac{-1}{3}, \dfrac{1}{4}$
    (c) $6, -3, 4$ (d) $\dfrac{\sqrt{29}}{2}, \dfrac{\sqrt{29}}{-4}, \dfrac{\sqrt{29}}{3}$

21. The length of perpendicular from the point $P(2, 1, -1)$ to the plane $x - 2y + 4z = 9$ is
    (a) $\sqrt{21}$ units   (b) $\dfrac{9}{\sqrt{21}}$ units
    (c) $\dfrac{13}{\sqrt{21}}$ units   (d) None of these

22. The distance between the parallel planes $x + y - z + 4 = 0$ and $x + y - z + 5 = 0$ is
    (a) $3\sqrt{3}$ (b) $\dfrac{4}{\sqrt{3}}$
    (c) $\dfrac{5}{\sqrt{3}}$ (d) $\dfrac{1}{\sqrt{3}}$

23. Equation of the plane passing through the points $(a, 0, 0)$, $(0, b, 0)$ and $(0, 0, c)$ is
    (a) $ax + by + cz = 0$ (b) $ax + by + cz = 1$
    (c) $\dfrac{x}{a} + \dfrac{y}{b} + \dfrac{z}{c} = 0$ (d) $\dfrac{x}{a} + \dfrac{y}{b} + \dfrac{z}{c} = 1$

24. The points $(2, 5, -4)$, $(1, 4, -3)$ and $(4, 7, -6)$ are
    (a) collinear
    (b) form an equilateral triangle
    (c) form an isosceles triangle
    (d) form a right angled triangle

Answer Keys

1. (c)   2. (c)   3. (c)   4. (d)   5. (b)   6. (c)   7. (c)   8. (a)   9. (c)   10. (c)

11. (c)   12. (d)   13. (c)   14. (a)   15. (b)   16. (b)   17. (c)   18. (a)   19. (c)   20. (c)

21. (c)   22. (d)   23. (d)   24. (a)

Solutions

1. Let $AB = \sqrt{(2-1)^2 + (3+1)^2 + (-5-3)^2}$

$$= \sqrt{1^2 + 4^2 + (-8)^2} = \sqrt{1+16+64} = \sqrt{81}$$

$$= 9 \text{ units}$$

2. $OP = \sqrt{(-8)^2 + 5^2 + (-6)^2} = \sqrt{125} = 5\sqrt{5}$ units

3. $x = \left\{\dfrac{2\times(-1)+3\times 5}{2+3}\right\} = \dfrac{-2+15}{5} = \dfrac{13}{5}$,

$y = \left\{\dfrac{2\times(-2)+3\times 4}{2+3}\right\} = \dfrac{-4+12}{5} = \dfrac{8}{5}$,

and $z = \left\{\dfrac{2\times 4+3\times 2}{2+3}\right\} = \dfrac{8+6}{5} = \dfrac{14}{5}$,

$\therefore$ Required point is $\left(\dfrac{13}{5}, \dfrac{8}{5}, \dfrac{14}{5}\right)$

4. Let the required ratio be $\lambda : 1$, then

$$\dfrac{9\lambda+3}{\lambda+1} = 5 \Rightarrow 9\lambda+3 = 5\lambda+5$$

$$\Rightarrow 4\lambda = 2$$

$$\therefore \lambda = \dfrac{2}{4} = \dfrac{1}{2}$$

$\therefore$ Required ratio $= \dfrac{1}{2} : 1 = 1 : 2$

5. y-axis makes angles of $90°, 0°, 90°$ with coordinate axes.

Therefore, the direction cosines of y-axis are $\cos 90°, \cos 0°, \cos 90° = (0, 1, 0)$

6. $l^2 + m^2 + n^2 = 1$

$\Rightarrow \cos^2\alpha + \cos^2\beta + \cos^2\gamma = 1$

$\Rightarrow (1-\sin^2\alpha) + (1-\sin^2\beta) + (1-\sin^2\gamma) = 1$

$\Rightarrow 3 - (\sin^2\alpha + \sin^2\beta)\sin^2\gamma = 1$

$\therefore \sin^2\alpha + \sin^2\beta + \sin^2\gamma = 2$

7. Direction cosines of line are

$$\dfrac{6}{\sqrt{6^2+2^2+(-3)^2}}, \dfrac{2}{\sqrt{6^2+2^2+(-3)^2}},$$

$$\dfrac{-3}{\sqrt{6^2+2^2+(-3)^2}}$$

$$\Rightarrow \dfrac{6}{\sqrt{36+4+9}}, \dfrac{2}{\sqrt{36+4+9}}, \dfrac{-3}{\sqrt{36+4+9}}$$

$$\Rightarrow \dfrac{6}{\sqrt{49}}, \dfrac{2}{\sqrt{49}}, \dfrac{-3}{\sqrt{49}}$$

$$\Rightarrow \dfrac{6}{7}, \dfrac{2}{7}, \dfrac{-3}{7}$$

8. Direction cosines of line are

$$\dfrac{2}{\sqrt{2^2+3^2+(-2)^2}}, \dfrac{3}{\sqrt{2^2+3^2+(-2)^2}},$$

$$\dfrac{-2}{\sqrt{2^2+3^2+(-2)^2}}$$

$$\Rightarrow \dfrac{2}{\sqrt{4+9+4}}, \dfrac{3}{\sqrt{4+9+4}}, \dfrac{-2}{\sqrt{4+9+4}}$$

$$\Rightarrow \dfrac{2}{\sqrt{17}}, \dfrac{3}{\sqrt{17}}, \dfrac{-2}{\sqrt{17}}$$

9. Direction ratios of the given line segment are

$(5-7), [-3-(-5)], (8-9)$

$\Rightarrow (-2, 2, -1)$

$\therefore$ Direction cosines of the given line segment are

$$\dfrac{-2}{\sqrt{(-2)^2+2^2+1^2}}, \dfrac{2}{\sqrt{(-2)^2+2^2+1^2}},$$

$$\dfrac{-1}{\sqrt{(-2)^2+2^2+1^2}}$$

$$\Rightarrow \dfrac{-2}{\sqrt{4+4+1}}, \dfrac{2}{\sqrt{4+4+1}}, \dfrac{-1}{\sqrt{4+4+1}}$$

$$\Rightarrow \dfrac{-2}{\sqrt{9}}, \dfrac{2}{\sqrt{9}}, \dfrac{-1}{\sqrt{9}}$$

$$\Rightarrow \dfrac{-2}{3}, \dfrac{2}{3}, \dfrac{-1}{3}$$

10. $\cos\theta = \dfrac{a_1 a_2 + b_1 b_2 + c_1 c_2}{\sqrt{a_1^2+b_1^2+c_1^2}.\sqrt{a_2^2+b_2^2+c_2^2}}$

$$= \dfrac{3\times 4+4\times(-3)+5\times 5}{\sqrt{3^2+4^2+5^2}.\sqrt{4^2+(-3)^2+5^2}}$$

$$= \dfrac{12-12+25}{\sqrt{9+16+25}.\sqrt{16+9+25}}$$

$$= \dfrac{25}{\sqrt{50}\sqrt{50}} = \dfrac{25}{50} = \dfrac{1}{2}$$

$$\Rightarrow \cos\theta = \dfrac{1}{2}$$

$$\Rightarrow \cos\theta = \cos 60°$$

$$\therefore \theta = 60°$$

11. Let the required direction cosines be l, m, n Then,

$$l - m + 2n = 0 \qquad \text{...(i)}$$

$$2l + m - n = 0 \qquad \text{...(ii)}$$

On solving (i) and (ii) by cross multiplication,
We get

$$\frac{l}{-1} = \frac{m}{5} = \frac{n}{3} = \frac{\sqrt{l^2 + m^2 + n^2}}{\sqrt{(-1)^2 + 5^2 + 3^2}} = \frac{1}{\sqrt{35}}$$

$$\Rightarrow l = \frac{-1}{\sqrt{35}}, m = \frac{5}{\sqrt{35}}, n = \frac{3}{\sqrt{35}}$$

12. Two lines with direction ratios (a_1, b_1, c_1) and (a_2, b_2, c_2) are parallel when $\frac{a_1}{a_2} = \frac{b_1}{b_2} = \frac{c_1}{c_2}$.

13. $\cos\theta = \dfrac{\left[3 \times 4 + 4 \times (-3) + 5 \times 5\right]}{\sqrt{3^2 + 4^2 + 5^2} \cdot \sqrt{4^2 + (-3)^2 + 5^2}}$

$$= \frac{12 - 12 + 25}{\sqrt{9 + 16 + 25}\sqrt{16 + 9 + 25}}$$

$$= \frac{25}{\sqrt{50}\sqrt{50}} = \frac{25}{50} = \frac{1}{2}$$

$$\Rightarrow \cos\theta = \cos\frac{\pi}{3}$$

$$\therefore \theta = \frac{\pi}{3}$$

14. $p = \dfrac{\left|2 \times 2 - 3 \times 3 + 4 \times (-1) - 10\right|}{\sqrt{2^2 + (-3)^2 + 4^2}}$

$$= \frac{|4 - 9 - 4 - 10|}{\sqrt{4 + 9 + 16}} = \frac{19}{\sqrt{29}}$$

15. Equation of xz-plane is $y = 0$

16. Equation of a plane parallel to yz-plane at a distance a from it is $x = a$.

17. $6x - 3y + 2z = 14 \qquad \text{...(i)}$

On dividing throughout by $\sqrt{6^2 + (-3)^2 + 2^2} = 7$,

We get, $\dfrac{6}{7}x - \dfrac{3}{7}y + \dfrac{2}{7}z = 2$

This is the normal form in which p = 2 units

18. $ax + by + cz + d = 0$

$$\Rightarrow ax + by + cz = -d$$

$$\Rightarrow \frac{x}{\left(\dfrac{-d}{a}\right)} + \frac{y}{\left(\dfrac{-d}{b}\right)} + \frac{z}{\left(\dfrac{-d}{c}\right)} = 1$$

$\therefore$ Given plane meets y-axis at $\left(0, \dfrac{d}{b}, 0\right)$

19. The required equation is

$$\frac{x}{2} + \frac{y}{3} + \frac{z}{4} = 1$$

20. $2x - 4y + 3z = 12$

$$\Rightarrow \frac{x}{6} + \frac{y}{-3} + \frac{z}{4} = 1$$

$\therefore$ Intercepts made by the given plane on coordinate axes are 6, –3, 4.

21. $P = \dfrac{\left|2 - 2 \times 1 + 4 \times (-1) - 9\right|}{\sqrt{1^2 + (-2)^2 + 4^2}}$

$$= \frac{|2 - 2 - 4 - 9|}{\sqrt{1 + 4 + 16}}$$

$$= \frac{|-13|}{\sqrt{21}} = \frac{13}{\sqrt{21}} \text{ units}$$

22. Let (x_1, y_1, z_1) be a point on the plane $x + y - z + 4 = 0$,

Then, $x_1 + y_1 - z_1 + 4 = 0 \qquad \text{...(i)}$

$\therefore$ Required distances = Distance of (x_1, y_1, z_1) from $x + y - z + 5 = 0$

$$= \frac{|x_1 + y_1 - z_1 + 5|}{\sqrt{1^2 + 1^2 + (-1)^2}} = \frac{|(x_1 + y_1 - z_1 + 4) + 1|}{\sqrt{3}}$$

$$= \frac{|0 + 1|}{\sqrt{3}} = \frac{1}{\sqrt{3}} \quad \text{[using equation (i)]}$$

23. This plane makes intercepts a, b, c with the coordinate axes.

$\therefore$ Its equation is $\dfrac{x}{a} + \dfrac{y}{b} + \dfrac{z}{c} = 1$

24. Let the given points be A, B, C.

Then $AB = \sqrt{(-1)^2 + (-1)^2 + (1)^2} = \sqrt{3}$,

$BC = \sqrt{3^2 + 3^2 + (-3)^2} = 3\sqrt{3}$

and $CA = \sqrt{2^2 + 2^2 + (-2)^2} = \sqrt{4 + 4 + 4} = 2\sqrt{3}$

$\therefore CA + AB = CB$

Hence, points A, B, C are collinear.

CHAPTER 12

Linear Programming

Summary

- **Linear Programming**

  Linear programming is a method which provides the optimization (maximization or minimization) of a linear function composed of certain variables subject to the number of constraints.

- **Applications of Linear Programming**
  - Used in finding highest margin, maximum profit, minimum cost etc.
  - Used in industry, commerce, management science etc.

- **Linear Programming Problem (LPP)**

  Linear Programming problem is a type of problem in which a linear function z is maximized or minimized on certain conditions that are determined by a set of linear inequalities with non-negative variables.

- **Mathematical Formulation of LPP**
  - **Optimal value:** Maximum or Minimum value of a linear function
  - **Objective Function:** The function which is to be optimized (maximized/minimized).
  - **Linear objective function:** $Z = ax + by$ is a linear function form, where a, b are constants, which has to be maximized or minimized is called a linear objective function.

    For example- $Z = 340x + 60y$, where variables x and y are called decision variables.

- **Constraints:** The limitations as disparities on the factors of a LPP are called constraints. The conditions x ≥ 0, y ≥ 0 are called non-negative restrictions.

- **'Linear'** states that all mathematical relations used in the problem are linear relations. Programming refers to the method of determining a particular program or plan of action.

- **Mathematical Formulation of the Problem**

  A general LPP can be stated as (Max/Min) $Z = c_1x_1 + c_2x_2 + \ldots\ldots + c_nx_n$ subject to given constraints and the non-negative restrictions.
  - $x_1, x_2, \ldots\ldots, x_n \geq 0$ and all are variables.
  - $c_1, c_2, \ldots\ldots c_n$ are constants.

- **Graphical methods to solve a Linear Programming Problem**

- **Corner Point method:** This method is used to solve the LPP graphically by finding the corner points.

  Procedure-
  (i) Replace the signs of inequality by the equality and consider each constraint as an equation.
  (ii) Plotting each equation on the graph that will represent a straight line.
  (iii) The common region that satisfies all the constraints and the non-negative restrictions is known as the feasible region. It is a convex polygon.
  (iv) Determining the vertices of the convex polygon. These vertices of the polygon are also known as the extreme points or corners of the feasible region.
  (v) Finding the values of Objective function at each of the extreme points. Now, finding the point at which the value of the objective function is optimum as that is the optimal solution of the given LPP.

- **General features of a LPP**
  - The feasible region is always a convex region.
  - The maximum (or minimum) solution of the objective function occurs at the vertex (corner) of the feasible region.
  - If two corner points produce the same optimum (maximum or minimum) value of the objective function, then every point on the line segment joining these points will also give the same optimum (maximum or minimum) value.

- **Different Types of Linear Programming Problems**
  - **Manufacturing problems**

    In order to make maximum profit, determine the number of units of different products which should be produced and sold by a firm when each product requires a fixed manpower, machine hours, warehouse space per unit of the output etc., in order to make maximum profit.
  - **Diet problems**

    Determining the minimum amount of different nutrients which should be included in a diet so as to minimize the cost of the diet.

➤ **Transportation problems**

To find the cheapest way of transporting a product from factories situated at different locations to different markets.

➤ **Allocation problems**

These problems are concerned with the allocation of a particular land/area of a company or any organization by choosing a certain number of employees and a certain amount of area to complete the assignment within the required deadline, given that a single person works on only one job within the assignment.

EXERCISE

1. For the constraint of a linear optimizing function $z = x_1 + x_2$, given by $x_1 + x_2 \leq 1$, $3x_1 + x_2 \geq 3$ and $x_1, x_2 \geq 0$.
   - (a) There are two feasible regions
   - (b) There are infinite feasible regions
   - (c) There is no feasible regions
   - (d) None of these

2. Which of the following is not a vertex of the positive region bounded by the inequalities $2x + 3y \leq 6$, $5x + 3y \leq 15$ and $x, y \geq 0$
   - (a) $(0, 2)$
   - (b) $(0, 0)$
   - (c) $(3, 0)$
   - (d) None of these

3. The intermediate solutions of constraints must be checked by substituting them back into
   - (a) Objective function
   - (b) Constraint equations
   - (c) Not required
   - (d) None of these

4. A basic solution is called non-degenerate, if
   - (a) All the basic variables are zero
   - (b) None of the basic variables is zero
   - (c) At least one of the basic variables is zero
   - (d) None of these

5. If the number of available constraints is 3 and the number of parameters to be optimized is 4, then
   - (a) The objective function can be optimized
   - (b) The constraints are short in number
   - (c) The solution is problem oriented
   - (d) None of these

6. Objective function of a linear programming problem is
   - (a) A constraint
   - (b) A function to be optimized
   - (c) A relation between the variables
   - (d) None of these

7. If the constraints in a linear programming problem are changed
   - (a) The problem is to be re-evaluated
   - (b) Solution is not defined
   - (c) The objective function has to be modified
   - (d) The change in constraints is ignored

8. Which of the following statements is correct
   - (a) Every linear programming problem admits an optimal solution
   - (b) A linear programming problem admits a unique optimal solution
   - (c) If a linear programming problem admits two optimal solutions, it has an infinites number of optimal solution
   - (d) The set of all feasible solutions of a linear programming is not a convex set

9. The minimum value of linear objective function $c = 2x + 2y$ under linear constraints $3x + 2y \geq 12$, $x + 3y \geq 11$ and $x, y \geq 0$, is
   - (a) 10
   - (b) 12
   - (c) 6
   - (d) 5

10. The maximum value of $P = x + 3y$ such that $2x + y \leq 20$, $x + 2y \leq 20$, $x \geq 0$, $y \geq 0$, is
    - (a) 10
    - (b) 60
    - (c) 30
    - (d) None of these

11. Inequations $3x - y \geq 3$ and $4x - y > 4$
    - (a) Have solution for positive x and y
    - (b) Have no solution for positive x and y
    - (c) Have solution for all x
    - (d) Have solution for all y

12. The constraints
    $-x_1 + x_2 + \leq 1$; $-x_1 + 3x_2 \leq 9$; $x, x_2 \geq 0$ define
    - (a) Bounded feasible space
    - (b) Unbounded feasible space
    - (c) Both bounded and unbounded feasible space
    - (d) None of these

13.

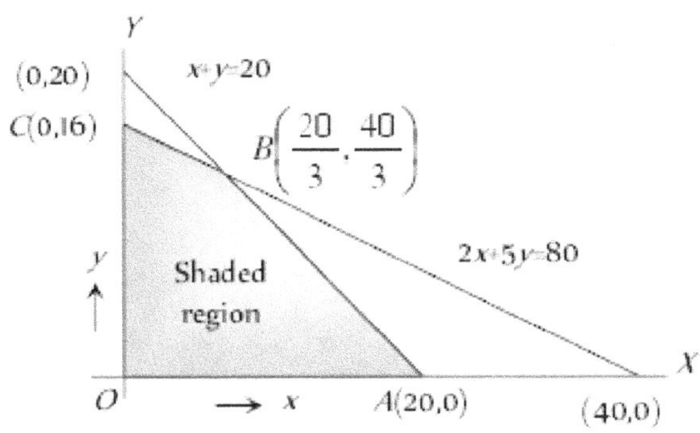

Shaded region is represented by

(a) $2x + 5y \geq 80$, $x + y \leq 20$, $x \geq 0$, $y \leq 0$

(b) $2x + 5y \geq 80$, $x + y \geq 20$, $x \geq 0$, $y \geq 0$

(c) $2x + 5y \leq 80$, $x + y \leq 20$, $x \geq 0$, $y \geq 0$

(d) $2x + 5y \leq 80$, $x + y \leq 20$, $x \leq 0$, $y \leq 0$

14.

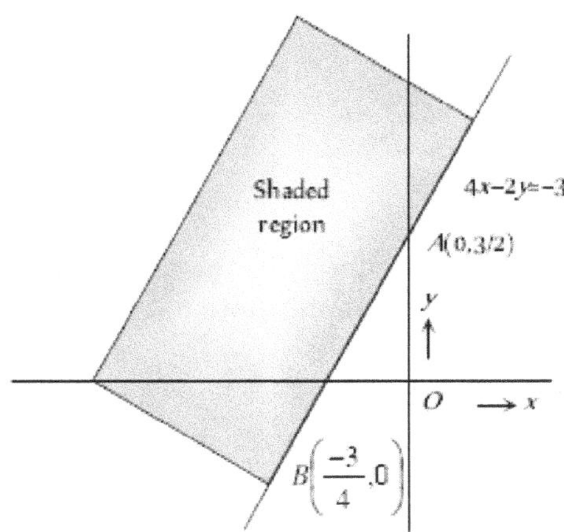

Shaded region is represented by

(a) $4x - 2y \leq 3$ (b) $4x - 2y \leq -3$

(c) $4x - 2y \geq 3$ (d) $4x - 2y \geq -3$

15. A firm makes pants and shirt. A shirt takes 2 hour on machine and 3 hour of man labour while a pant takes 3 hour on machine and 2 hour of man labour. In a week there are 70 hour of machine and 75 hour of man labour available. If the firm determines to make x shirts and y pants per week, then for this the linear constraints are

(a) $x \geq 0$, $y \geq 0$, $2x + 3y \geq 70$, $3x + 2y \geq 75$

(b) $x \geq 0$, $y \geq 0$, $2x + 3y \leq 70$, $3x + 2y \geq 75$

(c) $x \geq 0$, $y \geq 0$, $2x + 3y \geq 70$, $3x + 2y + \leq 75$

(d) $x \geq 0$, $y \geq 0$, $2x + 3y \leq 70$, $3x + 2y \leq 75$

16. The minimum value of the objective function Z = 2x + 10 y for linear constraints $x - y \geq 0$, $x - 5y \leq -5$ and x, $y \geq 0$ is

(a) 10   (b) 15

(c) 12   (d) 8

17. Maximize z = 3x + 2y, subject to $x + y \geq 1$, $y - 5x \leq 0$, $x - y \geq -1$, $x + y \leq 6$, $x \leq 3$ and x, $y \geq 0$

(a) x = 3   (b) y = 3

(c) z = 15   (d) All the above

18. Maximum value of 4 x + 5y subject to the constraints $x + y \leq 20$, $x + 2y \leq 35$, $x - 3y \leq 12$ is

(a) 84   (b) 95

(c) 100   (d) 96

19. The maximum value of Z = 4x + 3y subjected to the constraints $3x + 2y \geq 160$, $5 x + 2y \geq 200$, $x + 2y \geq 80$, x, $y \geq 0$ is

(a) 320   (b) 300

(c) 230   (d) None of these

20. The maximum value of $\mu = 3x + 4y$ subjected to the conditions $x + y \leq 40$, $x + 2y \leq 60$; x, $y \geq 0$ is

(a) 130   (b) 120

(c) 40   (d) 140

Answer Keys

1. (c)	2. (d)	3. (b)	4. (b)	5. (b)	6. (b)	7. (a)	8. (c)	9. (a)	10. (c)
11. (a)	12. (b)	13. (c)	14. (b)	15. (d)	16. (b)	17. (d)	18. (b)	19. (d)	20. (d)

Solutions

1. Clearly, from graph there is no feasible region.

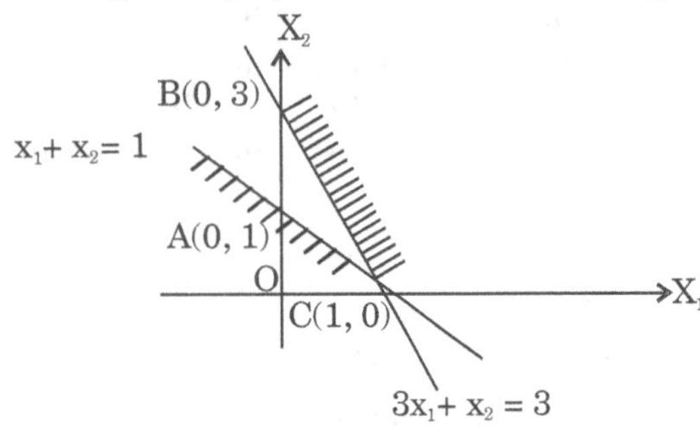

2. 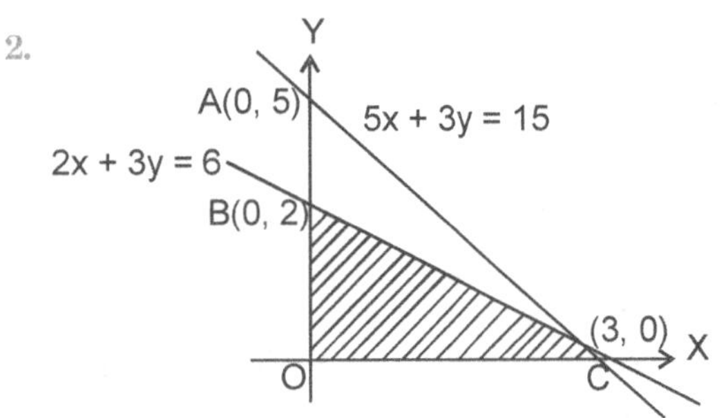

Here $(0, 2)$, $(0, 0)$ and $(3, 0)$ all are vertices of feasible region.

3. The intermediate solutions of constraints must be checked by substituting them back into constraint equations.

4. A basic solution is called non-degenerate, if none of the basic variables is zero.

5. If the number of available constraints is 3 and the number of parameters to be optimized is 4, then the constraints are short in number.

6. Objective function of a linear programming problem is a function to be optimized.

7. If the constraints in a linear programming problem are changed the problem is to be re-evaluated.

8. If a linear programming problem admits two optimal solutions, it has an infinite number of optimal solutions.

9. Minimum $(z) = 2(2) + 2(3) \Rightarrow c = 10$

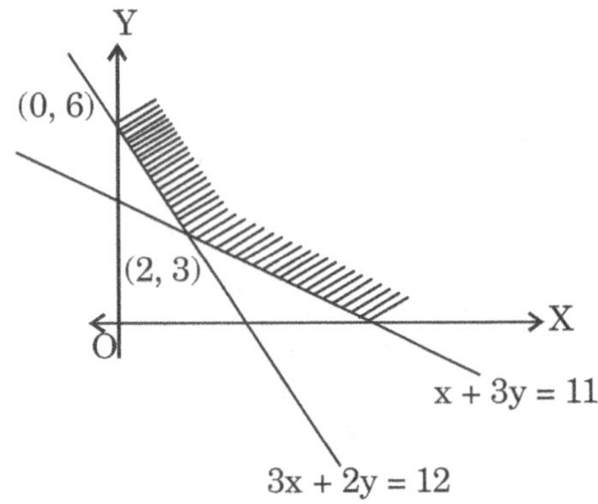

10. Obviously, $P = x + 3y$ will be maximum at $(0, 10)$

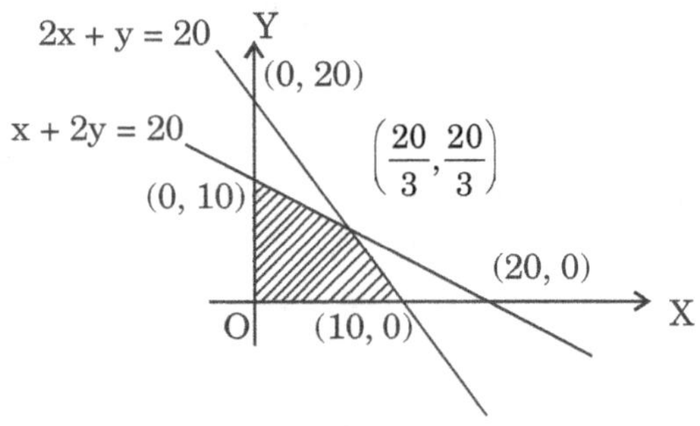

$\therefore P = 0 + 3 \times 10 = 30$

11. (a) Following figure will be obtained on drawing the graphs of given inequations :

From $3x - y \geq 3$, $\dfrac{x}{1} + \dfrac{y}{-3} = 1$

From $4x - y \geq 4$, $\dfrac{x}{1} + \dfrac{y}{-4} = 1$

Clearly the common region of both the inequations is true for positive value of (x, y). It is also true for positive values of x and negative values of y.

12. 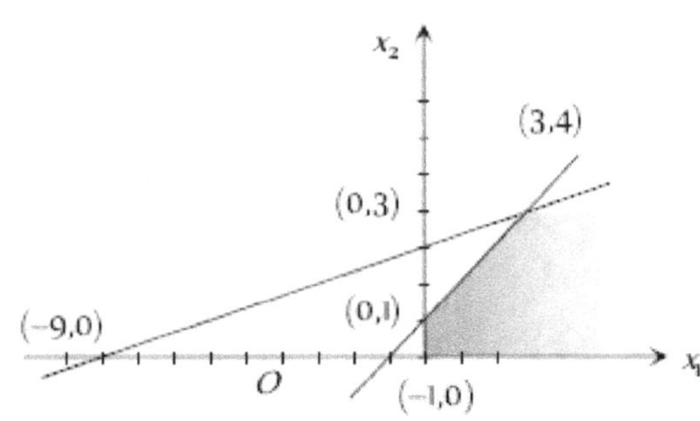

It is clear from the graph, the constraints define an unbounded feasible space.

13. In all the given equations, the origin is present in shaded area. Answer (c) satisfy this condition.

14. Origin is not present in given shaded area.
So $4x - 2y \leq -3$ satisfy this condition.

15.

	Working time on machine	Man labour
Shirt(x)	2 hours	3 hours
Pant(y)	3 hours	2 hours
Availability	70 hours	75 hours

Linear constraints are $2x + 3y \leq 70$, $3x + 2y \leq 75$ and $x, y \geq 0$

16. 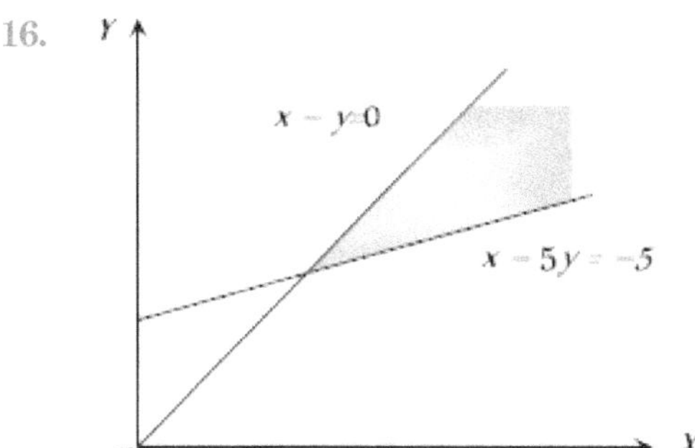

Required region is unbounded whose vertex is

$\left(\dfrac{5}{4}, \dfrac{5}{4}\right)$

Hence the minimum value of objective function is

$= 2 \times \dfrac{5}{4} + 10 \times \dfrac{5}{4} = 15.$

17. 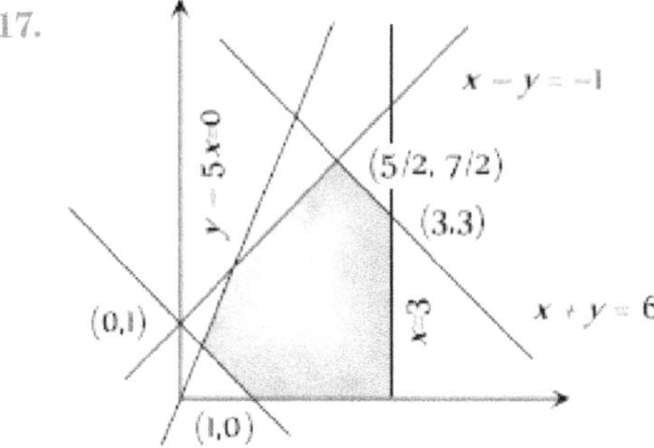

The shaded region represents the bounded region (3, 3) satisfies, so $x = 3$, $y = 3$ and $z = 15$.

18. 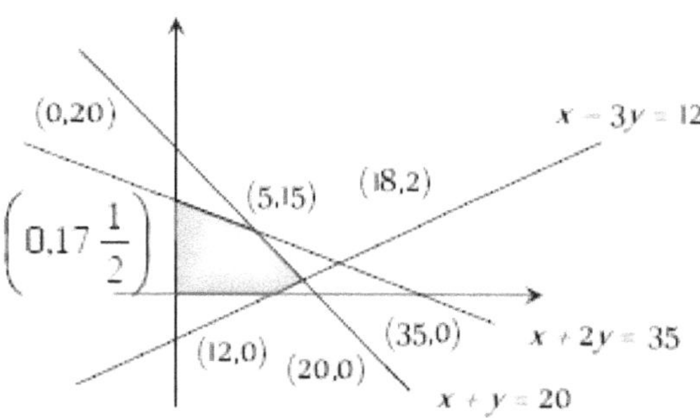

Obviously, max. $4x + 5y = 95$. It is at (5, 15).

19. 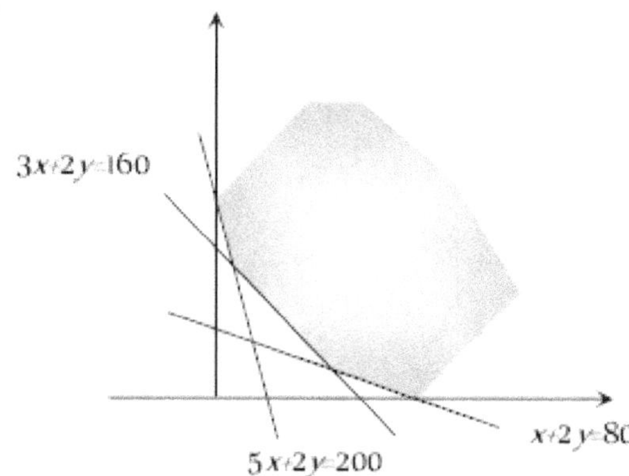

Obviously, it is unbounded. Therefore its maximum value does not exist.

20. 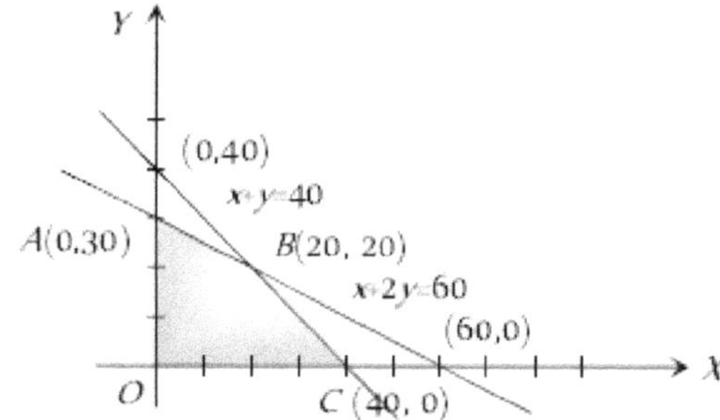

Obviously Max $\mu = 3x + 4y$ at (20, 20)
$\mu = 60 + 80 = 140$

CHAPTER 13

Probability

Conditional Probability and Independent Events

- **Probability:**
  Let S be the sample space and E be the event in an experiment.
  Then,

  $$\text{Probability} = P(E) = \frac{\text{Number of favourable event}}{\text{Total number of events}}$$

  $$= \frac{n(E)}{n(S)}$$

  Where, $0 \leq n(E) \leq n(s)$
  $\Rightarrow 0 \leq P(E) \leq 1$

  Hence, the probability of the occurrence of an event E is denoted by $P(E)$

  Now, $P(\overline{E}) = 1 - P(E)$ ($P(\overline{E})$ can also be written as $P(E')$)

  > **Mutually Exclusive Event:** The two events which cannot occur simultaneously are called mutually exclusive events.

  > Independent Events: If the occurrence or non-occurrence of one event is unaffected by the occurrence or non-occurrence of other, these events are called independent events.
  > Consider an example of drawing two marbles one by one with replacement from a jar containing 2 red marbles and 1 yellow marble
  > Now assume, X = the event of occurrence of a red marble in first draw
  > And Y = the event of occurrence of a yellow marble in second draw
  > So, here the probability of occurrence Y is not affected by that of X.
  > Hence, events X and Y are independent events.

  > **Exhaustive Events:** If the performance of random experiment always results in the occurrence of at least one of the given set of events, the set of those events will be known as exhaustive.

  > If their union is the total sample space
  > If event A, B and C are disjoint pairs i.e.,
  > Consider an example of throwing a die,
  > $A = \{1, 2, 3, 4, 5, 6\}$
  > Now assume X = the event of occurrence of an multiple of $2 = \{2, 4, 6\}$
  > Y = the event of occurrence of the number not divisible by $2 = \{1, 3, 5\}$
  > Z = the event of occurrence of multiple of $3 = \{3, 6\}$
  > Here X and Y are mutually exclusive but Y and Z are not.

- **Conditional Probability:**
  The probability of occurrence of event A when B has already been occurred is known as Conditional probability also called probability of occurrence of A w.r.t B.

  Some important formulae related to conditional probability

  > $P(A \mid B) = \dfrac{P(A \cap B)}{P(B)}$, $B \neq \phi$ i.e., $P(B) \neq 0$

  > $P(B \mid A) = \dfrac{P(A \cap B)}{P(A)}$, $A \neq \phi$ i.e., $P(A) \neq 0$

  > $P(\overline{A} \mid B) = \dfrac{P(\overline{A} \cap B)}{P(B)}$, $P(B) \neq 0$

  > $P(A \mid \overline{B}) = \dfrac{P(A \cap \overline{B})}{P(\overline{B})}$, $P(\overline{B}) \neq 0$

  > $P(\overline{A} \mid \overline{B}) = \dfrac{P(\overline{A} \cap \overline{B})}{P(\overline{B})}$, $P(\overline{B}) \neq 0$

  > $P(A \mid B) + P(\overline{A} \mid B) = 1$

  Some formulae

  > $P(A \cup B) = P(A) + P(B) - P(A \cap B)$ i.e.,
  > $P(A \text{ or } B) = P(A) + P(B) - P(A \text{ and } B)$

  > $P(A \cup B \cup C) = P(A) + P(B) + P(C) - P(A \cap B)$
  > $- P(B \cap C) - P(C \cap A) + P(A \cap B \cap C)$

➤ $P\left(\overline{A}\cap B\right) = P\left(\text{only } B\right) = P(B-A) = P$

   $(B \text{ but not } A) = P(B) - P(A\cap B)$

➤ $P\left(A\cap \overline{B}\right) = P\left(\text{only } A\right) = P(A-B) = P$

   $(A \text{ but not } B) = P(A) - P(A\cap B)$

➤ $P\left(\overline{A}\cap \overline{B}\right) = P(B-A) = P\left(\text{neither } A \text{ nor } B\right)$

   $= 1 - P(A\cup B)$

Baye's Theorem and Probability Distribution

- BAYES' theorem:

  ➤ If E_1, E_2, E_3 .... E_n are n non-empty constituting a partition of sample space S i.e., S_1, S_2, S_3 .... S_n are pair wise disjoint and $E_1\cup E_2\cup E_3\cup.....\cup E_n = S$ and A is any event of non- zero probability, then

  $$P(E\mid A) = \frac{P(E_i).P(A\mid E_i)}{\sum\limits_{j=1}^{n} P(E_j)P(A\mid E_j)}, i = 1,2,3,.......n$$

  ➤ For example,

  $$P(E_1\mid A) = \frac{P(E_1).P(A\mid E_1)}{P(E_1).P(A\mid E_1) + P(E_2).},$$
  $$P(A\mid E_2) + P(E_3).P(A\mid E_3)$$

  $i = 1,2,3,.......n$

  ➤ It is also known as the formula for the probability of cause.

  ➤ Prior probabilities are the probabilities which are known before the experiment takes place.

  ➤ $P(A\mid E_n)$ are called posterior probabilities.

- Random Variable:

  A real valued function defined over the sample space of an experiment is known as random variable. It is denoted by uppercase letters X, Y, Z etc.

➤ Discrete random variable : When only finite or countably infinite number of values can be taken by the random variable then it is called discrete random variable.

➤ Continuous random variable: When any value between two given limits can be taken by the variable then it is called continuous random variable.

If the values of a random variable together with the corresponding probability are known, then this is called the probability distribution of the random variable.

- Formulae:

  ➤ Mean or Expectation of a random variable

  $$X = X = \mu = \sum\nolimits_{i=1}^{n} x_i P_i$$

  ➤ Variance $= \left(\sigma^2\right) = \sum\limits_{i=1}^{n} P_i x^2_i - \mu^2$

  ➤ Standard deviation $= \sigma = \sqrt{\text{Variance}}$

- Bernoulli Trials:

  They are basically known as trials of a random experiment.

  If they satisfy the following conditions:

  ➤ There should be a finite number of trials.

  ➤ The trials should be independent.

  ➤ Each trial has exactly two outcomes: success or failure.

  ➤ The probability of success remains the same in each trial

- Binomial distribution:

  A Binomial distribution with probability of success in each trial as p and with n Bernoulli trials is denoted by $B(n, p)$

  n and p are the parameters of Binomial Distribution

  Therefore the expression $P(x = r)$ or $P(r)$ is called the probability function of Binomial Distribution.

Exercise

1. A dice is thrown. What is the probability of getting a prime number?

   (a) $\dfrac{1}{6}$ (b) $\dfrac{1}{3}$

   (c) $\dfrac{1}{2}$ (d) 1

2. If a fair coin is tossed twice, what is the probability of getting heads in both the trials?

   (a) $\dfrac{1}{4}$ (b) $\dfrac{1}{2}$

   (c) $\dfrac{3}{4}$ (d) 1

3. In a simultaneous throw of two dice, the probability of getting a total of 7 is

   (a) $\dfrac{7}{36}$ (b) $\dfrac{1}{7}$

   (c) $\dfrac{1}{4}$ (d) $\dfrac{1}{6}$

4. If E and F are mutually exclusive events, then P(E $\cap$ F) is

   (a) P(E). P(F) (b) P(E) + P(F)
   (c) P(E) – P(F) (d) 0

5. If E and F are mutually exclusive, then P(E $\cup$ F) = ?

   (a) P(E) + P(F) (b) P(E) × P(F)
   (c) P(E) – P(F) (d) None of these

6. For any two events E and F, P(E – F) = ?

   (a) P(E) – P(F) (b) P(E) – P(E $\cap$ F)

   (c) P(E) – P(E $\cup$ F) (d) None of these

7. If E and F be events in a sample space such that P(E) = 0.3, P(F) = 0.2 and P(E $\cap$ F) = 0.1, then

   P($\overline{\text{E}}$ $\cap$ F) = ?

   (a) 0.2 (b) 0.1
   (c) 0.4 (d) 0.05

8. If E and F are events such that P(E) = 0.4,

   P(F) = 0.8 and P$\left(\dfrac{\text{F}}{\text{E}}\right)$ = 0.6 , then P$\left(\dfrac{\text{E}}{\text{F}}\right)$ = ?

   (a) 0.4 (b) 0.2
   (c) 0.3 (d) 0.5

9. If E and F are independent events, then P(E $\cap$ F) =?

   (a) P$\left(\overline{\text{E}}\right)$ – P$\left(\overline{\text{F}}\right)$ (b) P(E) + P(F)

   (c) P(E) . P(F) (d) 0

10. If E and F are independent events, then

    P$\left(\dfrac{\overline{\text{E}}}{\overline{\overline{\text{F}}}}\right)$ = ?

    (a) $1 - \text{P}\left(\dfrac{\overline{\text{E}}}{\text{F}}\right)$ (b) $1 - \text{P(F)}$

    (c) $1 - \text{P(E)}$ (d) None of these

11. The probability of simultaneous occurrence of two independent event E and F is

    (a) P(E) + P(F)

    (b) P(E) – P(F)

    (c) P(E) . P(F)

    (d) P($\overline{\text{E}}$) . P($\overline{\text{F}}$)

12. If E and F are two events such that P(E $\cup$ F) = $\dfrac{5}{6}$,

    P(E $\cap$ F) = $\dfrac{1}{3}$ and P$\left(\overline{\text{F}}\right)$ = $\dfrac{1}{2}$, then the events E and F are

    (a) dependent

    (b) independent

    (c) mutually exclusive

    (d) None of these

13. The probability of a problem being solved by two students are respectively $\dfrac{1}{3}$ and $\dfrac{1}{2}$. The probability that the problem is being solved is

    (a) $\dfrac{2}{3}$ (b) $\dfrac{3}{4}$

    (c) $\dfrac{1}{3}$ (d) 1

14. If A and B are independent events such that P(A) = 0.4, P(B) = P and P(A $\cup$ B) = 0.6 then the value of P is

    (a) $\dfrac{1}{4}$ (b) $\dfrac{1}{2}$

    (c) $\dfrac{1}{3}$ (d) $\dfrac{1}{6}$

15. From a pack of 52 cards, two cards are drawn one by one without replacement. The probability that first drawn card is king and second is queen, is

  (a) $\dfrac{2}{13}$ (b) $\dfrac{8}{663}$

  (c) $\dfrac{4}{663}$ (d) $\dfrac{103}{663}$

16. A coin is tossed and a dice is rolled. The probability that the coin shows the head and the dice shows 6 is

  (a) 1/8   (b) 1/12

  (c) 1/2   (d) 1

17. For two events A and B, if $P(A) = P\left(\dfrac{A}{B}\right) = \dfrac{1}{4}$ and $P\left(\dfrac{B}{A}\right) = \dfrac{1}{2}$, then

  (a) A and B are independent

  (b) $P\left(\dfrac{A'}{B}\right) = \dfrac{3}{4}$

  (c) $P\left(\dfrac{B'}{A'}\right) = \dfrac{1}{2}$

  (d) All of these

18. From a pack of 52 cards two are drawn with replacement. The probability that the first is a diamond and the second is a king is

  (a) 1/26   (b) 17/2704

  (c) 1/52   (d) None of these

19. The probabilities of winning the race by two athletes A and B are $\dfrac{1}{5}$ and $\dfrac{1}{4}$. The probability of winning by neither of them, is

  (a) $\dfrac{3}{5}$ (b) $\dfrac{3}{4}$

  (c) $\dfrac{2}{3}$ (d) $\dfrac{4}{5}$

20. Let A = {2, 3, 4,......, 20}. A number is chosen at random from the set A and it is found to be a prime number. The probability that it is more than 10 is

  (a) $\dfrac{9}{10}$ (b) $\dfrac{1}{10}$

  (c) $\dfrac{1}{5}$ (d) $\dfrac{1}{2}$

Answer Keys

1. (c)   2. (a)   3. (d)   4. (d)   5. (a)   6. (b)   7. (b)   8. (c)   9. (c)   10. (c)

11. (c)   12. (b)   13. (a)   14. (c)   15. (c)   16. (b)   17. (d)   18. (c)   19. (a)   20. (d)

Solutions

1. S = {1, 2, 3, 4, 5, 6}

  Let E = {2, 3, 5}, then

$$P(E) = \dfrac{n(E)}{n(S)} = \dfrac{3}{6} = \dfrac{1}{2}$$

2. S = {HH, HT, TH, TT} and E = {HH}

  Then, n(S) = 4 and n(E) = 1

$$\therefore \ P(\text{Both heads}) = P(E) = \dfrac{n(E)}{n(S)} = \dfrac{1}{4}$$

3. Total number of possible outcomes = 6 × 6 = 36

  Let E = Event of getting a total of 7

  E = {(1, 6), (2, 5), (3, 4), (4, 3), (5, 2), (6, 1)}

  n (S) = 36 and n(E) = 6

$$\therefore \ P(\text{a total of 7}) = P(E) = \dfrac{n(S)}{n(E)} = \dfrac{6}{36} = \dfrac{1}{6}$$

4. E and F are mutually exclusive

  $\therefore \ E \cap F = \phi$

  $\Rightarrow P(E \cap F) = P(\phi) = 0$

5. If E and F are mutually exclusive,

  then, $P(E \cap F) = 0$

  $P(E \cup F) = P(E) + P(F) - P(E \cap F)$

  $\Rightarrow P(E \cup F) = P(E) + P(F)$

6. $(E - F) \cap (E \cap F) = \phi$

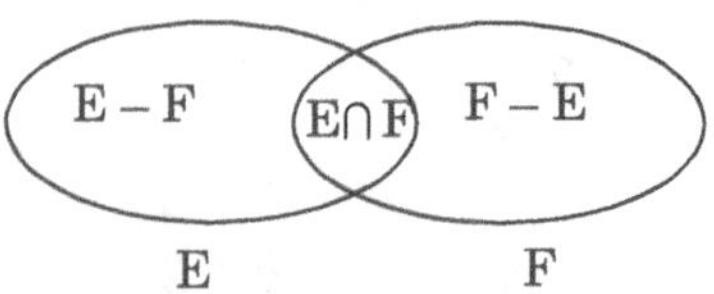

  and $(E - F) \cup (E \cap F) = E$

$\therefore \quad P(E) = P(E - F) + P(E \cap F)$

$\Rightarrow P(E - F) = P(E) - P(E \cap F)$

7. $\Rightarrow P(\overline{E} \cap F) = P(F) - P(E \cap F)$

$= (0.2 - 0.1) = 0.1$

8. $P\left(\dfrac{F}{E}\right) = \dfrac{P(E \cap F)}{P(E)}$

$\Rightarrow P(E \cap F) = (0.6 \times 0.4) = 0.24$

$\therefore P\left(\dfrac{E}{F}\right) = \dfrac{P(E \cap F)}{P(F)} = \dfrac{0.24}{0.8} = 0.3$

9. When E and F are independent events, then $P(E \cap F) = P(E) \cdot P(F)$

10. $P\left(\dfrac{\overline{E}}{\overline{F}}\right) = \dfrac{P(\overline{E} \cap \overline{F})}{P(\overline{F})}$

$= \dfrac{P(\overline{E}) \cdot P(\overline{F})}{P(\overline{F})} = P(\overline{E}) = 1 - P(E)$

11. $P(E$ and $F) = P(E \cap F)$

$= P(E) \cdot P(F)$

12. $P(F) = 1 - P(\overline{F}) = \left(1 - \dfrac{1}{2}\right) = \dfrac{1}{2}$

$P(E \cup F) = P(E) + P(F) - P(E \cap F)$

$\Rightarrow \dfrac{5}{6} = P(E) + \dfrac{1}{2} - \dfrac{1}{3}$

$\Rightarrow P(E) = \left(\dfrac{5}{6} + \dfrac{1}{3} - \dfrac{1}{2}\right) = \dfrac{4}{6} = \dfrac{2}{3}$

$P(E) \cdot P(F) = \dfrac{2}{3} \times \dfrac{1}{2} = \dfrac{1}{3} = P(E \cap F)$

Hence, E and F are independent events.

13. $P(E) = \dfrac{1}{3}, P(F) = \dfrac{1}{2}$

$1 + P(\overline{E}) P(\overline{F})$

$1 - \dfrac{2}{3} \times \dfrac{1}{2} = \dfrac{2}{3}$

14. $P(A \cap B) = P(A) \cdot P(B) = 0.4\,P$

$\therefore \quad P(A \cup B) = P(A) + P(B) - P(A \cap B)$

$\Rightarrow 0.6 = 0.4 + p - 0.4\,p$

$\Rightarrow 0.6\,p = 0.2$

$\therefore p = \dfrac{0.2}{0.6} = \dfrac{1}{3}$

15. $P = \dfrac{4}{52} \times \dfrac{4}{51}$

$= \dfrac{4}{663}$

16. $P = \dfrac{1}{2} \times \dfrac{1}{6} = \dfrac{1}{12}$

17. $P(A) = P\left(\dfrac{A}{B}\right)$

A does not depends on B therefore A & B are independent

$P\left(\dfrac{A'}{B}\right) = P(A') = 1 - P(A)$

$= 1 - \dfrac{1}{4} = \dfrac{3}{4}$

$P\left(\dfrac{B'}{A'}\right) = P(B') = 1 - P(B)$

$= 1 - P\left(\dfrac{B}{A}\right) = 1 - \dfrac{1}{2} = \dfrac{1}{2}$

18. $P = \dfrac{13}{52} \times \dfrac{4}{52} = \dfrac{1}{52}$

19. $P(\overline{A}) \cdot P(\overline{B}) = \left(1 - \dfrac{1}{5}\right)\left(1 - \dfrac{1}{4}\right)$

$= \dfrac{3}{5}$

20. $A = \{2, 3, 4, \ldots\ldots 20\}$

Prime number $= \{2, 3, 5, 7, 11, 13, 17, 19\}$

$P = \dfrac{4}{8} = \dfrac{1}{2}$